DATE			

APR - - 2023

Also by John Boessenecker

Badge and Buckshot: Lawlessness in Old California

The Grey Fox: The True Story of Bill Miner, Last of the Old-Time Bandits
(with Mark Dugan)

Lawman: The Life and Times of Harry Morse, 1835–1912

Against the Vigilantes: The Recollections of Dutch Charley Duane

*Gold Dust and Gunsmoke: Tales of Gold Rush Outlaws, Gunfighters,
Lawmen, and Vigilantes*

Bandido: The Life and Times of Tiburcio Vasquez

When Law Was in the Holster: The Frontier Life of Bob Paul

*Texas Ranger: The Epic Life of Frank Hamer, the Man Who Killed Bonnie
and Clyde*

*Shotguns and Stagecoaches: The Brave Men Who Rode for Wells Fargo in
the Wild West*

*Ride the Devil's Herd: Wyatt Earp's Epic Battle Against the West's Biggest
Outlaw Gang*

*Wildcat: The Untold Story of Pearl Hart, the Wild West's Most Notorious
Woman Bandit*

GENTLEMAN BANDIT

THE TRUE STORY OF
BLACK BART,
THE OLD WEST'S
MOST INFAMOUS
STAGECOACH ROBBER

JOHN BOESSENECKER

HANOVER
SQUARE
PRESS

**HANOVER
SQUARE
PRESS™**

Recycling programs
for this product may
not exist in your area.

ISBN-13: 978-1-335-44942-9

Gentleman Bandit

Hanover Square Press
22 Adelaide St. West, 41st Floor
Toronto, Ontario M5H 4E3, Canada
HanoverSqPress.com
BookClubbish.com

Printed in U.S.A.

Charles E. Boles, better known as Black Bart, the gentleman bandit.

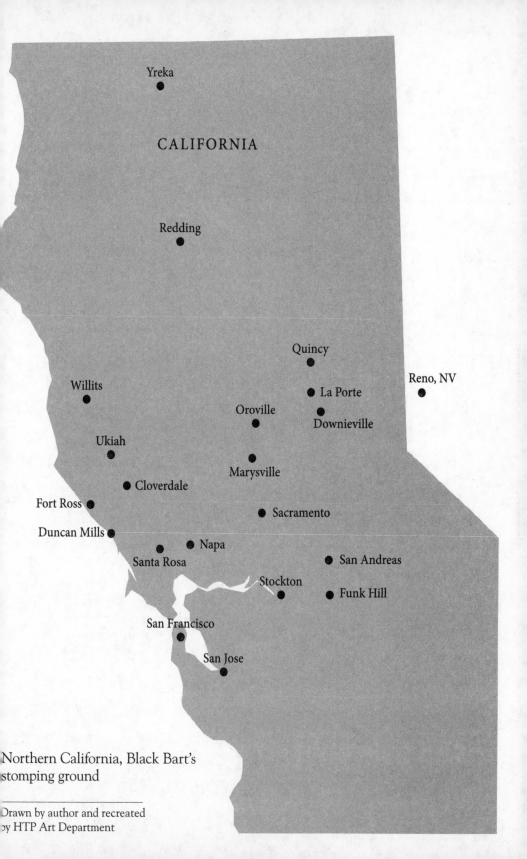

Yreka

CALIFORNIA

Redding

Quincy

Reno, NV

Willits

La Porte

Oroville

Downieville

Ukiah

Marysville

Cloverdale

Fort Ross

Sacramento

Duncan Mills

Napa

Santa Rosa

San Andreas

Stockton

Funk Hill

San Francisco

San Jose

Northern California, Black Bart's
stomping ground

Drawn by author and recreated
by HTP Art Department

For Bruce Levene

Table of Contents

1

You Fine-Haired Sons of Bitches

"Please throw down the box."

Stage driver John Shine nervously fingered the reins of his six-horse team as he stared down the yawning barrels of the highway robber's shotgun. The bandit had suddenly appeared in front of Shine as he was urging his horses up the long, gradual slope of Funk Hill in the foothills of California's Sierra Nevada Mountains. For a moment, Shine hesitated as he reached for the green Wells Fargo strongbox under his seat.

The bandit looked over his shoulder at the manzanita-choked hillside behind him and yelled, "If he dares to shoot, give him a solid volley, boys!"

Shine glanced up quickly and saw half a dozen rifle barrels protruding from the rocks and brush behind the bandit. They were aimed directly at his stage. The driver was certain that he was being held up by a large outlaw gang. He had no way of knowing that he was about to become the first victim of Black Bart, the Old West's greatest stage robber.

Earlier on that fateful morning of July 26, 1875, Shine had

stepped out of the stage depot in the gold town of Sonora and climbed onto the driver's seat of his "mud wagon." Fancy stagecoaches made by the Abbot-Downing Company of Concord, New Hampshire, had been used for two decades in the far west. But Concord coaches were expensive and hard to get. As a result, three-quarters of all stages on the frontier were inexpensive and uncomfortable mud wagons built by local wagon makers. Stagecoaches, including many mud wagons, could carry as many as ten passengers inside and another six on top. Valises and carpetbags were also carried on top, while trunks and large mailbags were placed in the rear boot, a platform with leather coverings at the back of the stage. As Shine hoisted the Wells Fargo & Company strongbox and the US mail pouch aboard, ten passengers crammed aboard his stage. Some took seats inside and others on top, directly behind the driver and also on the rear "dickey" seat.

Any coach that carried a strongbox filled with treasure would customarily be accompanied by a Wells Fargo shotgun messenger, or express guard. He rode on the front seat, known as the driver's box or the front boot, and sat next to the reinsman. Shotgun messengers were hired for their courage, skill with firearms, and willingness to fight if attacked by bandits. And contrary to popular belief, shotgun messengers did not guard stagecoaches and their passengers. They guarded Wells Fargo's express shipments. Shine's coach carried two Wells Fargo strongboxes. One was the standard wood and iron-strapped chest placed underneath the driver's seat. The other was a locked iron box, known as a "pony safe" because of its small size, bolted to the floor and concealed under the inside rear passenger seat. On this morning, the box under the driver's seat held only $174 in bills, while $655 in gold coin was locked in the pony safe. For Wells Fargo, it was a minor shipment, and as a result, no shotgun messenger rode on the stage. Shine gave the guard's usual seat to a woman passenger. That was considered the seat of honor.

A traveler on a Sierra Nevada stage once explained, "As every one knows, the most desirable of all places on a stagecoach is that known as the 'box-seat.' This is with the coachman; for, if he is intelligent, and in a good humor, he can tell you of all the sights by the way; with the personal history of nearly every man and woman you may meet; the qualities and 'points' of every horse upon the road; with all the adventures, jokes, and other good things he has seen and heard during his thousand and one trips, under all kinds of circumstances, and in all sorts of weather. In short, he is a living road-encyclopedia, to be read and studied at intervals, by the occupant of the 'box-seat.'"[1]

PHOTO BY DON GORDON.

The site of Black Bart's first stage robbery, on Funk Hill in Calaveras County, California.

John Shine, twenty-seven years old, was a very experienced driver. And he was no stranger to guns or to violence. In 1865, at just sixteen, he ran away from his father's homestead in Wisconsin, lied about his age, and joined the Union Army in Chicago. He served during the final months of the Civil War, then returned to the family farm. Three years later, seeking adventure, he traveled by steamship to California and worked as a gold miner in the Sierra Nevada foothills of Amador County. In 1869 he became a stagecoach driver, variously known as a whip, a reinsman, or a jehu, the last nickname derived from the chariot-driving biblical king of Israel. Each of the driver's reins, or ribbons, controlled one horse. The two animals at the front of the team were called the lead horses, or leaders; the pair closest to the driver were the wheel horses, or wheelers. A stagecoach driver also carried a whip, but he did not use it to flay the team. Instead, he would crack it above the animals' heads to urge them forward. It took extraordinary skill for a reinsman to manage a four- or six-horse team on twisting mountain roads. Stage drivers were hugely popular on the frontier because they were a primary connection with the outside world, and so widely respected that they were called "knights of the whip."

John Shine worked hard as a jehu, and in 1873 he managed to purchase a one-third interest in a large stage line headquartered in the prominent mining town of Sonora. Though he had become an owner, his principal job remained guiding coaches up and down the mountains between Sonora and the railhead in Milton. From Milton, a narrow-gauge railroad led thirty miles west to the city of Stockton, which in turn connected with the transcontinental railroad run by the Central Pacific. The stages on the Sonora-Milton route carried both passengers and gold from the mines in the Sierra Nevada foothills. Therefore, they were a favorite target of highway robbers.[2]

Shine's stage rolled out of Sonora, headed for Milton, forty miles west. Eight of the passengers were women and children. The only men aboard were John Olive, one of Shine's partners in the stage line, and a young gold miner from Sonora who carried a holstered six-gun. The two men rode inside the stage, and no one else was armed. As Shine called to his horses and chatted with the passengers, he guided the coach down the stage road that skirted tall hills richly covered with manzanita and scrub oak. The route followed modern-day Highway 49—named after the major gold rush year—to the Reynolds Ferry crossing on the San Joaquin River. The road down into the river canyon was steep and winding until it reached the ferry. Today Reynolds Ferry is covered by the huge New Melones reservoir. But in that era, it featured a pontoon boat that was pulled across the stream by ropes and workhorses, guided by a long wire cable.

Shine, much to the delight of the children, skillfully brought the coach aboard the ferry, soothed his horses as they drifted across the powerful stream, then eased his stage off the ramp on the opposite shore. From there it was a tough haul out of the river canyon and up Funk Hill, which is more mountain than hill. The stage road made a gradual three-mile ascent in a long curve around the side of Funk Hill, with its summit just to the right of, and about two hundred feet above, the roadway. As Shine's stage rounded the side of Funk Hill, moving at a crawl, a lone figure suddenly rushed from behind a boulder to his right. The man wore a long, white, soiled duster to conceal his clothes. A flour sack mask with eye holes covered his head. Shine noticed that the man's boots were wrapped with cloth in order to hide his tracks, and he had a lever-action Henry rifle slung across his back. But mostly he noticed the yawning bore of the bandit's double-barreled shotgun, and several rifle barrels aimed at him from the roadside brush.

Shine yanked the reins to calm his frightened team. Then he quickly complied with the bandit's orders to throw down the Wells Fargo express box and the mailbag. Inside the coach, the young miner drew his six-shooter. John Olive seized his hand and shoved the revolver downward so the robber would not see it.

"Put that damned thing away," Olive whispered hoarsely. "Do you want to get us all killed?"

The miner took his advice and holstered his pistol. Several of the women passengers gasped and shrieked in terror at the ghostly, shotgun-wielding apparition. One tossed her purse out the window. The highwayman picked it up and handed it back to her. Then he bowed deeply and spoke in a hollow, raspy voice.

"I don't want your money. I only want boxes."

An old engraving depicts Black Bart's first stage holdup.

<small>JOHN BOESSENECKER COLLECTION.</small>

The robber did not know that there was a Wells Fargo safe under the back seat. Thinking he had secured the entire express shipment, he called to Shine, "That will be about all, boys. Drive on."

Shine cracked his whip, and his coach lurched forward. He glanced over his shoulder and saw the bandit hacking at the strongbox with a hatchet. The jehu continued up the grade and around a bend until he was well out of sight. Then he jumped down from the front boot and started back toward the holdup site. Meanwhile the bandit was still chopping at the Wells Fargo box when a second stagecoach hove into sight. Its driver, Donald McLean, was bringing several passengers from Sonora to the Milton railhead. He had left Sonora well after Shine. The highwayman covered McLean with his shotgun and again politely demanded, "Please throw down the box."

"It is a private stage and carries no express box," McLean told him. The robber, instead of searching the coach or robbing the passengers, simply waved him on. McLean urged his horses forward, and farther up the grade he encountered Shine. The two drivers, with several male passengers, cautiously walked back to the holdup site. By the time they got there, the robber had vanished. The shattered express box, now empty, lay near the roadway. Next to it was the mail sack, cut open with a slit in the shape of a T and also empty. Registered letters were a favorite target of bandits, for they often held paper money or gold dust. Shine looked across the road at the rocks and the mesquite where the rifle barrels were still aimed toward the road. He approached cautiously and was flabbergasted to find that the rifles were actually sticks, cleverly positioned by the bandit.

Shine carried the strongbox and the mailbag back to his coach and continued another four miles to Copperopolis. He reported the holdup to the local Wells Fargo agent, then continued on to Milton with his passengers. The agent sent a telegram to Sheriff Ben K. Thorn in San Andreas, the seat of Calaveras County. Known since 1849 for its rich gold fields and rowdy mining camps, Calaveras ("skulls" in Spanish) had become even more famous after the 1865 publication of Mark Twain's popular short story "The Celebrated Jumping Frog of Calaveras County." Thorn was sheriff of Calaveras, and the holdup had occurred in his jurisdiction. A former forty-niner, he was one of the most famous lawmen on the Pacific Coast. Thorn first became a deputy sheriff in 1855 and won election as county sheriff in 1867. During his five-decade career, he tracked down and captured scores of dangerous outlaws.

Ben Thorn immediately mounted up, rode to the robbery site, and carefully looked it over. In the brush, he found the bandit's sawed-off, twelve-gauge shotgun. The robber had left it behind, taking his Henry rifle with him. This was deliberate, not careless. There was no firearm registration in that era, so the weapon was not traceable. A man carrying a shotgun was commonplace, like an ordinary duck hunter. However, a man carrying a shotgun and a Henry rifle would arouse suspicion. Sheriff Thorn conducted a vain manhunt for the cautious bandit. Wells Fargo offered a $250 reward, but the highwayman vanished.[3]

John Shine safely brought his passengers to the train depot in Milton. This was not his last adventure on the road. He was stopped two other times by stage robbers, and in 1876, Wells Fargo even presented him with a gold watch for foiling a holdup. He would live to old age, dying a wealthy man in Sonora in 1930. By then he had owned several different stage lines across the Sierra, operated a gold mine, won election as a state senator, and even served as US Marshal for Northern California. In later years, Shine told many stories of his life on the frontier, but his favorite was about that dramatic day on Funk Hill. "I was the first man Black Bart ever held up," he declared. "He didn't get anything, though. I gave him the wooden box, and he took it. I guess he hadn't heard that Wells Fargo had just started putting on steel boxes, which were carried inside."[4]

Wells Fargo's chief, and only, detective at that time was James B. Hume. Like his old friend Sheriff Thorn, he had come to California during the gold rush, failed at mining, and taken up a lifelong career in law enforcement. After serving as city marshal of Placerville—commonly known as Hangtown due to an 1849 triple lynching—he was elected sheriff of El Dorado County. Hume's prowess as a sleuth and thief-taker led Wells Fargo officials to appoint him as their chief special officer in 1873. During the next three decades, he would track down countless stage and train robbers and became the West's most famous express detective. But Jim Hume had no more success in identifying the lone highwayman than did Ben Thorn.[5]

Wells Fargo needed a great detective like Hume. The company had been founded at the height of the gold rush in 1852. During the 1850s, its messengers, mounted on horses or mules, brought newspapers and mail to lonely miners in the isolated gold camps. On the return trip, they carried gold dust and nuggets from the Sierra Nevada mining region to San Francisco for shipment to the East Coast. Unlike the US mail, Wells Fargo guaranteed delivery and promptly repaid any losses. As a result, the company grew rapidly, buying out smaller concerns and establishing offices in every new frontier boomtown. By the mid-1870s, it had more than four hundred offices throughout the West and carried express shipments on six thousand miles of stage lines and three thousand miles of railroads. And although the company did run a handful of stagecoach lines, in most cases it paid local stage companies to carry its ubiquitous strongboxes that were made of pine, strapped with iron, and painted green.

Each company office was run by an agent. Contrary to depictions in film and television, Wells Fargo agents were not detectives or secret agents. Most were merchants who owned a Wells Fargo franchise and ran the town's Wells Fargo office from their general store. The agents' main duty was shipping letters and packages; they did not investigate robberies. Such detective work was handled by men like Jim Hume. And because Wells Fargo shipped money, gold, and other valuables, it attracted highway robbers, commonly called road agents. Holdups of Wells Fargo shipments began in California in the mid- and late 1850s, then became increasingly common. Hume later reported that from 1870 to 1884, Wells Fargo was the target of 347 actual and attempted stage robberies in which six drivers and guards were killed and ten wounded. Detective Hume had plenty of cases to work on, and he soon forgot about the lone bandit on Funk Hill.[6]

Five months later, on a wet and bitterly cold December 28, 1875, stage driver Mike Hogan swung aboard his coach at the depot in North San Juan, situated in the Sierra Nevada Mountains fifteen miles north of Nevada City. He had seven passengers aboard, five men and two young women, plus a Wells Fargo box holding a small amount of cash. Hogan cracked his whip, and the coach started on the long downhill run to the river town of Marysville, forty miles distant. Two weeks earlier, Hogan, a former Marysville police officer, had been stopped by two highwaymen at a point eighteen miles from North San Juan. One repeatedly threatened to shoot before Hogan handed over the Wells Fargo box. Now, as he approached the holdup site, Hogan regaled his passengers with the story of the robbery.

Suddenly a masked man appeared before him and called out, "Halt, and throw out that box, quick!"

Hogan instantly complied, tossing out not only the express box but also the mailbags. Then the bandit waved him on. The entire incident had lasted only a moment. Hogan raced his coach five miles into Smartsville, where he turned his passengers over to another stage driver. Then he organized a well-armed, mounted posse and galloped back to the scene of the robbery. A local newspaper reported, "Hogan is probably getting mad. Two robberies in as many weeks is more than he can bear, especially as he is an active and experienced police officer. Hogan was but three hours behind the robbers, and as they cannot cross the river except only by the regular bridges, there is hope of his overtaking them." But Hogan and his possemen returned empty-handed. At first he claimed that his stage had been stopped by four highway robbers. But as a fellow stage driver later remarked, "When he found out it was only one man that robbed him, he was the laughingstock of the community."[7]

Five months passed. On the evening of June 2, 1876, stage driver A. C. Adams urged his team through the rugged Siskiyou Mountains in southern Oregon. His sixty-mile trip had begun

PHOTO BY DON GORDON.

The old stage road, now Penn Valley Drive, five miles east of Smartsville, where Black Bart pulled his second stagecoach robbery.

earlier that day in Jacksonville, Oregon, on the Siskiyou Trail that connected California with Oregon and roughly paralleled modern-day Interstate 5. Adams's coach carried three passengers on their way south to Yreka, California. The Wells Fargo box held less than $90. Adams made his way slowly through the darkness, the roadway illuminated by moonlight and the two oil lanterns mounted on each side of his driver's box. He crossed into California, then continued on a few hundred yards to Coles Station, the first stage stop south of the state line. There he watered his horses while the passengers got out and stretched their legs. Adams started out again and headed up a long grade two miles from Coles Station. It was ten o'clock when a figure stepped out of the heavy roadside timber.

"Stop and hand out the box!" the man shouted as he covered the driver with a double-barreled shotgun. He stood silhouetted with the bright moonlight behind him.

Adams reined in his team and instantly decided to play it dumb.

"What box?" he asked innocently.

"Throw it out!" the highwayman insisted.

Adams continued parleying with the bandit and asking him exactly what he wanted. The robber exploded in anger, cursing the jehu.

"I'll blow your head off if the box doesn't come out quick!"

That was enough for Adams, and he tossed the Wells Fargo strongbox and the mailbags onto the stage road.

"Drive on," ordered the bandit.

By now Adams was eager to comply, and the passengers were happy that they had been spared. According to a local journalist who later interviewed them, "After going about a hundred yards, Adams stopped his team and held a consultation with the passengers as to what was best to do, and as all the firearms the party could muster was a little four-chamber revolver, shooting a bullet about the size of a pea, they concluded nothing could be done." Adams brought his coach into the next settlement, Cottonwood Creek, and raised the alarm. At daybreak, two men rode to the scene, where they found the broken express box in a gully near the road. A deputy sheriff soon joined them, and they managed to track the road agent a short distance before losing the trail.

Wells Fargo officials offered a bounty of $250, plus a newly created standing reward from the State of California of $300 for the arrest and conviction of express robbers. A few days later, a stage line employee reported seeing a suspicious pedestrian on the stage road south of Roseburg, Oregon. He obtained a description of the stage robber's boot prints and concluded that they matched those of the man he had seen. He then sent a telegram to the sheriff in Roseburg, who promptly picked up the stranger and lodged him in jail. At Wells Fargo headquarters in San Francisco, Jim Hume received word of the arrest. After boarding a train for the railhead at Redding in Northern California, he continued on to Oregon by stagecoach, stopping on the way to inspect the tracks at the holdup site.

Although the Roseburg sheriff insisted that there was a match, Hume disagreed. The Wells Fargo detective closely examined the prisoner's boots and determined that they were not the same. Declared a Yreka newspaperman, "The boots on the man arrested did not correspond with the description telegraphed, and this Oregon officer made unnecessary cost in telegraphing and getting a detective here from below, beside doing great injustice to an innocent man." The prisoner was released. Hume, an expert in criminal investigation, was scrupulously honest, and during his long career, he would work just as hard to free an innocent man as he would to convict a guilty one.[8]

For more than a year, Detective Hume heard nothing of the lone highwayman. But he had little time to ruminate, for dozens of other stage robbers occupied his time. In 1876 alone, Hume helped hunt down the bandit gangs led by "Sheet Iron Jack" Allen, who robbed four coaches in Northern California; Tommy Brown, whose band shot and badly wounded a passenger in a stage holdup; Old Jim Smith, who had been a member of the notorious Tom Bell gang during the gold rush; and numerous others, including such noted road agents as Dick Fellows, Henry "Liverpool" Norton, and Ramon Ruiz. But before long, the elusive, shotgun-wielding robber would become a major thorn in Jim Hume's side.

On the afternoon of August 2, 1877, Ash Wilkinson supervised the routine loading of his six-horse coach in Mendocino on California's North Coast. Mendocino was a picturesque logging village situated on high bluffs overlooking the Pacific Ocean. The good-natured Wilkinson was a popular reinsman on the North Coast. A journalist friend once called him "one of the jolliest knights of the whipstock that ever mounted a box." Wilkinson boarded seven passengers and a Wells Fargo box holding about $300 in coin. Early that afternoon, his coach rolled out

REWARD

WELLS, FARGO & CO.'S EXPRESS BOX

on SONORA AND MILTON STAGE ROUTE, was ROBBED this morning, near Reynolds' Ferry, by one man, masked and armed with sixteen shooter and double-barreled shot gun. We will pay

$250

for ARREST and CONVICTION of the Robber.

JNO. J. VALENTINE, Gen. Supt

San Francisco, July 26, 1875.

The Wells Fargo reward notice that was issued after Black Bart's first stage robbery.

of Mendocino, headed for Duncans Mills, a railroad station on the Russian River, ninety miles south. His stage followed the coast while the passengers enjoyed breathtaking views of the Pacific as thundering waves crashed into the cliffs below. It was a two-day journey, and at Point Arena, they stopped and spent the night at the village hotel.

At daylight, Wilkinson started south again, passing through Fort Ross, which decades earlier had been a Russian trading post. From there the stagecoach continued south on the coastal road for three miles, where it dropped into Timber Gulch. Wilkinson walked his horses carefully down the deep ravine and around a sharp bend in the road that overlooked the Pacific Ocean. Suddenly a figure jumped in front of his lead horses. As the jehu later told a newspaperman, he quickly observed that the man stood "about five feet ten inches high, with an old slouch hat, masked, with a linen duster on and rags tied around his legs" and was "armed with a double barreled shotgun and a six-shooter."

"Stop and throw off the box!" the bandit shouted as he covered Wilkinson with his shotgun. Some of the passengers, on the other hand, later reported that he said in a polite tone, "Please throw out the box and the mail bags."

Wilkinson complied with alacrity, and the road agent waved the stage on. The driver continued on fourteen miles to Duncans Mills, where a small posse quickly organized and rode to the holdup site. A few feet from the roadside, they found the shattered express box and an old axe. Inside was a written list of items carried in the strongbox, known as a Wells Fargo waybill. On the reverse of the waybill, the highwayman had inscribed a brief poem:

I've labored long and hard for bread,
For honor, and for riches.
But on my corns too long you've tred,
You fine haired sons of bitches.

Beneath that, he added a postscript: "Driver, give my respects to our friend, the other driver, but I really had a notion to hang my old disguise hat on his weather eye." It was signed "Black Bart, the Po8," a poor pun for "poet." Each line had been written in a different hand so as to disguise its author. Clearly the bandit was taunting Wells Fargo. He had also apparently intended to stop the previous stage, but had been scared off by the other driver's "weather eye." In other words, the jehu had been too alert and watchful for Black Bart's liking. Ever after, the holdup site, situated on the steep slope above the raging Pacific surf, was known as Shotgun Point.[9]

At daybreak the next morning, a man matching the robber's description was spotted in Guerneville, on the Russian River eight miles inland from Duncans Mills. But again the highwayman quickly disappeared, though at least he now had a name. Jim Hume investigated the holdup without success. Most stage robbers were hardened, uncouth ruffians who stole the Wells Fargo box, the mail, and anything of value carried by the driver and his passengers. This mysterious bandit was unique, given his polite and gentlemanly demeanor and the fact that he never robbed anyone aboard the stage. Despite Hume's relentless detective work, it would be long years and a total of twenty-nine stagecoach holdups before he finally discovered the true identity of the lone bandit. By that time, Black Bart would be the most notorious—and prolific—stage robber in American history.

2

The Gold Hunter

Black Bart was the grandson of an English bastard. His family hailed from Shelfanger, a tiny village twenty miles south of Norwich in East Anglia, England. His grandfather, James, born in 1753, was the "base child" of Elizabeth Birch and a man named Bowles. Because his surname was registered both as Birch and Bowles in church records, James's natural father may have acknowledged him as his own son. James married at age twenty-three and sired several children, among them sons John, in 1789, and Leonard, born three years later. The family was illiterate, and its two surnames were spelled phonetically: Birch and Burch, Boles and Bowles.

John Burch—or Boles—became a farm laborer in the village of Bressingham, a few miles from Shelfanger. In 1811, when he was twenty-one, he married seventeen-year-old Maria Halls in Shelfanger. Despite living in poverty, they managed to raise seven children in Bressingham. The youngest, Charles E. Boles—destined to become America's greatest stage robber—

was born in 1829. Soon after, on October 25, 1829, Charles was baptized in the parish church of Bressingham.[1]

When Charles was an infant, his father John and uncle Leonard became determined to better their lives. In the early spring of 1830, a group of almost two hundred of their impoverished neighbors left for London, where they boarded sailing ships for America. The journey was funded by members of the local parish church, and not without controversy. One critic complained that the group's married men "had for a long time threatened to go themselves, and leave their families chargeable to the parish, unless they were furnished with the means of taking them also." Their sea voyage proved an ordeal, filled with sickness, hunger, and fear of the huge swells that frequently threatened to sink their ship. But they arrived safely in New York City, boarded a steamboat for Albany, and then proceeded by canal boat to Utica in upstate New York.[2]

One of their number wrote a letter home, describing the hardships of the journey and his dislike of New York State. He warned his friends and neighbors not to join them. But his letter arrived too late for John and Leonard Boles. They had already left Shelfanger with their wives and children and followed the same route, one hundred miles south to London. The youngest was Charles, less than a year old. From London, a sailing vessel took them across the Atlantic, and they arrived in New York City on July 1, 1830. Whether their passage was also paid for by the church is unknown. According to family tradition, the infant Charles came down with smallpox on the ship but soon recovered. True or not, Charles would develop a tough and healthy constitution.[3]

From New York, the Boles family took the same journey as their former neighbors from England. The Erie Canal was then only five years old, and it provided the best route west. John and Leonard Boles made their way to Jefferson County on the northern border of New York State. The brothers each managed to acquire a hundred-acre farm, where they began raising crops and dairy cows. John Boles's farmstead was located just south of Godfreys Corner, midway between the village of Plessis and the larger town of Alexandria Bay on the Saint Lawrence River. There John and Maria Boles had two more children, increasing their brood to nine. Charles was especially close to his sister Maria, born on the farm in January 1832 and two years his junior. As was customary, the eldest children, all teenagers, did farmwork. At Godfreys Corner stood a one-room schoolhouse, and there young Charles received a good grammar school education. He was bright and performed well in reading, writing, and penmanship. Though not particularly religious, he enjoyed studying the Bible.

Boles grew into a solid and powerful youth, his muscles honed by arduous years of farm labor. He was of average size for that era, five feet eight, one hundred fifty pounds, but with the strength of a much larger man. As one of his boyhood friends recalled, "Charley, as we usually called him, received a common school education and when grown up became better known than any other young man in this section on account of excelling in athletic sports, and was probably for his weight the best collar-and-elbow wrestler in Jefferson County." Collar-and-elbow wrestling originated in Ireland and was then a hugely popular sport. Also known as Irish Scuffling, the rules required the combatants to stay on their feet, and to throw the opponent while grasping his collar or elbow. Young Boles was a natural athlete and a great walker, able to cover dozens of miles a day on foot without tiring. He once boasted that he could easily walk fifty miles in one day. Charley became very popular, with a witty sense of humor and a penchant for reading books and writing rhymes. As another boyhood comrade explained, "He was a young man of excellent habits and greatly esteemed and respected by all who knew him."[4]

Boles disliked farming and always regretted that he did not

get more schooling. "I left home when a young boy," he recalled years later, "and I had no opportunities for education, a thing which I have regretted all through life." Nonetheless, his voracious reading helped turn him into a well-spoken, polite young gentleman. Charley loved to read the news in his spare time, and in mid-October 1848, a front-page headline in the local newspaper caught his eye: "THE GOLD MANIA IN CALIFORNIA." It featured a letter written by Thomas O. Larkin, a prominent Californian who had been US consul to California when the future state had been part of Mexico. Larkin's letter, sent by clipper ship around Cape Horn, had taken more than three months to reach New York. Larkin announced the discovery of gold, and reported that some men were digging up $400 a week—more than a working man could earn in a year. He described in detail how miners dug and panned for gold, and also used "gold rockers" to separate the precious metal from creek-side sand and gravel. Despite the apparent authenticity of the letter, the newspaper's editor cautioned his readers, "There is every reason to believe that the whole affair is one of the greatest humbugs of the age, got up by heartless speculators to induce emigration to the barren mountains and sterile plains of California."[5]

During the next six weeks, New York newspapers published more letters from distant California announcing a great gold strike. But these accounts were also met with widespread skepticism. Then, on December 5, 1848, all doubts were laid to rest when President James Polk, in his annual message to Congress, declared, "The accounts of the abundance of gold in that territory are of such extraordinary character as would scarcely command belief were they not corroborated by authentic reports of officers in the public service." These words set off one of history's greatest mass migrations. Gold fever swept America and then the world.

Charley Boles, then nineteen, had grown to hate the drudgery of farmwork, and he longed for a life of freedom and adventure. Now he could not restrain himself. His thoughts can only be imagined, but as one young man of the day recalled, "A frenzy seized my soul… Piles of gold rose up before me at every step; castles of marble…thousands of slaves bowing to my beck and call; myriads of fair virgins contending with each other for my love—were among the fancies of my fevered imagination. The Rothschilds, Girards, and Astors appeared to me but poor people; in short, I had a very violent attack of the gold fever."[6]

Though most gold seekers in the Midwest joined wagon trains to California, those on the eastern seaboard took sailing ships from New York or Boston. The voyage was a long one, down the coast of South America, around Cape Horn, and north to California. It took from three to six months, and the cheapest ticket for a steerage passenger was $200. Young Boles did not have that kind of money—equivalent to $7,000 today—so he decided to travel overland on horseback. The three-thousand-mile trip was wrought with many dangers: hunger, exposure, dehydration, sickness from cholera-contaminated water, and attacks by Plains Indians. But Charley was undaunted. In the spring of 1849, as soon as the winter snow melted, he and his nineteen-year-old cousin David Boles started west, mounted on old farm plugs.

Almost ten years earlier, Charley's brother William, fifteen years his senior, had moved west and settled in Farmington, a village in the southeastern corner of Iowa. Charley and David headed for Iowa, and it took them several months and nine hundred miles of hard riding before they reached William's home. The brothers had not seen each other in years, and their reunion must have been a happy one. While in Farmington, Charley became seriously ill from malaria, which at that time was prevalent in Iowa and Missouri. He gradually recovered, but by then it was too late in the season to start across the western plains. He and David spent the winter with William, his wife, and their four children. One of Charley's friends later said that in the spring of 1850, the Boles boys "started across the plains for California, and after four months of great hardships arrived there."[7]

They most likely crossed the Sierra Nevada Mountains through Beckwourth Pass, named after the famed African American mountain man Jim Beckwourth. The pass, located northwest of what is now Reno, Nevada, led directly into present-day Butte County in California's Northern Mines. Charley and David reached the gold fields in the summer of 1850. The mining region was teeming with excitement and exploding with growth. When gold had been discovered in 1848, California's population consisted of more than one hundred thousand Native Americans and about fourteen thousand others, most of them Latinos who disliked their former Mexican rulers and called themselves Californios. By the end of 1848, ten thousand men had flocked to the gold fields; a year later, the number was forty thousand. They were overwhelmingly young and male, and had left their mothers, sisters, daughters, and sweethearts back home. Soon after the Boles boys arrived, California became a state, and within two years, its population mushroomed to more than two hundred fifty-five thousand.

The mining region, known variously as the Mother Lode or El Dorado, was enormous, extending across much of the western foothills of the Sierra Nevada Mountains. The Northern Mines were situated north of the Mokelumne River, an area drained by the Cosumnes, American, Bear, Yuba, and Feather Rivers. The Southern Mines constituted the country south of the Mokelumne River, including the Calaveras, Stanislaus, Tuolumne, and Merced Rivers.

Emigrants like the Boles boys, who came overland and crossed the Sierra Nevada, found themselves smack in the middle of the Northern Mines. Tent encampments and small settlements had sprung up quickly at the most promising sites. The towns of Downieville, Nevada City, Grass Valley, Auburn, and Placerville became important centers of mining and commerce. Marysville, at the mouth of the Yuba River and accessible by riverboat from San Francisco, was the principal entrance to the Northern Mines. In the Southern Mines, Mokelumne Hill, Murphys, Columbia, Sonora, and Mariposa were among the principal camps. The San Joaquin River port of Stockton was the main entrance to the Southern Mines. Far to the north was yet another El Dorado, the Trinity River mines, and its main towns of Shasta and Weaverville.

In the gold camps, tents and log cabins clustered precariously on the steep slopes of ravines, creeks, and rivers. Summers were dusty, dry, and hot, with temperatures that often exceeded one hundred degrees. Winters were wet, muddy, and bitterly cold, with snow flurries, ice, and hail. Most of the miners lived and worked together in small companies, frequently made up of their comrades from home. Their lives were primitive and comforts few, with exorbitant prices for scarce supplies and food. The common currency was gold dust, and miners carried their dust in small buckskin pouches called "pokes." With very few women in the Mother Lode, most miners were forced for the first time to perform all domestic chores for themselves: washing, cooking, housekeeping, and sewing patches onto their tattered clothing.

Charley and David began digging and panning in Butte County. They found that hunting for gold was backbreaking, often unrewarding, and frustrating. In the first year of the gold rush, miners readily found small nuggets in rivers and creeks, where they had been washed loose from deep deposits upstream. Those nuggets and flakes were known as placer gold. The forty-niners used tin wash pans to scoop up sand and gravel from streambeds, swirling the water until it left the heavier pieces of gold at the bottom of the pan. Soon they built gold rockers, in which water and sand were mixed in a wood box like a child's cradle. The cradle was rocked back and forth, causing the muddy sand to drain out through holes in one end, thus separating the gold. The next invention was the "Long Tom," a huge rocker, up to fifteen feet long, with water fed into it by a flume at the top. Later, more efficient sluice boxes became popular, and the Boles boys, like all placer miners, used them extensively. Sluice boxes were long wooden troughs with steplike slats, or "riffle" bars. Water ran through the sluice while miners shoveled in sand and river rock; the water poured down the sluice box, leaving small particles of gold that collected on the riffle bars.

One of Charley's boyhood comrades from Jefferson County had also joined the gold rush. He recalled that the Boles boys "engaged in mining with moderate success." Like most gold seekers, they were constantly looking for a better claim or a big strike. In the fall of 1850, Charley and David heard that their New York friend had a mining claim at Union Bar, on the North Fork of the American River. Union Bar was a small camp of tents and rude cabins clustered along the river, occupied by about

HALLMARK PHOTOGRAPHIC COLLECTION.

California gold miners working a Long Tom sluice box in about 1852.

sixty gold seekers. Today the site is buried under Folsom Lake, east of Sacramento. As Charley's friend explained, "They came to our cabin on Union Bar, and finally decided to remain with us, which they did and we all worked together until the fall of 1851, when we started for home." The young men were tired, disillusioned, and homesick, for very few gold miners struck it rich. Most quickly left the placer mines and sought work in more traditional occupations. Perhaps just as significantly, Charley and his comrades found that women were extraordinarily scarce in the mining region, which was then 97 percent male. The Boles boys, their friend from New York, and several companions headed to San Francisco, where they boarded a ship for Panama. After crossing the Isthmus to the Caribbean, they took another ship to New York City and arrived back in Jefferson County in January 1852.[8]

Charley Boles had had his first taste of adventure, and he wanted more. His visit to the family farm didn't last long. As his boyhood chum recalled, "After remaining with his father about three months, Charley again started for California." This time he was accompanied not only by his cousin David Boles, but also by his thirty-year-old brother, Robert, and several comrades. By that time, travel to California had become much faster, with steamships bringing thousands of gold seekers annually to the new El Dorado. The shipping magnate Cornelius Vanderbilt had established a new line of steamers to Nicaragua, with a land crossing to the Pacific. The cost was also much cheaper, less than $100 for a ticket in steerage. Charley and his companions boarded one of Vanderbilt's steamships and departed New York City in early April 1852.

Their voyage took them down the eastern seaboard to the Caribbean, where the ship stopped for coal in Havana, Cuba. From there it continued on to San Juan del Norte (now Greytown), at the mouth of the San Juan River on the coast of Nicaragua. The passengers disembarked and then boarded small steamboats that took them up the San Juan River to Lake Nicaragua. It was a one-hundred-twenty-mile trip on a waterway that sliced through the steamy jungle, with Nicaragua on the north shore and Costa Rica on the south. A US naval officer who visited a few months before Charley's arrival described Vanderbilt's operation. "His steamers are long, narrow propeller affairs, which do not draw more than three feet at most, even when loaded. There are three of them here now. They go up to the falls, which are more than half way up to the lake, and then the passengers get out and walk around to another boat above, which takes them to the opposite side of the lake." After reaching Lake Nicaragua, the riverboats continued thirty-five miles across the lake to its west shore. There the Boles boys and the rest of the passengers disembarked and swung onto mules for the final ten-mile ride to the Pacific Coast port of San Juan del Sur.[9]

Unknown to Charley and his companions, the greatest danger in crossing the Nicaragua jungle came from mosquitos infested with malaria. Probably because he had already survived a bout of malaria in Iowa, Charley may have developed an immunity to it. Neither Robert nor David Boles was so fortunate. Both were apparently bitten by mosquitoes, though it took two weeks for any symptoms to appear. By that time, the Boles boys were aboard the Vanderbilt steamship *Pacific*, bound for California. The *Pacific*, built in New York City less than two years before, was a side-wheeler, 223 feet long. She steamed out of San Juan del Sur on the night of April 29, 1852, crammed with four hundred passengers, among them sixty women and fifty-five children. Most of the women and children were the families of lonely gold hunters who had beseeched their wives to join them in California.

On the trip north to San Francisco, five passengers died, primarily from dysentery and typhoid fever. It was an ominous sign. The *Pacific* finally docked in San Francisco on May 13, just over a month after the Boles boys had left New York. Charley was fascinated with San Francisco, the world's biggest boomtown. When gold was discovered in 1848, it was a tiny village of eight hundred people. By 1850 it had exploded into a roaring port town of twenty-five thousand living in tents and wood-frame houses, with modern, four-story brick buildings erupting everywhere. More than five hundred vessels had been abandoned in San Francisco's harbor; their crews had jumped ship and headed for the Mother Lode country. When Charley's group arrived in 1852, the city had thirty-five thousand residents, many employed by hardware merchants, banks, shippers, express companies, lumber dealers, and the myriad other businesses connected with the gold mines. Dozens of saloons, fandango houses, gambling halls, and bordellos served the transient populace.

By the time of their arrival on the *Pacific*, David Boles was deathly ill from malaria. He struggled for three weeks, but there was little Charley could do. David died less than a month later, on June 9, 1852. After burying him in Yerba Buena cemetery, the grieving Charley and Robert left San Francisco and headed for the mining region. As much as Charley liked the excitement of the burgeoning city, he wanted to make his fortune as a gold miner. But by this time, Robert Boles was suffering badly from malaria. As their New York friend later explained, "Robert lived but a short time after arriving in the mines, making a sad ending to all their hopes of acquiring wealth and then returning home to spend their remaining years in the quiet enjoyment of home life."[10]

Charley spent most of the next year mining in Placer County, northeast of Sacramento. He had little success, and drifted from one mining camp to another. He dug for gold throughout the Mother Lode country, from Tuolumne County in the south to Shasta and Trinity Counties near the Oregon border. He became intimately acquainted with the backwoods, trails, and wagon roads that connected the far-flung tent encampments and boomtowns. This knowledge would prove of great value to him in his later career. But Charley Boles was no gold rush desperado. Those who met him found a well-educated, well-read young man who did not imbibe to excess or frequent gambling halls and brothels.[11]

Drinking, brawling, and whoring were the hallmarks of many a forty-niner. But Charley seemed to be cut from a different cloth. No doubt he carried a Colt revolver and a bowie knife—almost all men did in California, for there was very little law enforcement in the early years of the gold rush. Men—and the fledgling state's few women—knew that they were responsible for their own self-protection. Heavy drinking, coupled with an armed populace, led to astronomical homicide rates, among the highest in the history of peacetime America. In the 1850s, California saw murder rates twenty to thirty times greater than the current national rate. But despite being exposed to such violence, there is no evidence that Charley ever took part. Instead he was nothing but a peaceful and law-abiding citizen.[12]

By 1854, Boles had, once again, failed to strike it rich and he decided to head home. Lacking the money to pay for steamship passage, he crossed the Sierra Nevada on horseback. Charley then made his way east across the high desert, the Rocky Mountains, and the Great Plains, retracing the overland route he had taken west four years earlier. His destination was the homestead of his brother William in Farmington, Iowa, where he planned to stop and rest before continuing on to New York.

By this time, the gold rush had marked Charley Boles indelibly. It made him tough and self-reliant, able to withstand extreme hardship and privation. He could live outdoors for months at a time, withstand searing heat and freezing cold, and subsist on meager food and little water. Though he remained a gentleman, the gold rush left him with a wanderlust, a rootless yearning for distant lands and raw adventure. At the same time, it scarred him with an insatiable desire to get rich quick, without settling in for the long haul. His experiences in the California gold rush would mark and define him for the rest of his days.

3

The Rifleman

Charley Boles rode relentlessly across the Great Plains, an eighteen-hundred-mile journey that led to his brother's homestead in Iowa. In Farmington he settled down for a spell and helped out on William's farm. If he had any idea of drifting on, that was soon discouraged by a slender, dark-haired nineteen-year-old named Mary Elizabeth Johnson. Like Charley, she was a native of New York State. She had come to Iowa in 1856 with the family of her older sister, Louisa, and her husband, Moses Booth. Charley and Mary became romantically involved, and after a whirlwind courtship, she found herself pregnant. That was shocking in an era in which middle-class women did not have premarital sex. Whether Charley ever truly loved her would never be clear, but they married in Farmington on November 27, 1856. By the time the couple exchanged vows, Mary was four months along.[1]

With a wife and unborn child to support, Boles knew he had to stop drifting and earn a proper living. He had only two skills—farming and mining—and there were no gold mines in

Iowa. He and Mary moved two hundred miles north to prime farmland at New Oregon, Iowa, not far from the Minnesota state line. There his new brother-in-law, Moses Booth, had acquired a large farm. New Oregon was situated on the Turkey River, two miles south of present-day Cresco. The village of New Oregon no longer exists, but in 1856, it was a busy farming community of eight hundred people, with stores, a schoolhouse, a church, and even a weekly newspaper. In New Oregon, the Boleses were joined by Charley's youngest brother, Hiram, age twenty-three. Hiram had brought some money with him from New York, and in April 1857, the Boles brothers purchased two parcels of farmland in New Oregon, at a bend in the main road just south of the Turkey River bridge. The price was a bargain by modern standards: $1.25 an acre.

Two weeks later, on April 26, 1857, Mary gave birth to a daughter, Ida Martha Boles. The couple's exuberance over their first child was soon dampened, for Charley and Hiram encountered financial problems in New Oregon. A storekeeper, Almeson Sadler, had extended credit to Hiram, but he was unable to pay. In 1858, Sadler brought a lawsuit against Hiram, obtained a judgment, and seized his parcel of farmland. Charley came to his brother's rescue, and in May 1859, he paid Sadler the amount due, just under $100, and Sadler deeded the farm to Charley. For a struggling farmer like Boles, that was a major expense.[2]

While Hiram stayed behind to work the homestead, Charley and Mary left Iowa and moved to his father's farm at Godfreys Corner, New York. Cross-country travel was becoming easier, and they probably took a wagon or stagecoach to Chicago, and then boarded a train on the newly constructed railroad to New York. On May 17, 1859, at the John Boles homestead, Mary gave birth to their second child, a daughter they named Eva Ardella. But Charley was still overcome with wanderlust, and he despised farming. Mary had a dowry, for Charley soon borrowed $400 from her, which was probably every cent she owned. In the spring of 1860, he returned to Iowa, where he signed a deed transferring ownership of his farmland to Mary in exchange for the $400. Though Boles apparently deeded the farm to her as security for the $400 she loaned him, he had originally acquired the property for less than a quarter of that sum. What Charley did with the money is unknown, but Mary's decision to trust her husband would turn out to be the biggest mistake of her life.[3]

The next year, Boles returned to Godfreys Corner and moved his family to Decatur, Illinois. Decatur, the seat of Macon County, was a busy farming and railroad town of about four thousand people, situated one hundred eighty miles south of Chicago. Why Charley chose to settle in Decatur is unclear, but he probably had friends or relatives there. He and Mary soon managed to buy an eighty-acre farm near Warrensburg, ten miles northeast of Decatur. The family lived in a wood-frame house on the property. The building was divided into two homes, and in the other lived twenty-eight-year-old Reuben Bills and his wife, Linda. The Boles and Bills families soon became close friends. In the Warrensburg house, Mary and Charley welcomed their third daughter, Frances Lillian, whom they called Lillie, on June 6, 1861. But the looming Civil War would soon permanently change Charley's life as a struggling farmer.[4]

When the rebellion erupted that year, Northerners like the Boles family thought the conflict would be short and easily won. Young men rushed to join up, motivated by patriotism and a sense of adventure. Charley, at thirty-one, was older than most of those who volunteered. Because he had a wife and three children to support, he did not enlist. Then the Battle of Bull Run, fought six weeks after the birth of his daughter Lillie, shocked the Northern public. The Union forces were defeated, and it became evident that the nation was in for a long and bloody war. President Abraham Lincoln called for five hundred thousand volunteers, but Charley either resisted any desire to join up or was dissuaded by his wife. He was also decidedly apolitical. Even

The Charley Boles farmhouse near Decatur, Illinois. This photo was taken some years before it was torn down in 1979.

though his father and his uncle Leonard had become natural-ized American citizens, Charley never did so. He later said that although he ascribed to the principles of the antislavery Repub-lican Party, he did not seek US citizenship and did not vote.[5]

During the following year, the war spread, and thousands of young soldiers died. At first for Charley and his neighbors in Macon County, the battles fought in Virginia were far removed from rural Illinois. Then the Western Theater of the Civil War, in which Union forces first drove south into Kentucky and Ten-nessee, brought the conflict closer to home. In the Battle of Shiloh in April 1862, almost twenty-four thousand men were killed, wounded, or missing in action. The Tennessee carnage was stunning, with more casualties than the Revolutionary War, the War of 1812, and the Mexican War combined. Two months later, on July 2, President Lincoln issued a new call for legions of volunteers to serve three-year enlistments.

No longer could Charley Boles resist. Whether he was moti-vated by loyalty to the Union, wanderlust, hatred of farm labor, or an unhappy marriage, he went into Decatur on August 13, 1862, and enlisted as a private in Company B of the 116th Illinois Volunteer Infantry Regiment. As one of his fellow Macon County volunteers explained, "In August of 1862 a wave of patriotism was sweeping all over the loyal North. The magnitude of the war was beginning to be realized, and five hundred thousand additional troops had been called for. Men were enlisting in Decatur and in every village of Macon County." Their headquarters was Camp Macon, in the county fairgrounds just outside of Decatur. The nine-hundred-eighty-man regiment was recruited and led by Colonel Nathan W. Tupper, whose brother had been killed at Shiloh. Charley's company, one of ten in the regiment, consisted of a captain, two lieutenants, five sergeants, eight corporals, and seventy-eight privates. "On August fifteenth we went into camp in the fairgrounds, which, now much enlarged, we know as Fairview Park," recalled one volunteer years later. "There were two other companies in camp when we arrived, and others came in soon after. We began playing soldier at once, with constant drilling, frequent marching, guard mounting, and all the rest of it."[6]

Charley and his fellow volunteers spent the next two months in military training, marching, and marksmanship at Camp Macon. At the time, modern repeating rifles that fired metallic cartridges were new, expensive, and difficult to obtain. And the army's single-shot, muzzle-loading rifles could not be manufactured fast enough to equip the huge numbers of volunteers. As a result, Boles and the other privates were issued old flintlock muskets that had been converted into percussion firearms. Each man also received a belt with a cartridge box and sling, a percussion cap box, a bayonet with a scabbard, a knapsack, a blanket, and a canteen. Their leather cartridge boxes held forty rounds, each one a paper cartridge with a lead minié ball and a charge of gunpowder. Inside the cartridge box were two tin containers that protected the charges from sparks that could make them explode. Charley Boles would learn about that danger firsthand.

Firing the antiquated, single-shot muskets was extremely cumbersome. A rifleman first removed a paper cartridge from the box and tore it open with his teeth. He then poured the gunpowder down the barrel of the rifle and pushed in the minié ball. After pulling out the ramrod, he shoved it down the barrel and packed the charge in tightly. Then he replaced the ramrod, cocked the hammer, pulled out a percussion cap from his cap box, and placed it on the nipple below the hammer. Only then was the musket ready to fire. An experienced rifleman could fire two, perhaps three, shots in one minute, provided that his gun did not jam or misfire due to poor gunpowder or an over-heated barrel. For weeks, Boles and the rest practiced loading and firing until they became reasonably adept.

Charley was older, better read, and better traveled than most of his fellow recruits. Many of them were raw-boned farm boys who had never strayed fifty miles from Macon County. Charley, on the other hand, had traveled across the Western frontier, sailed the Atlantic, the Caribbean, and the Pacific, and seen Cuba, Central America, and California. His age, maturity, and life experience quickly became evident. In later years, veterans of the 116th recalled him fondly. One, Thomas Littleton, described an incident that took place during their initial training at Camp Macon. Littleton, when off duty, left camp for a visit into Decatur. "One night I was in an oyster saloon and a feller named Cook come in there, and this Cook was drunk and he said to me, 'What in hell you doin' here?' and he hit me over the head with a chair. I was knocked against the wall, but I grabbed a cheese knife to defend myself when a feller stepped up to Cook and says, 'You leave that young feller alone.' Now that was my first meeting with Boles."[7]

One of the men who enlisted with Charley as a private in the 116th was German-born Christian Riebsame, who would later be promoted up through the ranks to captain of Company B. Years later he recalled that Boles "was a man of wonderful bravery and courage, and one of the best soldiers that I ever knew." Riebsame added, "He was a short, thick-set man with rather light hair, and very large mustache and goatee. He was of a reticent and solitary disposition and seemed to enjoy his own company, yet he was quite highly respected by his comrades. He was of fair average character with the rest of the regiment and his bravery was undisputed. He was not a drinking man." Another of Charley's comrades said, "He was a good soldier, a good mixer, and everybody seemed to like him." Boles maintained his skill as a collar-and-elbow wrestler, and became known in his regiment as "Wrestling Charley."[8]

During the next few weeks, men continued to join up, and the regiment was mustered into Federal service on September 30, 1862.

JOHN BOESSENECKER COLLECTION.

Charley's friend Sergeant Christian Riebsame. He was later promoted to captain of Company B of the 116th Illinois.

Once the training was complete, they marched into Decatur and boarded Illinois Central Railroad trains for a two-hundred-mile ride south to Cairo, Illinois. Recalled one, "We left Decatur for the seat of war on November the eighth, in thirty-six common box cars, and never thought of grumbling because we were not furnished with passenger coaches." Said another, "The hardest time that I ever saw was when we left Decatur, women and children stood on the side of the streets crying and shaking hands with us." One can only imagine the emotions of Mary Boles as she watched her husband's train slowly disappear down the tracks, not knowing if she would ever see him again.[9]

In Cairo the next day, they boarded steamers and headed down the Mississippi River to Memphis, Tennessee. The steam vessels were commercial side-wheel riverboats converted into troop transports. Charley's friend, Private Reuben Bills, described their journey to Memphis in a letter to his wife, Linda. "We had a right smart trip on the way down. It is the most ill begotten, desolate, heathenish country from Cairo to Memphis that I ever saw. I didn't see one decent looking house on the whole route. We loaded our guns when we started from Cairo, they said we might have to use them shooting at Secesh [Secessionists] on the road." But Boles and his comrades saw no action on their trip south.[10]

When they reached Memphis, which had been captured from Confederate forces four months earlier, Charley and his comrades disembarked at the steamboat landing. The regiment then marched into camp, where they joined General William Tecumseh Sherman's 15th Army Corps that now occupied the city. They made camp in Memphis for a few weeks, then left on November 26 as part of General U. S. Grant's Central Mississippi Campaign, dubbed the "Tallahatchie March." Reuben Bills related their departure from Memphis: "We marched from here with forty thousand men, all in fighting trim, besides two regiments of cavalry and five or six batteries of artillery, and we met General Grant on the road with 75,000 more, so you see we had some punkins of an army. I wish I had the ability to describe an army like ours on the march, but I can't do it. People there at home have no idea of the vastness of [an] army with all the men, horses, mules, and wagons. Our train after we got on the road fairly reached fifteen or twenty miles. The road was literally full and running over with men on foot, on horseback, in wagons." Bills added that "we didn't have much to eat, and what we did have was nothing but mush and stinking bacon, and sometimes we had to use water that the cows in Illinois wouldn't drink."[11]

Because of his rugged life on the Overland Trail and in the California gold fields, Charley was used to such primitive conditions. But still, a rifleman's life was incredibly difficult. As one Illinois volunteer wrote to his brother back home, "Do you think you could even take your rifle and walk from fifteen to twenty miles a day with nothing to eat but a piece of wormy cracker and two or three cups of coffee in twenty-four hours? Say nothing about sleeping on the ground often without anything but a blanket to protect you from the rain. If you should eat nothing but bread and water for two or three days and a little fat pork, take a blanket and lay out in the grass under the apple trees, if it rains all the better, then you can imagine what soldiering is."[12]

Charley and his comrades marched south into Mississippi for seventy-five miles. However, the 116th failed to engage the Confederates and soon returned to their camp in Memphis. By this time, they learned something more than remarkable: one of the riflemen in Company A was actually a woman. She was known only as Kate, and was the paramour of one of the lieutenants in the company. Kate marched with the men and even did picket duty. Private Henry Bear of Company A explained in a letter home, "She goes in men's clothes. She has been with the regiment ever since we left Memphis. She used to be an occupant of the Brick [a brothel]. There is a few in our company that would like to have such rips as her in camp, and on account of them our lieutenant was talked to as was some of the rest. You could hardly tell her from a man. I did not notice her til in camp on the Tallahatchie and then I would not have if someone had not showed her to me." Bear explained that the colonel of the 116th reprimanded Kate's beau. Apparently she left the company in Memphis, for Bear made no further mention of her in his letters home.[13]

In Memphis, Charley and the rest lounged about in camp and waited for orders. On December 16, Reuben Bills wrote to his wife, complaining that it had been raining all day. "Charles Boles and Fred [Fuller] and I laid abed till three o'clock in the afternoon and then it cleared up. We are all thinking of sending our overcoats home before we start. We don't use them so I think we had better send them home than to throw them away. I want you should keep it till I come home for I shall need it then. I don't know how we will send them yet but Charley will know before he writes, so Mrs. Boles can let you know about it."[14]

They did not stay in camp long. On December 20, 1862, the 116th, as part of a force of thirty-two thousand men of the 15th Corps, boarded steamers and headed down the Mississippi River. General Grant's plan was to seize the heavily fortified city of Vicksburg, Mississippi. The Confederate stronghold's artillery, mounted on bluffs above the Mississippi River, prevented Union vessels from passing to the south. Grant understood that control of the Mississippi River was key to winning the Western Theater of the Civil War. He planned to make a diversionary march from the north, hoping to draw the rebels out of Vicksburg to meet him, while Sherman would lead an assault from the west.

Vicksburg was protected by vast swamps to the north and by the Mississippi River on the west. General Sherman's huge force of infantrymen, which included the 116th, was supported by seven US Navy gunboats. The day after Christmas, the steamers proceeded several miles up the Yazoo River, where Boles and the rest disembarked three miles north of Vicksburg. The main natural barrier between them and Vicksburg was the Chickasaw Bayou, a stream that was chest-deep and fifty yards wide. On the other side was a high levee and bluffs mounted with rebel artillery and rifle pits.

The next day, the brigade that included the 116th was held in reserve while other brigades probed and then attacked the Confederate positions. For two days, Sherman's men were repelled by heavy rebel artillery fire. Finally, on December 29, Sherman ordered a bombardment of the rebel defenses followed by a massive assault. The center of the attack across Chickasaw Bayou was led by the 6th Missouri Infantry, supported by the volunteers of the 116th Illinois and the 8th Missouri, and regulars of the 13th US Infantry. Other Union brigades attacked on the left and right flanks. The Federal soldiers met heavy resistance as they advanced. The 6th Missouri managed to wade across Chickasaw Bayou but then got pinned down by heavy fire from the levee above them. Charley and the rest of the 116th moved forward to assist the Missourians, but they came under blistering rebel fire before they could cross the bayou.[15]

Reuben Bills later said that he and Charley took cover behind the trees. As he wrote to his wife, "We were stationed in the woods on one side of a bayou and they [Confederates] were on the other side behind a high levee. I got behind a big gum tree within forty rods of them. I kept my eyes peeled and when they showed their lousy heads above the levee I let them have a load. We soon put a stop to their fire. I suppose you know all about it by this time, for Charley wrote from the battlefield."[16]

Henry Bear of the 116th described what happened next. "When they began to pour in their heavy fire we all fell to our bellies. We was there within eighty yards of them and could not fire for fear of hitting our men so there we all lay from half past twelve til after dark, and it a-raining half of the afternoon and them all the time pouring in a storm of bullets. We would not

Charley's friend, neighbor, and fellow soldier, Reuben Bills. He was killed in the Battle of Arkansas Post in 1863.

dare leave for they would have crossed the levee and taken the 6th prisoners sure. [We] waited til it got dark and then the 8th and 13th regulars commenced firing as hard as they could, for what I know up in the air, and they [the rebels] were afraid to poke their heads above their works. So under our fire the 6th escaped what was feared their certain destruction. Wonderful to relate, the balls did not kill any of us. I can't tell how it came, for they struck all around, right in front of my head and over our backs into the trees and bushes.

"It was a hot place, sure. I don't want to get in any hotter, at least I want, if I do, to have a chance to shoot too. We fell back a hundred yards after dark. It rained like forty all night. We stuck our guns, our bayonets, in the ground and sat down against trees til morning. Early in the morning they commenced firing at us again." By then it became obvious to Boles and the rest that the assault was impossible. The men of the 6th Missouri managed to retreat across the bayou, having lost fifteen killed and sixty-three wounded. Private Bear wrote two days later, "Last night we throwed up breastworks to protect the artillerists from the fire of the sharpshooters. We can see that they were not idle either. They was pounding all night. We can see this morning a heavy cannon right in front of us. They have one of the strongest natural works here in the whole South. With but very little work they can make it almost impregnable. I believe if we had crossed that levee we would never have got back."[17]

The attack proved a failure, and General Sherman ordered his troops back to the riverboats. The Battle of Chickasaw Bayou was the opening salvo of the Vicksburg campaign, a six-month effort to dislodge the Confederates from the fortress city and free up the Mississippi River to Union traffic. Boles became particularly impressed by the use of "Quaker guns," mainly employed by Confederates but sometimes by Union forces. Facetiously named after pacifist Quakers, they were dummy cannons carved out of logs and placed on gun carriages or atop earth fortresses. At a distance they looked like the real thing and frequently prevented enemy assaults. Charley, in his later career as a stage robber, would make his own Quaker guns.

Though Boles and the 116th had their baptism of fire at Chickasaw Bayou, Charley did not cover himself in glory. Years later, his sergeant, Isaac Jennings, recalled that as they prepared to board a steamer to retreat, Private Boles disobeyed a direct order. Sergeant Jennings ordered Charley and another private to act as rear guards. He directed them to face the enemy and provide cover for the company in case the rebels opened fire as they boarded their steamboat. As Jennings later declared, "Boles and another refused to mount guard. Two other men were called and Boles and the other were not reported." Charley's apparent eagerness to seek the safety of the riverboat seems to have outweighed his willingness to protect his comrades.[18]

This would not be the last selfish decision in his life. But in the bloody months to come, Charley Boles would demonstrate dauntless courage under fire, coupled with an unwavering and selfless devotion to duty. Such conflicts in character would both define him and become hallmarks of his life.

4

The Charge of the Light Brigade

On New Year's Day 1863, Charley Boles and the rest of the 116th, fresh from being repulsed at Chickasaw Bayou, boarded riverboats and floated down the Yazoo River to its confluence with the Mississippi. The Illinois volunteers had received orders to attack another Confederate stronghold, Fort Hindman, a huge earthworks at Arkansas Post in southeastern Arkansas. It was constructed on a bluff above the Arkansas River, twenty miles from its junction with the Mississippi. The fort was manned by five thousand rebel soldiers and helped protect Arkansas from Union invasion. From the mouth of the Yazoo River, Charley's regiment steamed one hundred fifty miles up the Mississippi and finally up the Arkansas River to Fort Hindman. They were part of another massive invasion force: thirty-three thousand soldiers transported on fifty steamers and supported by nine iron-clad gunboats.

On Friday evening, January 9, 1863, Boles and thousands of fellow riflemen began climbing out of their boats at a plantation on the Arkansas River, two miles below Fort Hindman. The

Union force was so large it took all night for the troops to dis-
embark. In the morning they began marching up the riverside
toward Fort Hindman. The Union brigades attacked, forcing
the Confederate soldiers from their trenches, and then they surrounded the fort. Charley and his comrades in the 116th were
ordered to prepare for an assault on the east side of the earthen
fortress. They were accompanied by the 113th Illinois and the
6th and 8th Missouri infantry regiments, which formed a brigade
of about four thousand men that was part of General Sherman's
15th Army Corps. The next day, Union gunboats opened a dev-
astating barrage on the fort, the precursor to a massive infantry
attack the following morning. Charley's thoughts can only be
imagined as he and the other volunteers huddled in the dark that
night, not knowing what fate held in store for them at daybreak.

One of the Illinois volunteers, Captain George Clark, gave an
electrifying description of their actions. "Saturday night we lay
on our arms, in line of battle, under fire of the enemy's cannon,
but all the damage they did us was in keeping us awake a part of
the night. All Saturday night the rebels were busy throwing up
breastworks. Sunday morning we moved up still closer to their
works, planted our batteries and perfected our plan of attack—
the enemy all the time being also busy completing their defenses
on the west, which they succeeded in making very strong. About
one o'clock in the afternoon of Sunday the ball was opened by
the gunboats opening a furious cannonading, seconded by the
land batteries, and returned briskly by the enemy. The sight
was truly grand and terrific, and the contest grew warmer and
warmer, and the batteries and the gunboats advancing steadily
all the time.

"After about forty minutes the cannonading was ordered to
cease on our part, and our infantry forces advanced to charge
upon the enemy's works. Then commenced rapid musketry firing, and the bullets rained down upon us in a leaden shower, but
our boys kept on advancing and holding every inch of ground

they gained, and steadily driving the enemy before them and into their line of defenses. And here let me say that the 113th and 116th Illinois, armed as they were with inferior guns, exhibited a bravery and cool courage for which Illinois may well feel proud. There was not a man among them all that for an instant wavered or fell back, and if their old, treacherous guns did not snap the cap the first time, they tried them, again and again, until they would go, and when one of their comrades fell who had a good gun, the ones who had poor guns would exchange pieces and go into them again. Our lines slowly, but surely and steadily, advanced upon the enemy's works, until we fought them at pistol shot, and if one of the Butternuts [Confederates] put up even his hand or head, he was riddled with balls."[1]

Charley and the rest of the 116th were at the forefront of the fighting. Henry Bear later said that they took cover during the forty-minute Union artillery barrage. "Then we made a charge of a half mile to within 150 yards of their breast works. After we got that close we could keep their artillery silent. We got behind logs, stumps, and torn-down chimneys. We were firing all the time. I shot thirty-two rounds. The balls came close to my head but did not hit me."[2]

One rebel shell fired from the fort exploded in the midst of Company B, killing a lieutenant and a private. Shrapnel from the exploding shell slammed into two more men, one of them Sergeant Isaac Jennings. As one of the soldiers recalled, "Jennings was wounded in the leg and a piece of the shell struck his rifle and twisted it into a worthless bit of steel." Jennings later said that the shrapnel "bent the barrel in the form of a letter S, besides shattering the stock and wounding other soldiers in Company B" and that he "fell to the ground covered with blood." Jennings was carried off the field, still clutching his rifle, which he kept for the rest of his life.[3]

Then Charley and the others in Company B crawled forward on their bellies, firing at the rebel defenses. They suffered tremendous casualties. Of the hundred men in the company, only twenty-five came out unscathed. Captain Clark explained, "We shot down all their artillery horses and completely silenced all their cannon by killing off all their cannoneers, and at last, finding their case a hopeless one, they hoisted the white flag all along their lines at just thirty minutes before five o'clock p.m. You ought then to have witnessed the scene and heard the shouts of our boys; shout after shout went up and made the very air tremble. We had fought them in their own stronghold, upon their own chosen ground, they behind strong entrenched positions, we in the open field, and after three and a half hours hard fighting, they were ours. Glory to God in the highest, and all honor and praise to our brave lads who bravely maintained on that day the old stars and stripes."[4]

One of Boles's friends, Private John Bradon, recalled that Charley suffered his first battle wound in the assault. "A spent ball hit him on the left foot and barely made an abrasion of the skin. That never hurt him." Boles's comrade and neighbor Reuben

JOHN BOESSENECKER COLLECTION.

The Battle of Arkansas Post, where Charley and many of his comrades in Company B were wounded in January 1863.

Bills was not so lucky—he died from the Confederate fire. As was customary, his body was not sent back to Decatur; instead he was buried in Little Rock, Arkansas. Because so many men had been killed or wounded, Charley's friend Sergeant Christian Riebsame found himself in charge of Company B.[5]

Following the Battle of Arkansas Post, Boles and the rest boarded the steamboats and returned to Vicksburg. There they undertook their deadliest assignment of the war, one that did not involve fighting rebel soldiers. The Mississippi River made a horseshoe bend opposite Vicksburg. During the previous summer, Union forces had begun digging a canal that would cut across the bend and allow its riverboats to bypass the Confederate guns at Vicksburg. Though more than four thousand soldiers and freed slaves worked on the canal, they were forced to give up due to low water and widespread dysentery and malaria. But in early 1863, General Grant gave orders to finish the canal. On January 22, two of Sherman's divisions, including Boles and the 116th, landed opposite Vicksburg and traded their rifles for shovels.

Charley must have despised this work, for it was no different than shoveling manure and digging irrigation ditches. As Henry Bear explained, "We have to dig by regiment two hours at a time. We come on every six hours. Two brigades works at a time. It is pretty hard work but I would sooner dig than fight if it will accomplish anything." A warm, constant rain fell, and the exhausted men were invaded by swarms of mosquitoes. Said Bear, "I have not been in a tent since we came here." He added that they were within range of the Confederate cannons. "We can see Vicksburg plain from here. They can just about reach us with their solid shot but not, I think, with their shells."[6]

The soggy soldiers fashioned shelters with their blankets or dug muddy caves to sleep in. Many of the men fell ill from malaria and dysentery. Those who died were buried on the levee just yards from the soldiers' camps. By the middle of March, the 116th had managed to dig seventy feet of canal, nine feet deep and seventy feet wide. But just as in the prior summer, the undertaking failed. This time the river flooded and destroyed the canal. Charley's hardy constitution and apparent immunity to malaria served him well. He was lucky, for one hundred soldiers of the 116th, more than one-tenth of the entire regiment, died in less than two months on Grant's Canal. Their shallow graves on the levee were soon washed away by the surging Mississippi.[7]

On March 19, 1863, Boles and those of the 116th who were fit for duty climbed back onto the troop transports. They had been ordered to take part in what became known as the Steele's Bayou expedition. US Naval gunboats and two troop transports had been trapped by six hundred rebel soldiers in Steele's Bayou, north of Vicksburg. The Union plan had been for the boats to bypass the heavy guns of Vicksburg by steaming down Steele's Bayou and then south to the Yazoo River, bringing them just north of the fortress city. But the bayou was so narrow and shallow that as the vessels inched their way through, the Confederates felled trees across the water and trapped the boats.

The 116th, with the 6th and 8th Missouri, a total of eight hundred men, came to the rescue by riverboat transport. They disembarked and marched twenty-two miles across the swamps, repeatedly exchanging fire with rebels who tried to block their way. On March 22, Charley and the rest reached the trapped riverboats on Steele's Bayou. The rebel forces had increased to five thousand, eager to capture the invaluable gunboats. The 116th and the Missouri boys soon received infantry support, led personally by General Sherman, and managed to hold off the Confederates while the Federal vessels withdrew. Though the rescue was successful, the Steele's Bayou expedition, like the Battle of Chickasaw Bayou, proved yet another dismal Union failure in the ongoing effort to capture Vicksburg.[8]

Charley Boles had "smelt powder" and was now a combat veteran. His intelligence and schooling distinguished him from his fellow riflemen. As John Bradon recalled, "When he was in the army he was known as a good penman and a man of considerable education." And Captain Harvey Mahannah of the 116th said, "We knew him as a good fellow and a splendid soldier," adding, "He was perhaps about five feet eight or nine inches in height, not heavy, but a well-knit frame, a man capable of enduring much fatigue." As Mahannah remembered, "During his service with the regiment there was nothing of an unusual nature to make him more prominent than the other members of his company, except that he was apparently better educated than the majority of the men. He was quiet, gentlemanly always, and a good soldier."[9]

Because General Grant's efforts to approach Vicksburg by rivers and bayous had failed, he decided to attack the city from the north and the east. On April 29, Boles and the rest of the 116th returned to Chickasaw Bayou with nine other regiments carried by ten troop transports and supported by eight gunboats. They were to make a diversionary attack on the bluffs north of Vicksburg while Grant's command attacked the fortified town of Grand Gulf, thirty miles downriver from Vicksburg. The Vicksburg bluffs were topped with artillery batteries that commanded the Yazoo River. The 116th was assigned to assault Haynes Bluff, the heavily guarded northernmost set of hills that protected Vicksburg. The transports steamed up the Yazoo River to Chickasaw Bayou, where the men disembarked below Haynes Bluff and its adjacent hill, Snyder's Bluff.[10]

As one of the Illinois volunteers noted in his diary, "After an hour of slow steaming we came in sight of Snyder's Bluff, the gunboats *Choctaw, DeKalb, Black Hawk* and *Tyler* took their position in the bend. The transports remaining on the right bank of the river. The first two mentioned boats commenced feeling for the batteries on the hill with an occasional response. We had nothing to do, and the plantation we landed by was well stocked with cattle, though deserted. Companies were sent out to bring in the cattle and load them aboard our boat. Half of the cattle escaped before they came near our boat and the balance, about eighteen head, were got to the gang planks and were surrounded entirely by bayonets, but they were afraid to go aboard, and being pricked considerably, the largest one made a dash into the crowd and cleared the way. The balance followed, and it was a comical sight. Four or five were shot and five or six got on the steamer alive."[11]

That night Boles and his comrades had fresh beef for dinner, a welcome relief from their usual fare of coffee, hardtack, and bacon. They made camp for the night, and at daybreak began the assault. While Charley and the rest hugged the ground, the gunboats opened a heavy barrage on the bluffs. Rebel cannons returned the fire, hitting one of the ironclads, the *Choctaw*, more than fifty times. At three in the afternoon, the 116th advanced on Haynes Bluff. Because the attack was a mere diversion, they did not make an all-out infantry assault, but instead took cover and drew the rebels' fire. The feint worked, for they managed to keep the Confederates busy for two days while Grant's forces attacked and captured Grand Gulf. The town's rebel defenders retreated to Vicksburg.[12]

Then Boles marched with the 116th back to the troop transports, and the boats slipped down the Yazoo to its confluence with the Mississippi. The volunteers were sent into camp at Milliken's Bend, the Union Army headquarters located twenty miles upriver from Vicksburg. On May 7, after resting for a few days, they started on a long journey that skirted Vicksburg to the south. The 116th and other regiments first marched through the swamps for four days, then crossed the Mississippi by boats near Grand Gulf. From there they trudged northeast fifty miles toward Raymond, Mississippi. Because their rations were so meager, the soldiers frequently foraged for food and supplies. In other words, they stole from Southern civilians. One of the Illinois volunteers said that while stopping in the settlement of

Cayuga, "we ransacked a formerly ransacked country store, but found nothing except a little hardware." They arrived in Raymond on May 14, two days after Union forces had captured the town after a sharp fight. Now General Grant, after seizing the state capital at Jackson, began a final assault on Vicksburg.[13]

The 116th joined Grant's columns, and on the morning of May 16, 1863, they approached Champion Hill, twelve miles northwest of Raymond, on the road that led to Vicksburg. Charley and his regiment had marched a huge southern loop, from a starting point twenty miles northwest of Vicksburg to Champion Hill, twenty-two miles east of the fortified city. They were now part of a force of thirty-two thousand men that converged in three columns on Champion Hill, which was defended by an army of twenty-three thousand Confederates from Vicksburg. If the Federals could defeat the rebels at Champion Hill, they would be able to advance on Vicksburg from the east.

One of the volunteers described what happened. "We marched four miles and encountered the enemy in force at Champion Hill. Our regiment ran about a mile under a burning sun to get into position, and threw out skirmishers to protect the right flank of the army. We quickly got into the thickest of the fight and opened fire. The battle soon raged with terrific fury. As reinforcements came up on both sides, the rapid volleys of musketry soon blended into one continual roar, only interrupted by the bursting of shells and the constant discharges of artillery from both armies. The enemy had concentrated his force on our right, and was making desperate efforts to drive us back; but [our] division was not to be moved. The rebels moved up under the brow of a hill, evidently intending to make a desperate effort to take one of our batteries. I could not help but admire the fine style they moved up, and the splendid colors they carried. There was a short pause, and then came the order to charge.

"The brigade immediately moved forward, under a deadly shower of grape and musketry, and opened a terrific fire upon the stubborn foe. At first, he stood his ground manfully, but finally wavered and broke. Our brigade here captured about a thousand prisoners, and several pieces of artillery. It was a horrid sight to see the battlefield after the fight was over, covered with the dead and wounded of both armies. We pursued the enemy about two miles and bivouacked almost worn out by the heat and fatigues of the day. How little the folks at home, seated by their comfortable hearthstones, realize of the heart-sickening horrors of this unnatural war!"[14]

Charley Boles was in the thick of the fighting. A fellow soldier vividly explained the action. "Our division reached Champion Hill about two p.m., and filed into a field on the right of the road. We were drawn up in a line facing the woods through which ran the road we had just left. It was by this road the rebels came out of Vicksburg to whip us. We had orders to lie down. The command was obeyed with alacrity, for bullets were already whizzing over our heads. I never hugged Dixie's soil as close as I have to-day. We crowded together as tight as we could, fairly plowing our faces into the ground. Occasionally a ball would pick its man in spite of precaution, and he would have to slip to the rear. Soon we got orders to rise up, and in an instant every man was on his feet. If the former order was well obeyed, the latter was equally so.

"The enemy charged out of the woods in front of us in a solid line, and as they were climbing the fence between us, which separated the open field from the timber, [a] battery, stationed in our front, opened on them with grape and canister, and completely annihilated men and fence and forced the enemy to fall back. Such terrible execution by a battery I never saw. It seemed as if every shell burst just as it reached the fence, and rails and rebs flew into the air together. They, finding our center too strong, renewed their charge on our left, and succeeded in driving it a short distance, but their success was only for a moment, for our boys rallied, and with reinforcements drove them in turn.

We now charged into the woods and drove them a little ways, and as we charged over the spot so lately occupied by the foe, we saw the destruction caused by our battery, the ground being covered thickly with rebel grey. When we reached the woods we were exposed to a galling fire, and were at one time nearly surrounded but we fought there hard until our ammunition was exhausted, when we fixed bayonets and prepared to hold our ground. A fresh supply of ammunition soon came up, when we felt all was well with us again. Meanwhile the right of our line succeeded in getting around to their left, when the enemy retreated towards Vicksburg, lest they should be cut off."[15]

The Union victory at Champion Hill proved to be pivotal in the Vicksburg Campaign. The rebels retreated fourteen miles to Big Black River Bridge, where they prepared to make a desperate stand in defense of Vicksburg. They took up strong positions on the high ground above the west bank of the Big Black River, then set fire to the bridge to keep Union forces from crossing it. But their efforts were in vain. The next day, May 17, Federal artillery rained havoc on the rebels, who fell back following a concerted charge by the Union troops. In two hours of fighting, the Confederates lost about fifty men killed and more than one thousand seven hundred captured. They retreated to the earth fortifications that surrounded Vicksburg. In the Battle of Big Black River Bridge, Boles and his comrades came under fire, but their regiment lost no men.[16]

The Union columns advanced on Vicksburg, which was now completely surrounded. On May 19, in the hope of avoiding a lengthy siege, Grant quickly ordered three brigades to attack the Stockade Redan, located on the northeast perimeter of Vicksburg. The Stockade Redan was an earth and log fortress perched on a hill and protected by a deep ravine choked with felled timber, the branches sharpened like giant barbed wire. Its walls were seventeen feet high, with a deep ditch around the base. The 116th and three other regiments—the 6th Missouri, a detachment from the 113th Illinois, and a battalion of the 13th US Infantry—made up one of the brigades assigned to attack the earthworks. Because so many men had been lost to bullets and illness, the four regiments had less than half their strength, some only a quarter.[17]

Following an intense bombardment of the Stockade Redan, Boles and the rest lined up behind the crest of a ridge about three hundred yards from its north face. At two o'clock, Charley and his fellow infantrymen charged up a hill overlooking the ravine, where they came under a heavy rebel fusillade. The 8th Missouri provided covering fire while the rest of the Union riflemen rushed down into the gulch. Boles found that the Confederates had filled the ravine with booby traps. They had strung telegraph wire between the tree limbs and hidden sharpened stakes under the grass. As the Union advance slowed to a crawl and men struggled to get through the ravine, the Confederates poured down a murderous barrage from the Stockade Redan. Henry Bear described the slaughter. "Sixty or seventy was hit in the regiment out of 240. Some of the boys went clear to the breast works but could not get over. It was awful. I don't want to see another such a time. It was fallen timber for five hundred yards. I fell five times going down the first hill on account of my lame leg catching in the brush. I don't see how any escaped at all for the bullets were flying thick as hail."[18]

Riflemen from the 116th managed to get close to the fortress walls, but by nightfall so many soldiers had been shot they had to withdraw. The charge was a complete failure. The Union forces lost 157 killed and 777 wounded. The 116th alone lost almost a third of its men—six killed and sixty-four wounded. But General Grant was undeterred. Three days later he ordered a four-hour bombardment of Vicksburg, followed by a mass assault on the numerous earth fortifications along a three-mile front on the eastern border of the city. Once again Charley and the 116th were detailed to help attack the Stockade Redan.

Their brigade's charge began at ten that morning, May 22, led by one hundred fifty volunteers—all unmarried men—who carried scaling ladders and long boards. The men rushed forward through open ground and, under heavy fire, crossed the ravine and began throwing together a rude bridge over the ditch at the base of the wall. Soon half of them were dead or wounded, sprawled in bloody heaps. The rest of the brigade followed as bullets, grapeshot, and canisters ripped into their ranks.[19]

An Illinois artilleryman offered a firsthand account of the deadly assault. "As the men came in plain sight, led by their officers, swords in hand and men following with boards to cross the trench, we saw the whole charge. And though the bullets were flying thick overhead, we watched the party until we saw the flag planted on this side of the fort in front of the port embrasure and some five or six men lying close against the fort over the ditch. The rebels, not daring to expose themselves enough to fire at the men on their works, our troops kept up a brisk fire from the hill immediately in front of their works.

"We all admired the bravery of the men that lay by near the flag, exposed as they were to the shots of the enemy and our men too. After the storming party had reached its place and a regiment had got safely behind the brow of the hill next to their works, we had to fire pretty high and slow, our ammunition being nearly exhausted. We had to reserve our fire for such times as when a rebel regiment would start to cross the road over the hill in plain sight, then we opened fire on them along the whole line with artillery for the purpose of keeping them down and preventing them from firing on our men. Regiment after regiment crossed in this manner, but none but the storming party were on the enemy's works and none crossed over to them...

"At about 3 p.m. another storming party was to go in. We did not look up to watch it, soon after saw another flag on the works and nearly all of the men that were there dropped into the trench or were so wounded as to be unable to move."[20]

Charley Boles took part in the assault on the Stockade Redan at Vicksburg, May 19, 1863.

By this time, Charley's brigade was joined by another led by General Thomas Ransom. The fighting was so intense that many of the officers, including three colonels, were killed or wounded. The attack stalled. Then, in one of the most dramatic incidents of the Vicksburg Campaign, General Ransom ran through a hail of lead to the front of the two brigades. He seized the colors and yelled, "Forward, men! We must and will go into that fort! Who will follow me?"

Boles and the rest, screaming like demons, followed him across the ravine, but they were unable to breach the high walls of the Stockade Redan. After half an hour of desperate fighting, General Ransom cried, "Men of the second brigade, we cannot maintain this position. You must retire to the cover of that ravine, one regiment at a time, in order!"

He ordered one regiment to stay behind and provide cover fire, then coolly directed the other regiments to withdraw. "Move slowly," Ransom shouted. "The first man who runs or goes beyond the ravine shall be shot on the spot. I will stand here, and see how you do it."

At that, Charley and the rest retreated, first through the ravine and then across a quarter mile of open ground to safety. Once again, the assault had been a failure all along the Union lines, leaving heavy casualties: 502 dead, 2,550 wounded, and 147 missing in action. Because the 116th and the other regiments had been so depleted, their actions so gallant, and their losses so great, one early writer dubbed the assault on the Stockade Redan "The Charge of the Light Brigade."[21]

Charley Boles, in near-constant combat, had proved that he had plenty of what his fellow soldiers called "sand." Declared his friend Christian Riebsame, "He was a man of wonderful nerve and courage, and in every fight in which the company participated he was always at the front."[22]

5

Wounds of War

Charley Boles had spent most of his adult life behind a shovel, planting crops and digging for gold. As much as he despised manual labor, now his life depended on it, for the siege of Vicksburg had begun. The failure of the assaults of May 19 and 22, 1863, prompted General Grant to reduce his losses by blockading the city and attempting to starve the rebels out. He ordered his men to dig an extensive network of trenches surrounding Vicksburg. Boles and the rest of the 116th excavated a series of eight-foot-wide rifle pits below the Stockade Redan, all the while dodging Confederate sniper and artillery fire. Once again, Charley found himself reduced to shoveling dirt, but it was surely preferable to making suicide charges.

His comrades found him diligent, reliable, and a gentleman always. As one private recalled, "We slept in the same tent for many months. Boles was a good soldier. He was brave, hardy, could endure long marches, had few bad habits and was generally liked. He did not use tobacco [and] never was profane." Dr. Joseph Hostetler, the regimental surgeon for the 116th, knew

him well, and years later declared, "A finer soldier than Charley
Boles never carried a gun." Hostetler said that he remembered
Boles "particularly by the rhymes he used to write. Boles was
a favorite in the army from his gentlemanly demeanor and affable, social ways."[1]

Charley and many of his fellow volunteers admired General Grant, whom they found humble and unassuming. During
the siege, their commander made regular visits to the trenches.
"General Grant came along the line last night," one of the Illinois
infantrymen wrote in a letter home. "He had on his old clothes
and was alone. He sat down on the ground and talked with the
boys with less reserve than many a little puppy of a lieutenant."[2]

The siege of Vicksburg lasted five weeks and featured heavy
Union shelling of the city. It also featured good-natured and
sometimes humorous exchanges between the opposing soldiers
from their respective rifle pits. On the night of June 20, following a heavy but ineffective Union bombardment of Vicksburg,
soldiers of the 116th began talking with the Confederates in
their trenches sixty yards distant. One of the Illinois volunteers
called out, "Hallo! I say, rebs!"

"Hallo yourself," came the Confederate reply.

"How do you make it over there?"

"Oh, bully. How do you get along?"

"Fine, very fine," the Illinois man responded. Referring to the
bombardment, he asked, "Where have you been all forenoon?"

"We crawled into our holes."

"And pulled the holes in after you, did you not, to keep our
shells out?"

"Some of us did. I say, Yank, your artillery men were all
drunk this morning, were they not?"

"No doubt some of them were, for we have plenty of whiskey. Do you get any?"

"No, that is played out long ago," the rebel replied. "If you
will save your three drams tomorrow and fetch them to the

rifle pits, I will come half way and give you twenty dollars in greenbacks for it."

"No doubt you would, but you know your supplies are cut off, and I dare not do it."[3]

Despite the amiable chatter, the riflemen of the 116th did not hesitate to fire at any rebel cap that appeared above the trenches. On June 27, Confederate General Martin Green became frustrated that his men were increasingly afraid to rise up and return the Union fire. Green shouted to his men, "A bullet has not been molded that will kill me!"

He then seized a musket and peered over the breastworks toward the Federals. Instantly a sharpshooter from the 116th fired a single shot, striking General Green in the neck and killing him. He was one of two Confederate generals slain during the siege of Vicksburg.[4]

By this time Charley's innate leadership qualities had not gone unnoticed, and four days later, on July 1, 1863, he received promotion to first sergeant of Company B. "By bravery upon the field of battle and efficiency in every way as a soldier, he was promoted to a sergeancy," Christian Riebsame later said. "In Sherman's army, in which the 116th was during the war, promotions were not made except upon merit, and no one disputed the fact that Boles deserved the promotion that he received."[5]

Just three days afterward, the thirty thousand Confederates in Vicksburg surrendered. The Fourth of July victory turned out to be one of the most important of the war, for it split the South in two and dealt a major blow to the Confederacy. But Boles and the 116th had no time to celebrate. The following day, they started on a march eastward as part of a huge force under General Sherman. A rebel army of thirty thousand was approaching Vicksburg from the rear, and Charley surely believed that yet another bloody battle awaited them. But when faced with Sherman's fifty thousand men, the Confederates retreated and escaped.[6]

On July 25, following an unsuccessful pursuit of the rebel army, the 116th went into camp on a plantation near the Big Black River battlefield site. They were joined by the rest of General Sherman's 15th Army Corps, and the spot became known as Camp Sherman. Here Boles and his comrades got two months of much-needed rest. Then, in late September, word arrived of the stunning Union defeat in the Battle of Chickamauga, more than four hundred miles northeast. Following that battle, the Federal troops retreated fifteen miles north to Chattanooga, Tennessee, where they were besieged by the Confederate army. Now Charley and his fellow volunteers received new and urgent marching orders. Sherman's 15th Army Corps, consisting of four divisions numbering twenty thousand men, including the 116th, were to relieve the beleaguered Union forces at Chattanooga. On September 27, they began hiking into Vicksburg, where they boarded steamboats up the Mississippi to Memphis. From there, Boles and the rest proceeded east by railroad to Corinth, Mississippi, where they disembarked and marched two hundred twenty miles further east to Chattanooga.

Because Sherman's army was so large, and the railroad tracks so war-damaged, it took almost two months for the soldiers to reach Chattanooga. Then, at 1:00 a.m. on November 24, 1863, Charley's regiment, with their old companions from the 6th Missouri, made a daring nighttime raid down the Tennessee River. They manned the muffled oars of 116 pontoon boats and silently rowed three thousand troops to the mouth of South Chickamauga Creek, just north of Chattanooga. "The rebels had three batteries planted along the riverside in full view of us," one of Charley's comrades, Private William Craig, recalled. "We crawled to our boats and started down the river four miles, then started across on the rebel side. We passed all of the batteries and they never knew it. They could have killed every one of us if they had known it."[7]

Boles and the rest captured the rebel pickets at Chickamauga

Creek without firing a shot. Then they used the pontoon boats to erect a fourteen-hundred-foot-long bridge across the Tennessee River, thus enabling the Union forces to cross the river into Chattanooga. Sherman's infantry and artillery crossed the bridge in time to take part in the Battle of Missionary Ridge. Charley's friend, Captain Harvey Mahannah, later told a journalist that their raid down the Tennessee River "was the most thrilling experience he had during the war."[8]

From the river, Boles and his comrades advanced toward the left flank of Missionary Ridge, a four-mile-long promontory that overlooked Chattanooga and was controlled by the Confederates. At the base of the ridge, the 116th engaged in a heavy skirmish with the rebels, then dug in for the night. The next morning, November 25, a massive Union assault of fifty-six thousand men began along the high ridge that was defended by forty-four thousand rebels and their artillery. The 116th helped attack Tunnel Hill, at the far left, or northern, tip of Missionary Ridge. The hill was topped by cannons and a railroad tunnel filled with rebel troops. One of the volunteers described their charge. "As we crossed the field the rebels swept the field with the batteries, and solid shot, grape, and shell flew about us in a most unbecoming manner over our heads, and but few in the ranks were struck. However, their shells fell very close to our heads, just missing us. One exploded so near us that I felt the heat of it very plainly."[9]

Sherman's assault on Tunnel Hill quickly proved both imprudent and ill planned. "The bugle sounded the 'charge' and with a whoop and a cheer our men sprang forward, receiving a terrible fire from the enemy, of both infantry and artillery as they passed through and beyond," one of the Illinois soldiers remembered. "Dropping behind trees, stumps, rocks, or anything that would shield [us] from the enemy's fire, there waited the promised support, which never came... The enemy outnumbering us two to one, and being behind strong works, and having two batteries of artillery bearing on the line of approach, the attempt to take the hill was abandoned." Recalled another, "The rebs made a bulge on our line and came swarming out of the tunnel and going around in rear of our line. The order was then given for the boys to 'save themselves and get out of here.' The boys threw their blankets, haversacks, and canteens and ran for dear life, the rebs firing at them as they ran and calling for them to halt, stop, and surrender."[10]

Charley and the rest of his regiment retreated to the Tennessee River and avoided capture. Sherman's attack on Tunnel Hill was a failure, resulting in almost two thousand casualties. Nonetheless, the Federal divisions fighting just south of them routed the Confederates from Missionary Ridge and lifted the siege of Chattanooga. It was one of the great Union triumphs of the Civil War. But once again, the 116th had no time to celebrate, for General Grant ordered Sherman and his 15th Corps to relieve a besieged Union force at Knoxville, Tennessee. Boles

JOHN BOESSENECKER COLLECTION.

Charley Boles and his regiment fought in the Battle of Missionary Ridge, November 25, 1863.

and his fellow riflemen, with meager supplies, promptly started a hundred-mile march northeast in freezing weather.

Years later, Christian Riebsame vividly recalled their trip. "Pen and pencil cannot portray the sufferings of the 15th Corps on that memorable campaign, where an ear of horse corn or a piece of moulded hardtack after a forced march constituted the day's meal. You would build a fire at night, hugging it closely, only to freeze the other side of you, then turn and thaw this side out. And when utterly exhausted you laid down to alleged rest, only to wake up after a fitful sleep to discover that you edged up to the embers too close and that your scant clothes were partly consumed."[11]

The rebels, learning of Sherman's approach, abandoned Knoxville and retreated north toward Virginia. The 116th then marched back to Chattanooga with the 15th Corps, where they boarded railroad boxcars and continued another seventy miles southwest to Larkinsville, Alabama. On January 9, 1864, they set up canvas tents on an abandoned plantation and went into winter quarters. There Charley's record of courage and leadership brought him another promotion. On January 28, he received a battlefield commission as second lieutenant of Company B. "He was promoted to be second lieutenant," explained his chum John Bradon, "but the company was so small that only one lieutenant was allowed." By this time the 116th, which once numbered one thousand men, had been reduced by casualties and disease to only 382. As a result, Boles was never mustered in as a lieutenant and instead continued to serve as sergeant.[12]

In the winter camp, Charley spent much of his spare time writing letters home. Unfortunately, none of those letters survived. He also loved playing card games with the men of his regiment. As Private Bradon said, "He was a great gambler and generally successful. He talked a great deal of his family and was apparently very fond of his wife and children." Captain Mahannah recalled, "He was especially fond of playing poker." Captain Riebsame agreed. "He played a good hand at poker and was inclined to sporting [gambling]." And another of the privates explained, "He had the reputation for being the best poker player in the regiment."[13]

Charley's addiction to gambling would become one of the greatest defects in his character. William Craig could have been thinking of Boles when he wrote a letter home. "The boys was paid off," he said. "They was paid nearly two hundred dollars and the most of them has gambled it all away." In another letter, Craig complained to his wife, "This rebellion will be the ruination of thousands of men. They have become hardened to everything... It is so surprising to see men when they draw their money sit right down and lose it all when I know that they have families at their homes that needs all that they can get but it is not the case with me."[14]

The Union soldiers were so poorly supplied that they often made foraging expeditions to get food. Late in January, they undertook a hunt for supplies, as Private Craig explained soon after. "We just have come off of another little trip of 125 [miles]. We was gone fifteen days. We had a very pretty little march. We got out all the forage that we wanted. There had never been no soldiers in that part of the country but rebels, so we took a great many prisoners, and bandards [contrabands, or escaped slaves] came to us starved and naked. It is hard to see the suffering of the southern people. Both men and women and children. Thousands of them must starve. I don't see any other remedy for them. The Union troops have taken everything that is edible so they can't help but suffer."[15]

Foraging was allowed by Federal law, and it had two military objectives. One was that it kept the Union soldiers fed, for often they had so little food, they had to steal to eat. Second, and just as important, it was a way to destroy rebel morale and weaken the Confederacy. Yet for Charley Boles, foraging—or stealing—would, like his penchant for gambling, become ingrained in his character.

The 116th remained in winter camp through the spring. In April, Charley was granted a furlough. He boarded a train for Decatur, where he had a happy reunion with Mary and the children. Their daughter Ida was seven, Eva almost five, and Frances almost three. He had not seen them in eighteen months, and they must have been delighted by his visit. He learned that Mary volunteered one to two days a week for the war effort, making clothing for the troops and preparing food for hospitalized soldiers. While Charley was home for a few weeks, he and Mary conceived their fourth child, a boy whom they would christen Arian. But all too soon, he had to return to his regiment in Larkinsville, Alabama. For General Sherman's invasion of Georgia was already underway.[16]

On May 2, 1864, Boles and the 116th, as part of the 15th Corps, started a long march to Georgia. First they walked north for several days until they reached the Tennessee line, near Chattanooga. There they joined an enormous Federal force and started south. Sherman's plan was to attack the Confederate army at Dalton, Georgia, which blocked the main route to Atlanta. The rebels quickly retreated sixteen miles south to the town of Resaca, where they spent two days digging rifle pits and earthworks. On May 8, the 116th and the rest of the 15th Corps passed through Snake Creek Gap in the mountains northwest of Resaca. Sherman's strategy was to circle around Resaca and attack the rebels behind their front lines.

That night, one of the Illinois volunteers noted in his diary, "We traveled today over a better country than I have seen for five months. The Yanks were never seen here before. All the negroes and stock have been run off. A little shooting commenced in the front today, and we passed a deserted signal station and picket post. Saw some rebs on a mountain south of us just before we went into camp."[17]

The next morning, as Charley and the rest moved out of Snake Creek Gap, a battle broke out with Confederate cavalry that had been sent forward to slow their advance. The Union forces prevailed, and the rebel cavalrymen fell back to the earthwork defenses at Resaca. There, sixty thousand Confederates were spread along four miles of battlefront. They faced a much larger Union Army of almost one hundred thousand. On May 14, two Union columns attacked Resaca from the north, while the 15th Corps assailed the rebels' right flank. Boles and the 116th, together with several regiments, joined together to assault a heavily defended ridge known as Bald Hill, just west of Resaca. One of the infantrymen who was just in advance of the 116th recalled, "The air was a hissing, shrieking, seething inferno of shot and shell. It seemed for a space of two hours and a half that no living thing could survive that horrible carnival." After desperate fighting, the rebels started to pull back, and the Federal soldiers shouted to the men behind them, "Come on! The Johnnies are retreating!"

Charley and the 116th were behind the other regiments rushing up the hill. They ran forward to support the attack. "We called out to them to load, and as they came scrambling up the hill, every one of them had managed, somehow, to shove a load into his gun," the infantryman explained. "When they arrived at the top of the hill they ran right into the enemy, and it was a good thing that they had their guns loaded. They poured a deadly fire into the enemy." Within moments, the 116th and the rest of its brigade reached the top of the hill, firing as fast as they could. "That settled the question for the Johnnies. They did retreat in earnest, and that was the last we saw of them in close proximity that day. They kept up desultory firing til long into the night, but that finally ceased."[18]

After two days of attacks and counterattacks, in which the Confederates stubbornly held off the Yankees, the rebels finally abandoned the battlefield and withdrew to the south. The Battle

JOHN BOESSENECKER COLLECTION.

The Battle of Resaca, in which Charley Boles took part. Eleven days later he was badly wounded at Dallas, Georgia.

of Resaca resulted in more than four thousand Union dead and wounded, and almost three thousand casualties on the Confederate side. As the first major engagement of the Atlanta campaign, it demonstrated that the outnumbered Southern army could slow, but not stop, the invasion of Georgia.

From Resaca, the 116th marched south with the 15th Army Corps toward Atlanta. They moved slowly, taking ten days to walk fifty miles. The huge Union force was checked by rebel resistance and skirmishes. The Confederates then retreated to the small town of Dallas, thirty miles northwest of Atlanta. There forty thousand rebels dug in and awaited a massive Union onslaught. Once again, the 116th was ordered to help attack the Confederate right flank. On May 26, the 15th Corps, accompanied by General Sherman, approached the outskirts of Dallas. They advanced into a large field in front of thick woods, separated by a long fence. Not a rebel was in sight, so Sherman stopped to confer with four of his generals and their staffs. Suddenly a Confederate soldier, concealed behind the fence, opened fire with his pistol, but missed. He then ran for the timber.[19]

Charley and the rest of the 116th started in pursuit, moving into the forest as a scouting party. They quickly found the woods alive with rebel soldiers. A blistering fight erupted as Boles and the others exchanged fire with the rebels concealed behind trees. A heavy rifle ball slammed into Charley's abdomen near the left hip, knocking him to the ground. He had been wounded in action a second time, and much more seriously. "He came very near being killed at Dallas," recalled his comrade Private Bradon. "A ball that day struck Boles' cartridge box which had just been filled. It went through the box, through his belt, pants and shirt, inflicting a flesh wound to the left of the navel. This left a scar which I suppose remains with him still." But Charley had much more than a flesh wound, for the rebel bullet tore into his abdomen. His comrades carried him off and took him to a field hospital, where doctors removed the slug. He spent more than three months in recovery. While Boles was laid up in the hospital, the 116th went on to take part in the bloody battles of Big Shanty, Kennesaw Mountain, Ezra Church, Atlanta, and Jonesborough.[20]

Charley finally returned to his regiment in Atlanta on September 5, 1864. Three days earlier, following a five-week siege, the city had fallen to Federal troops in one of the most important Union victories of the Civil War. The 116th remained in camp in Atlanta for more than two months. Then, on November 15, 1864, after the Federal soldiers burned many of the city's strategic buildings and commercial properties, they started east on Sherman's historic March to the Sea. Sherman's army consisted of sixty thousand infantry and cavalry, with two thousand five hundred supply wagons and six hundred ambulances for the wounded. His plan was to cut the Confederacy in half, destroy railroads, bridges, mills, cotton gins, and agriculture, and deliver a fatal wound to Southern morale. Sherman's men would move fast, without waiting for supply trains, and live off the land. Foragers, known as bummers, would appropriate anything they needed from the civilian populace: food, drink, feed, horses, cattle, and other livestock.

On their march through Georgia, Boles and the 116th met mostly light resistance. A week after leaving Atlanta, they trooped into the town of Gordon, where they began tearing up the tracks of the Georgia Central Railroad. Then they continued east twenty-five miles, reaching Ball's Ferry on the Oconee River on November 25. The rebels had dug in across the river to keep the ferry from falling into union hands. Charley, with the 116th and two other regiments, attacked the Confederates and forced them to retreat. But such combat was rare, for most of the soldiers' time was spent destroying railroads, burning buildings, and foraging for food, supplies, and feed for the army horses.[21]

"Each brigade foraging party consisted of about fifty men, well organized and officered," explained one of the men in the 116th. "These parties would be dispatched before daylight, with a knowledge of the intended route and the place of camping. They would proceed on foot five or six miles from the route, visiting every farm and plantation within range. Often a squad would procure a family carriage or wagon, load it with bacon, meal, sweet potatoes, poultry—in fact, anything good to eat. With this they would regain the main road, usually in advance of the train. When the latter came up, the supplies gathered would be delivered by each party to its brigade commissary, who took them in charge, and from time to time issued them to the men in the regular way. The foragers always carried their muskets ready for use in an instant, if necessity should arise. Now and then the foragers stirred up a small body of rebel cavalry, but as a rule they met no serious resistance."[22]

But near the end of Sherman's march, Private Craig gave a far less sanitized account of their foraging expeditions. "The country that we have traveled over in the last eight months is destroyed totally. Sherman told us to burn everything and you may depend there was nothing left. Neither stock of any kind that we could eat we shot down and left them laying. Houses we burned and fencing and large cotton factories we burned. We burned the houses, and the women and children standing outside crying. Neither clothes nor nothing to eat."[23]

On December 10, Sherman's army approached Savannah on the Georgia coast. US Naval ships were offshore with much needed food and supplies, but the route was blocked by Fort McAllister, an earthworks defended by two hundred thirty rebel troops and twenty-two heavy cannons. The fort was situated near the mouth of the Ogeechee River, ten miles south of Savannah. Three days later, Charley and his comrades marched fifteen miles from their position in the rear and then assembled at a point two miles from Fort McAllister. At the same time, Union scouting parties captured the rebel pickets and removed many "ground torpedoes," or land mines, from the approaches to the fort. The 116th Illinois and eight other regiments moved up to a position five hundred yards from Fort McAllister.

The nine regiments were so depleted that they numbered only about three thousand men, about one-third of full strength. But that weakness was compensated by modern armament.

Many soldiers in Charley's regiment no longer carried the antiquated cap-and-ball muskets that they had been issued back in Decatur. Instead they now toted newly invented arms that fired metallic cartridges: the seven-shot Spencer repeater and the sixteen-shot, lever-action Henry rifle, precursor to the Winchester. One Union soldier boasted that their Spencer rifles were "good for any two rebs in Dixie."

Federal skirmishers advanced, took up positions behind logs and trees, and laid down a heavy fire on Fort McAllister. They shot at any Confederate cannoneers who dared peer over the fort's parapets to aim their guns. Then, at exactly 4:45 p.m., bugles blared, and Boles and his fellow riflemen charged forward on foot. Each soldier was spaced apart so as to reduce casualties from shot and shell. Under heavy rebel fire, they climbed through a tangled mass of felled trees, ditches, and ground torpedoes. They fired their repeating rifles as fast as they could work the actions and advanced to the position of the skirmishers, who then rose up from cover and joined in the assault. By the time they reached the parapets, dozens of Federals had been killed or wounded by the land mines.

It was all over in fifteen minutes. The Confederates were overwhelmed by the rapid attack and the superior firepower. A war correspondent who watched the assault wrote that the Union riflemen "surmounted the crest and palisades, shot and bayoneted the gunners who refused to surrender, at their posts, and planted the Stars and Stripes upon the work in triumph." He concluded, "Perhaps in the history of this war there has not been a more striking example of the evidence of quick, determined action. Had we waited, put up entrenchments, shelled the place, and made the usual approaches, we should have lost many more lives and time that was invaluable. As it is, our entire loss is not more than ninety men killed and wounded."[24]

A week later, on December 20, the Confederate forces fled Savannah, and the following day, the city surrendered. There Charley and the 116th got a few weeks of rest. He was delighted to receive a gift from Mary in the mail. It was a small pocket Bible, which she had inscribed to him on the flyleaf, "This precious bible is presented to Charles E. Boles, First Sergeant, Company B, 116th Illinois Volunteer Infantry, by his wife as New Years gift. God gives us hearts to which His [illegible] faith to believe. Decatur, Illinois, 1865." Below that she signed her name. Even happier news arrived soon after, when he got word that their son, Arian, was born on January 8, 1865.[25]

On January 16, Boles and the 116th boarded a ship in Savannah and steamed fifty miles north to Beaufort, South Carolina. Their orders were to join the Campaign of the Carolinas, General Sherman's plan to link up with the Union Army in Virginia.

Charley Boles was one of the Union riflemen who assaulted Fort McAllister on the Georgia coast.

From Beaufort, they marched inland with other regiments for twenty miles to Pocotaligo, where they had a sharp skirmish with rebel troops. The Confederates were greatly outmanned. Charley and his comrades pursued the enemy through marshes and across creeks and rivers, frequently trading fire with small bands of Southern infantry and militia. A month later, when they emerged from the muddy swamps, their uniforms were in tatters, and many were barefoot. Boles and the rest then arrived at the outskirts of Columbia, the state capital, which surrendered on February 17. Many of the Federal troops celebrated by going on an extended drunk. Charley was not one of them, as his friend John Bradon recalled. "I never saw him drink anything until after we had taken Columbia, South Carolina, and then he only drank a little wine."[26]

Sherman's army marched out of Columbia a few days later, leaving parts of the city in flames. They continued north in two columns, crossing into North Carolina, where they finally met heavy rebel resistance. A twenty-thousand-man Confederate force had dug in near the village of Bentonville. On March 19, 1865, an attack by one Union column was turned back by the rebels. However, the next day, the 116th and the rest of the 15th Corps arrived on the battlefield and after heavy fighting managed to rout the rebel army. This was the last combat Charley Boles saw in the Civil War.

His regiment continued north and helped capture the town of Goldsboro. It became evident to Charley and his comrades that the war was coming to a close. On April 9, Private Craig wrote a letter home from Goldsboro. "And today there was two brigades came in to our lines and gave themselves up. They was cavalry. They brought their guns and horses and they said that there was more coming in a few days if our field officers would pardon the high officers in the southern states we would have peace before tomorrow night, but Lincoln won't do it. Neither would I, but that makes them fight longer and I would do the same."[27]

The same day, Confederate forces under General Robert E. Lee surrendered at Appomattox Court House in Virginia, effectively ending the Civil War. The following day, the 116th started yet another march, this one to the state capital in Raleigh, which surrendered without a fight on April 13, 1865. By this time, the regiment had only three hundred fifty men. With General Sherman and his army of sixty-five thousand, Boles and the 116th marched two hundred sixty miles north to Washington, DC. On May 24, 1865, in one of the proudest moments of Charley's life, he paraded down Pennsylvania Avenue in the Grand Review of the Armies. For two days, huge crowds of deliriously happy spectators, including President Andrew Johnson and General U. S. Grant, cheered on two hundred thousand victorious, combat-tested veterans.

Two weeks later, on June 7, the 116th finally got orders to return home. Charley and the rest boarded a railroad train and headed for Camp Butler in Springfield, Illinois. On June 15, their train stopped briefly in Decatur, but they could not stay. "This regiment on passing through Decatur were greeted with a perfect ovation from the citizens who turned out en masse to greet them," a local journalist reported. The 116th continued on to Springfield, where they remained in Camp Butler for more than a week before they were issued their final army pay. Now Boles and his comrades entrained back to Decatur. On his way home, Charley had plenty of time to reflect on his military career.[28]

The Civil War had changed him forever. He had seen bloody combat in numerous skirmishes and a dozen major engagements: Chickasaw Bayou, Arkansas Post, Steele's Bayou, Champion Hill, Black River Bridge, Vicksburg, Missionary Ridge, Resaca, Dallas, Ball's Ferry, Fort McAllister, and Bentonville. He had twice been wounded in action, and years later would claim that he actually had been wounded three times. At some point he lost two upper and two lower front teeth, and perhaps that happened in the war. Boles was battle hardened in the extreme. He could shoot a musket or rifle with deadly accuracy and face gunfire without flinching. He had slept outdoors and on the ground for almost three years, surviving bullets, starvation, illness, freezing weather, and countless exhausting marches through mud and dust, through rain, sleet, and snow. He could tramp tirelessly with full pack and rifle and could easily cover fifty miles a day. He could survive on scant food and little drink.

During the California gold rush, Boles had first learned how to survive extreme conditions. The gold rush had also made him a rootless adventurer, wanderer, speculator, and risk-taker who—as it would soon develop—was ill-suited for a domestic life with a spouse and children. During the Civil War, he learned how to live with death and near-constant violence. Taking extreme risks became part of his character, for he knew that his life could end at any moment. And during those army campaigns, especially the March to the Sea, he had learned to forage—to pillage and steal with abandon.

Charley Boles was not a stage robber born. He was a stage robber made—made by the gold rush and the Civil War.

6

I Have Had a Rough Life of It

Amid swirling clouds of locomotive steam and smoke, Charley Boles and his comrades swung down from the railroad passenger cars in Decatur. Once again they received a hero's welcome from grateful crowds at the depot. Mary was ecstatic to have her husband back, alive and well. And Charley, excited to see his brood again, held their infant boy, Arian, for the first time. The seemingly happy family climbed into a wagon and drove to their farmhouse north of town. There Boles traded in his blue uniform for work clothes and returned to a humdrum life of tilling the soil.

Years later, one of his friends recalled, "He tried farming there until he found that it meant only starvation, and then he went West. His wife was a smart, capable woman, who could earn a living by dressmaking. Boles had some education, but he had not learned a trade, and his army life did not increase his earning powers. The only thing he knew much about was mining, and it was agreed between him and his wife that he should go back to the mines and try to make a stake." Yet that is not exactly what happened. As two of his comrades from the 116th later told a Decatur journalist, "When the war was over he came home, but didn't remain here long as he and his wife quarreled and separated. Boles left Decatur."[1]

They quarreled over Charley's insistence that he make his fortune as a gold miner, and Mary's desire that he stay home, work hard, and help raise the children. Mary lost the fight, and in December 1865, just six months after his return, Charley boarded a train for the East Coast. There, probably using what was left of his army pay, he booked passage on a California-bound steamship and repeated the same trip that he had made in 1852. This time Boles landed in Panama and crossed the Isthmus, an act that demonstrated the extreme risk-taking that had come to imbue his character, for both his brother and cousin had died from malaria after doing exactly the same thing fourteen years earlier. Charley then boarded the steamer *Golden City*, owned by the Pacific Mail Steamship Company, and sailed north to California. He landed at the Pacific Mail wharf in San Francisco on February 11, 1866.[2]

Charley's excitement at being back in San Francisco quickly dissipated. He found that the days of the wandering forty-niner with his mule, pickax, and gold pan were long gone. The gold rush was over, and mining had become big business. Hardrock mining companies dug tunnels deep into the mountains to extract gold that was embedded in rock and quartz. Hydraulic miners employed giant water nozzles to wash hillsides away. Water-powered stamp mills crushed rock and quartz so that the gold could be removed. Boles wanted to be a mine owner, not a laborer. Greatly disillusioned, he soon left California and returned to Decatur. There he sold his homestead, and with Mary and the four children, moved back to New Oregon, Iowa, by the end of 1866. Mary still owned the farm there that she had purchased for $400, and her sister Louisa lived nearby.[3]

Charley was well regarded in New Oregon. One of his neighbors recalled him as "a nice, honorable man, and finely educated." Charles E. Booth, Louisa's son, later said, "I always thought him a model man, strictly honest and upright in all his dealings." But Boles had no intention of spending his days behind an Iowa plow. A new gold rush was underway in Montana Territory, and he became determined to join it. On March 25, 1867, Mary sold her property in New Oregon for $780, a tidy profit. She used the money to buy a smaller farm with a house, and apparently gave some cash to Charley. A few weeks later, on May 1, he left alone for Montana. His wish for adventure, wealth, and risk overcame any sense of responsibility for his family. And three years of facing Confederate gunfire seems to have led him to believe that he was entitled to his freedom.[4]

Charley made his way west to Montana's mining region, a thousand-mile journey. Most likely he boarded a steamer at Sioux City, Iowa, and proceeded up the Missouri River to the navigation headwaters at Fort Benton, Montana. From there he took a stagecoach—or walked—one hundred thirty miles south to Helena, a boomtown of about three thousand. He spent the summer of 1867 there hunting for gold, but soon found that the good mining claims had all been taken. Charley sent regular letters to Mary, and she later said that he would write as often as four times a week. Mary wrote back, but by that time he had moved on, and her messages languished in the unclaimed letters box in the Helena post office.[5]

Boles drifted south another one hundred twenty miles to Virginia City, Montana. A rowdy mining town of about five thousand people, Virginia City was then Montana's territorial capital. Its most famous resident had been Henry Plummer, who, despite being sheriff, also headed a large gang of highwaymen. They committed numerous robberies and murders until a vigilance committee sprang up and declared war on the bandit gang. Between December 1863 and February 1864, the Montana vigilantes captured and hanged twenty-two desperadoes in one of

America's most prolific lynching sprees. Henry Plummer and two of his henchmen died on the sheriff's own gallows.

For Charley Boles, committing highway robberies was the furthest thing from his mind. He continued prospecting for gold in the streams and hills, and spent that winter in Virginia City. He had minor success and sent some of his earnings home by way of money orders issued by Wells Fargo & Company's Express. By 1869, Charley had moved north to the little camp of Silver Bow, seven miles west of Butte. He acquired a partner, a tough thirty-seven-year-old Welshman named Harry Roberts who had also served in the Union Army, though not in the same regiment as Boles. The two built a cabin at Silver Bow and spent their days toiling over their Long Toms and sluice boxes.[6]

Virginia City, Montana, as Charley Boles saw it in the late 1860s.

Roberts was a popular figure in Silver Bow and later became a teamster and wagon boss. "Harry Roberts was one of the best known men in the west, and for many years had charge of large freighting outfits long before the country had become accessible by railroad," recalled a pioneer journalist. "Generous, true hearted, and honest as the day is long, Roberts had a friend in every man with whom he had any connections." But unlike

Boles, Roberts was a heavy imbiber and could be quarrelsome when drunk. Those traits would, many years later, lead to a violent and tragic conclusion to his life on the Montana frontier.[7]

Though Charley was an inveterate letter writer, only one missive from his Montana sojourn has survived. He penned it on April 4, 1869, while on a visit to Helena and following a very harsh winter. "My own dear Mary and little ones," he began. "I am indeed thankful for the very kind and loving letter just received from you, my dear wife. This is another beautiful Sabbath morning and I am happy to tell you I am well. Oh my dear I was so happy to hear that you were also well. I write every week as regular as God sends them and you I know have got plenty before this but the late snow blockade prevented them going sooner."

Mary had apparently asked him for money, for Charley then veered off into a long explanation of how he had borrowed cash from two fellow miners. Both had returned to their homes in Illinois, and Boles claimed that he lacked the funds to repay them. But then, in his next breath, he admitted that he did have money. "Now I will tell you what I have just done," he wrote. "As I told you in my last letter I would tell you today what I would do this summer. Well I have just bought a claim; paid $260 for it in dust. Now it all depends on how it pays, about my coming home this fall. So I remain in the same place in the same claim and in the same cabin and with the same partner. I pay as it comes out. I pay him half I get out of the ground until the claim is paid for. So I will have half I take out to pay expenses and to send home if needed. But it may not pay me, can't tell until we dig.

"But my dear I don't want to work for any man if I can help it. I will have a wood cabin, stove and everything handy, mining tools too, sluice boxes and can be where I am handy for mail. Quite an item with me I assure you. So if it pays reasonably well we will both come home in the fall. I hope you will not blame me if I fail and be sure not to put it down too strong that I am coming in the fall, but my darling I will if I can and for you only to know how very much I do want to see you all. My dear, at all events I will try and furnish you with what money you will need and use all you need to make you comfortable and happy and you can depend upon regular mail here often. I think the Union Pacific Railroad is about completed to our nearest point, which is about 480 miles from Helena City. Wells Fargo & Co. will go through to the station in 60 hours soon. So you see our mail will not be too long on the road from here after.

"Well my dear, kiss the little ones for me and tell them papa is aching to get hold of them once more. Now my dear, after once more telling you how dearly I love you I will close. So may God bless you all and keep you safe til I return to you again. Good bye, as your ever loving husband. C.E. Boles."[8]

Charley and his partner, Harry Roberts, continued to work their claim until 1871. According to Boles family lore, recalled by a descendant in the 1930s, he wrote letters to Mary from Montana claiming that he had been defrauded. Supposedly several men employed by Wells Fargo offered to buy his small mining claim. He refused, but they persisted. When he would still not cooperate, they somehow shut off Charley's supply of water. Without water for his sluice boxes, he was forced to abandon his placer mine. As the story went, he wrote letters home bitterly complaining about the affair and threatened ominously that he was "going to take steps," but did not elaborate. This event supposedly triggered his hatred of Wells Fargo and his subsequent pillaging of the company's express shipments.[9]

However, there are several problems with this story. First, the Boles family did not have copies of any letters describing these events. Second, Wells Fargo was an express company, not a mining company. It briefly ran stage lines in Montana, but the company's main business was shipping gold out of the territory and bringing letters, currency, and valuables in. Wells Fargo did not own or operate gold mines anywhere in the West. And more significantly, Wells Fargo had no presence in either Butte or Silver Bow County in 1871. There was not a Wells Fargo office within seventy miles of Silver Bow. The county's principal settlement, Butte, did not have a Wells Fargo office until 1877. Therefore, there were no Wells Fargo men in the county who could have defrauded Boles. The story is a romantic family yarn offered to provide an excuse for his long career of banditry.[10]

Charley's letters to Mary were filled with expressions of love and affection. Perhaps his sentiments were sincere, but his actions spoke louder than his words. He did not return to her, though she firmly believed that he would. When the census taker visited her Iowa home, she named Charley as the head of the household and identified his occupation as a miner. Mary later said, "My last letter from him was dated August 25, 1871, at Silver Bow, M.T." She told a journalist that Charley wrote that he "had settled up his business and was coming home to bring them to Montana, as he had made sufficient money for them to live comfortably." He even provided the date he would start for home, but he never appeared. By then Mary was deep in mourning. Their youngest child, Arian, age six, had died in her humble New Oregon farmhouse on August 12, 1871.[11]

Mary was strong and resilient, and she managed to cope with this double loss by a combination of courage and self-delusion. Mary convinced herself, and the entire Boles family, that her husband had not abandoned her, but instead had been captured by Indians or killed by bandits. Her nephew Charles Booth later expressed the family's shock. "I never saw a man who seemed to love his family more than he did his," Booth wrote. "He always wrote to them twice a week, until his mysterious disappearance." Booth explained the source of Mary's certitude. "The proprietor of the house where he boarded in Helena wrote to his wife that Boles had started for home in company with another man. She immediately came to the conclusion that this party had mur-

MARC C. REED COLLECTION.

Charley's wife, Mary Johnson Boles, in about 1870.

dered her husband for his money. She advertised for him in all
the papers in the Territory and finally sent a search party over
the country but to no avail." That was an expense she could ill
afford. Mary struggled to support her daughters, who attended
the New Oregon grammar school. In 1871, to make ends meet,
she began to take in boarders.[12]

The following year, the Boles family suffered more heart-
ache. Charley's uncle Leonard Boles, now eighty, lived with his
son Robert and Robert's family on a farm near Theresa, New
York, six miles south of Plessis. At two o'clock in the morning
of March 18, 1872, a fire suddenly broke out in the large, two-
story farmhouse. A woman friend who was visiting awoke to
the flames and threw her two children from an upstairs window into a snowbank below. She then leaped out the window

and saved herself too. Leonard was not so lucky. As he tried to descend the stairs, he was overcome by smoke and fell. He managed to break the glass of a window and climb outside. Robert rushed frantically through the house to save his wife and two children. His clothes burst into flames, and his fourteen-year-old son dragged him outside. Though his children were both unharmed, Robert died in great agony a few hours later. Leonard did not survive his injuries either; he lingered for three weeks before he too died.[13]

The tragic fire may have been too much for Charley's elderly parents. Six months later, in September 1872, his mother, Maria, died, age seventy-eight. Eleven days after that, his father, John, eighty-four, also passed away. John's last will and testament listed Charley as deceased, and he left most of his estate to his four living children. But he also provided gifts of $50 to each of his grandchildren, plus a total of $400 to provide help to Mary and her three daughters. However, the executor, Charley's brother Hiram, paid Mary only $80. A year later, she engaged a lawyer who filed a successful lawsuit in the Jefferson County probate court. In 1874, an embittered Mary sold her Iowa property and moved with her children three hundred miles down the Mississippi River to the picturesque town of Hannibal, Missouri, the boyhood home of Mark Twain. It was also the home of her brother Henry Johnson and his wife. There Mary lived on the brink of poverty, eking out a living as a seamstress.[14]

By this time, Charley had left Montana and severed any connection with his family. He even began using the last name of Bolton. Wells Fargo's chief detective, James B. Hume, later explained, "He went from Montana to Salt Lake [City] and remained in the land of the Mormons for two years." Exactly what Boles did in Utah during that time is a mystery. Then he drifted west to the Comstock Lode mining region south of Reno, Nevada. A journalist who later interviewed Charley wrote that he "went to Virginia City. He had held small stock in the Com-

stock and other mines, and lost a little. To hang on to mining
stock was a 'dead shot' to break any man, so he sold out when
the assessments came in." What Charley meant was that mining stock on the Comstock Lode was extremely unstable, and
he sold his stock as soon as he could unload it. Finally, in 1874,
Boles continued west on the Central Pacific Railroad to his favorite city, San Francisco.[15]

Charley found San Francisco more intriguing than ever. Its
population had boomed to about two hundred thousand, with
modern conveniences everywhere: hundreds of multistory brick
buildings, paved roads, streetcars, gaslights, and running water.
The city's busy port and convenient location had helped trans-
form it into the financial, industrial, political, cultural, and edu-
cational hub of the Pacific Coast. San Francisco had also become
the West's center for art, architecture, theater, literature, and
music. At various times in that era, it was home to luminaries like
authors Mark Twain and Robert Louis Stevenson, actors Edwin
Booth and Lotta Crabtree, and a large school of artists that included Albert Bierstadt and Thomas Hill. Wealthy railroad men,
steamship owners, financiers, and mining magnates—known
as nabobs or nobs in popular slang—built opulent mansions on
Nob Hill. Men made and lost fortunes speculating on gold and
silver mines in the city's stock exchange.

For Charley Boles, San Francisco was a far cry from the rustic
wood cabins and muddy trails of Montana Territory. And surely
he noted that there were attractive women everywhere, from
the middle-class homes perched on the steep slopes of Telegraph
Hill to the rowdy saloons, dance halls, and bordellos in the red-
light district, known as the Barbary Coast. Just three city blocks
separated those two worlds. Charley, by his own account, never
visited brothels or gambling dens. But though the city had far
more women in 1875 than it did in the gold rush, they were still
scarce, for San Francisco was then only one-third female. And

few of them were interested in a forty-five-year-old ex-farmer, shabbily dressed and almost penniless.

Charley, surrounded by signs of affluence, could only ruminate on his own misfortunes. He had failed as a gold miner in California in 1850, and failed again two years later. He had failed as a farmer in New York, Iowa, and Illinois. He then failed as a miner in Montana. By nature and by life experience, Boles was an adventurer, wanderer, speculator, and risk-taker who should never have married and had children. He had abandoned his wife and family and had failed as a husband and as a father. He had even assumed a false name. At the same time, he was hugely and justifiably proud of his service in the army. It had been the highlight of his life. He had served with honor, courage, and distinction. He had repeatedly risked his life in bloody combat, had been wounded twice, and for all that, he had received no reward for his sacrifice. He surely believed that he deserved financial success. He was entitled to it.

During the war, he and his comrades had made countless foraging expeditions. When they needed food or supplies, they simply took them. Thus, stealing was nothing new to him. So in San Francisco, Charley decided to earn his fortune in a different way. He later refused to reveal publicly why he turned to a career of stage robbery. "I have had a rough life of it," he said, and blamed "an uncommon circumstance which brings me into this condition. An uncommon and mysterious one— one which no man living, except myself, knows, and no man shall ever know."[16]

But one of his friends later provided Charley's version of how he became a highwayman. "He was traveling about, looking for something to do, and had spent his last dime. Being hungry, he walked up to a ranch house where the people were eating dinner, determined for the first time in his life to ask hospitality of a stranger. He was not a lazy, dirty tramp, but a traveler, out of money and hungry."

When the owner of the ranch met him at the door, Boles said, "I have walked some distance, and being quite hungry, I would like to have dinner with you. I have no money."

"Wait here," the rancher replied, and stepped inside. Charley took a chair on the front porch and waited, and as he sat there, several dogs came sniffing around him. Soon the rancher returned with some scraps of food in a tin plate, and handed it to Charley. Boles quietly received the plate, then placed it down in front of the dogs.

"Isn't it good enough for you?" demanded the rancher.

"No," Charley replied. "I do not think such hospitality good enough for anybody."

The rancher responded in a surly tone, "I don't believe in encouraging tramps."

Boles stood up and exclaimed, "This is the first time I ever asked anybody to give me anything, and it will be the last. Hereafter, when I want anything, I shall demand it and take it."

Explained Charley's friend, "He left the place, and further up the road he found another ranch. Nobody was in the house, but through the window he saw food on the table. He went in, ate all he wanted, and left a note, saying that he had taken a dinner, and telling the owner to send his bill if he wanted pay for it, giving his proper address. Of course, he never heard any more of it."[17]

Charley Boles had come to a fateful turning point in his life. Over and over again, success had eluded him. Since nothing else had worked, now he would steal it.

7

The Poet Highwayman

In San Francisco, Charley Boles became a new man. No longer was he a farmer in hobnailed boots, a rifleman in a muddy uniform, or a gold hunter in a shabby miner's frock. He suddenly began dressing in the height of fashion, sporting a salt-and-pepper wool suit with double-breasted coat, a silk tie with gold stickpin, and a diamond ring on one finger, all topped off with a stylish bowler hat. He stepped briskly across the city's cobblestone streets with a gold-headed walking stick swinging jauntily from his right fist. Though he was a loner, his gentlemanly manners and quick sense of humor soon attracted a small circle of friends and acquaintances. They ranged from the owner of his favorite restaurant, Jacob M. Pike, to the colorful and hugely popular fire chief of San Francisco, David Scannell.

To San Franciscans he was Charles E. Bolton, but at various times he claimed to be C. E. Benton, Harry Barton, and Charley Barlow. Boles told people that he was a prosperous stock speculator and mine owner with claims in the Sierra gold country and in Nevada's Comstock Lode. He spent much of his time in what was called Pauper Alley—a section of narrow Leides-dorff Street, between California and Pine. It was situated just off Montgomery Street, which later became known as "Wall Street of the West." Montgomery Street was—and still is—the center of San Francisco's financial district. It featured the head-quarters of major banks, mining companies, stock brokerages, real estate agencies, and shipping corporations. Pauper Alley, so named after the silver market crash known as the Panic of 1873, connected San Francisco's two stock exchanges.[1]

Charley found it an exciting place, rife with the wild hope of quick riches. As one observer wrote a few years later, "Pauper Alley used to be an exhilarating sight. It was literally thronged—densely packed with noisy, excited, but good-humored opera-tors; messenger boys tearing through the crowd, breathless, as though on errands of life and death…half the windows of the alley open, lined with spectators to see the fun; the saloons all thronged; a dense stream of thirsty humanity endeavoring to enter, and an equally dense stream seeking to make their exit; the bootblacks all scrubbing for their lives; their patrons enthroned, sleek, close-shaved, red-faced and jolly, for in Pauper Alley, prosperity patronizes the barber, bar, and bootblack… Groups of men studied [ore] specimens over their drinks, carried them in their pockets, and buttonholed their friends in order to ex-hibit them. There were samples of silver and gold bearing rock everywhere: in cabinets, in the exchanges and saloons, on the counters, in banks, and used as paper-weights in the offices of mining secretaries." He concluded by offering a description of its cash-hungry denizens, one that could have applied to Char-ley Boles: "If the truth must be told, they are a pretty hard lot in Pauper Alley."[2]

Several of Charley's San Francisco comrades later told a news-paperman, "He was a man of prepossessing manners, fluent and extremely entertaining in conversation. He claimed to have been a captain in the late civil war, and loved to recount to listeners, some of whom were old soldiers, the events of his

BRUCE LEVENE COLLECTION.

Charley Boles looked every inch the man he pretended to be: a prosperous mining inves-
tor in San Francisco.

military career." Given that Charley was a brevet first lieutenant
and a combat veteran, there was no need for him to exagger-
ate. Yet his apparent need to achieve success at any cost seems
to have taken over all aspects of his life, including the retelling
of his Civil War service.[3]

Charley roomed at various city hotels and boardinghouses
and frequently took trips out of town. He would leave his belongings behind in a trunk and tell his comrades that he had to
make a visit to one of his mines. He would be gone for a week
or a month, then return to his haunts in the financial district.
Boles did not drink, frequent saloons and gambling houses, or
patronize bordellos, of which San Francisco had scores. To all
outward appearances, he was simply one of thousands of respectable businessmen in the bustling young city by the bay.

The reason for Charley's sudden financial success would not become evident for years. But it began in the spring of 1875. In that era, San Francisco's newspapers, ever engaged in bitter circulation wars, gave extensive coverage to crime reports. Sensational stories of murders, shootings, brawls, and robberies filled their columns. Charley was a voracious reader of the San Francisco and Sacramento papers, and he followed the many accounts of stagecoach holdups. In November 1874 the dailies reported a double robbery on the stage road from Sonora to Milton. A gang of six masked highwaymen stopped the coach of John Shine, but he was not carrying an express box. They let him drive on, and when the next stage came along, they stopped it and looted the Wells Fargo shipment. It later developed that the gang was led by Ramon Ruiz, a notorious bandido. Several months later, in March 1875, Ruiz and two of his gang stopped a coach on Funk Hill, not far from Reynolds Ferry in Calaveras County. This time they escaped with more than $6,000 from Wells Fargo. That was a small fortune, worth more than $150,000 today.[4]

Boles must have studied the news reports of the Funk Hill robbery. He knew the area well, because more than twenty years earlier, he had prospected for gold in Calaveras County. Charley then planned his first holdup carefully. He likely took a steamer across San Francisco Bay and up the San Joaquin River to Stockton, then walked fifty miles to Funk Hill. Mimicking the Quaker guns he had seen in the Civil War, he whittled tree branches into mock rifle barrels and cleverly placed them amid the roadside rocks and brush. On July 26, 1875, he stopped John Shine's coach and stole Wells Fargo's treasure, then hiked out of the mountains and back to San Francisco. Years later, Boles recalled that he first headed south, forded the San Joaquin River near Grayson, then crossed the Coast Range through Pacheco Pass. With his Henry rifle slung over his back, he looked like a common traveler or hunter. In rural California in that era, sheriffs and constables were few and far between, and many men carried firearms for self-protection. On the way, he stopped at a house to eat and rest. There, as he later told a newspaperman, "a woman wanted to buy his gun." Charley responded that he "would not sell it, but would give it to her."

She replied, "No, I will buy it." The woman offered $10 and handed him a $20 gold piece. Charley gave her in change a $10 bill he had stolen from the express box. Then he continued on foot to San Jose and up the San Francisco Peninsula to his boardinghouse in the city. His two-hundred-fifty-mile walk, while impressive, was nothing compared to the marches he had made in the Civil War. Boles had wisely chosen to avoid riding horseback. In that era, everyone knew horseflesh, and witnesses often paid more attention to a saddle animal than to the man riding it. Therefore, a mounted fugitive was easier to identify. And Charley's ability to walk great distances made it possible for him to avoid well-traveled roads and trails and helped him evade capture for years to come.[5]

Boles started out slowly as a road agent. During the next two years, he held up only three more stagecoaches: Mike Hogan's stage from North San Juan in December 1875; A. C. Adams's coach on the Oregon-California line in June 1876; and Ash Wilkinson's rig on the Sonoma Coast in August 1877. By that time, he had found a clever moniker for his newfound identity as a lone highwayman. One of his favorite short stories was "The Case of Summerfield," written by a San Francisco lawyer named William H. Rhodes who used the pseudonym "Caxton." "The Case of Summerfield" was an early work of science fiction, about a man who discovered a way to set water on fire, and anyone obtaining his secret could destroy the world. It was first serialized in the *Sacramento Union* in 1871 and then widely reprinted by newspapers throughout the US and even in Australia. In 1876, "The Case of Summerfield" was released by a San Francisco publisher as part of an anthology of Rhodes's works.

One of several villains in the story was a stage robber named Bartholomew Graham, alias Black Bart.[6]

In Charley's first four robberies, he took only about $600 from Wells Fargo. That was hardly enough money to support his gentleman's lifestyle over a period of two years. However, in all of the holdups, he also stole the US mail. As Wells Fargo detective Jim Hume later said, "Black Bart told me that in his first twenty-seven robberies he realized more from the mails than from the express." Given Boles's comfortable situation in San Francisco, he must have taken a few thousand dollars from the mailbags. With this money, he lived in quiet prosperity in the city. Charley also made numerous visits by train to Sacramento, which he apparently used as a base for some of his stage robbing expeditions. As a Sacramento journalist later reported, "His face is well known at the depot dining rooms, for he traveled back and forth from San Francisco frequently."[7]

In July 1878, Boles made one of his customary trips out of San Francisco. He crossed the bay by ferry and then boarded an eastbound railroad train in Oakland. In his bedroll, he concealed a double-barreled sawed-off shotgun, which he broke down into two pieces, barrel and stock, for ease of carrying. At the depot in Sacramento, he changed trains and headed to Oroville, seventy miles north. Oroville, the seat of Butte County, was a bustling Sierra foothills town of one thousand five hundred people that served as a major shipping point for gold from the Northern Mines. Charley remembered Butte County well, for it was there that he had first dug for gold after arriving in California in 1850. From the train depot in Oroville, he walked northeast twenty miles into the mountains and made camp in the brush a mile east of Berry Creek. He knew that rich shipments of gold were regularly sent to Oroville by stage from the mining town of Quincy, high in the Sierra Nevada.

Early in the morning of July 25, 1878, the Oroville-bound coach rolled out of Quincy with Charles Seavy at the reins. His three passengers settled in for a long ride. The remote, winding wagon road from Quincy to Oroville, now Highway 162, was a one-day, sixty-five-mile trip. At three o'clock that afternoon, as Seavy carefully descended a hill a mile outside of Berry Creek, Boles suddenly jumped in front of his team.

"Throw out the box!" Charley demanded as he covered the jehu with his shotgun.

Seavy was so startled, and so busy reaching for the Wells Fargo box, that he did not get a clear view of the highwayman. Later, when his fright wore off, he amusingly recalled that the gun barrels looked three inches wide and that he had "a vivid remembrance of the appearance of the nineteen buckshot at the bottom of the shotgun." The passengers, however, got a good look at the road agent. They later said that he was "a tall, slim man, with iron gray hair and whiskers, probably full beard, vest and shirt, Kentucky jean pants, and long legged boots. He was armed with a shotgun and had a revolver in his belt. His face was concealed with a white cloth." Although in prior holdups Boles had worn a flour sack over his head, this time he only covered his face.

Seavy quickly tossed down the Wells Fargo strongbox, which held $400 and a $200 diamond ring. Then Charley called to the jehu, "Drive on."

As the coach rattled off, Boles broke open the box, removed its contents, and left inside a scrap of brown paper with another bit of doggerel, each line written in a disguised hand. He had apparently composed it in his camp the night before.

Here I lay me down to sleep
To wait the coming morrow.
Perhaps success, perhaps defeat,
And everlasting sorrow.
Let come what will, I'll try it on,
My condition can't be worse.

And if there's money in that box,
Tis munny in my purse.

At the bottom he signed it, "Black Bart, the Po8."

Charley broke down the shotgun, wrapped it in his blanket roll, and vanished into the brush. Meanwhile, Seavy whipped up his team and raced one mile into Berry Creek, a tiny mining camp and stage stop. There two of his passengers borrowed a rifle and returned to the holdup site. They made a long search but found no trace of the bandit or the express box. However, the next day, a California Indian passed along the road, spotted the shattered box, and brought it and the scrap of paper to local lawmen. Before long, the poem ended up in the hands of Jim Hume, who found it far from amusing.[8]

Charley's success encouraged him to try another holdup. From Berry Creek, he hiked south into the Feather River Canyon, crossed the stream, and continued on to the stage road that ran between Oroville and the mining town of La Porte, located high in the Sierra Nevada. Five days later, on July 30, Boles undertook a repeat performance. Early that morning, a coach driven by David Berry had left La Porte, headed for Oroville. One of the passengers was thirty-five-year-old Mary Wheeler, wife of the Wells Fargo agent in La Porte. She occupied the seat of honor next to Berry. Because the express box held only about $50, no shotgun messenger was aboard.

The stagecoach had made it about five miles from La Porte when Berry spotted a man walking along the side of the road. It was Charley Boles, clutching his shotgun closely in front of him so it could not be seen from behind. The poetic highwayman suddenly whirled around and stepped in front of the lead horses. He wore a mask and aimed his shotgun at the driver.

"Throw down the box," Boles ordered. Mary Wheeler reached under the seat, pulled out the treasure box, and hurled it at the bandit.

"Take it, you scoundrel, if it will do you any good," she exclaimed. Then Charley ordered the reinsman to drive on. In all of his twenty-nine holdups, this plucky woman was the only passenger who had enough nerve and fortitude to berate Black Bart.[9]

A posse soon arrived on the scene, but they found no trace of the bandit. George Hackett, a Wells Fargo shotgun messenger, rode up from Marysville to investigate the robbery. He was certain that both holdups had been pulled by the same man, but he had no better luck than the posse. A few days later, on August 2, several citizens arrested two ex-convicts, William Howard and William Robinson, not far from La Porte. They carried a pair of shotguns that were identified as those stolen in a burglary at a nearby ranch. Howard, a graying forty-seven-year-old, bore some resemblance to the road agent. The suspects were lodged in the county jail at Quincy, but when stage driver Seavy could not identify them, the grand jury refused to indict the pair. They were then taken to Marysville to face the burglary charges. Though Howard and Robinson were innocent of the stage robberies, they both pleaded guilty to stealing the shotguns and were sent to San Quentin prison. They were among the first of numerous men who would be wrongly accused of committing a Black Bart holdup.[10]

Wells Fargo officials quickly announced an $800 reward, comprised of $300 offered by the express company, $300 by the state of California, and $200 by the US Post Office Department. That sum was equivalent to more than $20,000 today. Jim Hume issued a detailed wanted circular that for the first time identified the slippery highwayman as Black Bart. "Arrest Stage Robber!" the notice announced in bold print. "These circulars are for the use of officers and discreet persons only." Hume described the holdups and the poems left at two of the robbery sites. He even paid a wood engraver to reproduce Black Bart's handwriting onto the wanted notice. Hume's circular concluded, "It will be seen from the above that this fellow is a character that would be remembered as a scribbler and something of a wit or a wag and would be likely to leave specimens of his handwriting on hotel registers and other public places. If arrested, telegraph the undersigned at Sacramento. Any information thankfully received. J.B. Hume, Special Officer Wells Fargo & Co."[11]

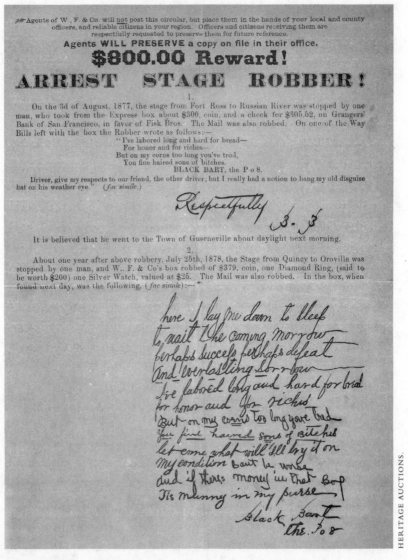

Detective Hume's detailed wanted circular that, for the first time, identified the slippery highwayman as Black Bart.

Despite the heavy reward, the elusive Charley Boles safely slipped back to San Francisco. But the booty from his two Oroville holdups did not last long. Instead of again trying his hand in the Sierra Nevada, he returned to the North Coast, this time to remote Mendocino County. Unlike Sonoma County, Mendocino, its northern neighbor, had no railroad. Charley most likely took a northbound train to Cloverdale, the end of the line, and then walked another thirty miles north to Ukiah, the Mendocino County seat. He had learned that both US mail and Wells Fargo shipments were regularly brought to Ukiah by stages from Arcata on the Pacific Coast, one hundred seventy miles to the north. Because in that isolated region the stage line was the main connection with the outside world, each coach carried numerous heavy sacks of mail.

Boles lay in wait on the stage road fourteen miles north of Ukiah, in Walker Valley. It was an ideal place for a holdup, where a fifteen-foot-high boulder was perched on the slope next to a sharp bend in the road. There, six-horse teams had to move slowly around the curve, and a coach could easily be halted. From the top of the boulder, Charley could see wagons and stages approaching from a mile in either direction, north and south. On the morning of October 2, 1878, the southbound stagecoach approached, with Alex Fowler at the ribbons and no passengers aboard. Boles quickly stepped out from behind the boulder, his shotgun leveled at the jehu.

"Throw out the Wells Fargo box and the mail bags!"

As Fowler yanked on his reins, he saw that the bandit had a flour sack mask over his head and his feet wrapped with cloth. The reinsman reached under his seat and tossed down the strongbox and one mail pouch. But Boles knew he was holding out.

"Throw out the rest of the mail," Charley ordered. As Fowler later recalled, the bandit said that he "knew something about the mail matter coming over the road."

Fowler promptly complied and tossed down the other mailbags. Boles ordered him to drive on, then chopped open the

Wells Fargo box with an axe. Charley was disappointed to find that it held only $40. He cut open the sacks of mail, but they apparently held little of value. He then disappeared into the brush. Ever after, the huge boulder at the holdup site would be known as Robber's Rock, and years later, as Black Bart Rock.[12]

Boles was determined to make his trip to the North Coast profitable, so he hiked east twelve miles across the mountainous country until he reached a second stage road. This one ran through the Round Valley Indian Reservation and south to Potter Valley, then to Ukiah. He stationed himself on the road about ten miles north of Potter Valley. Along the way, Charley had picked up some peaches. He sat under a tree, eating the fruit and leaving a stack of peach pits on the ground.

Black Bart Rock, fourteen miles north of Ukiah, where Charley Boles robbed his seventh stagecoach.

The next morning, Boles stopped the southbound mud wagon driven by Nat Waltrip. Like Fowler, Waltrip carried mail and Wells Fargo's express but no passengers that day. The road agent, shotgun in hand, ordered, "Throw out the box!"

Waltrip reached down, pulled out the treasure box, and then rested it on the front wheel, saying, "Come and take it."

"Throw it out!" Charley barked, and Waltrip obeyed. Then Boles told him to toss down the mailbags. He quickly inspected them and saw that one contained only newspapers. Waltrip recalled that "the robber said he had no use for [it], and volunteered to put it back in the wagon, which he did," and at the same time kept his shotgun aimed at him. After Charley replaced the sack in the stage, Waltrip sarcastically responded, "I'm much obliged."

"You are welcome," was the bandit's equally sarcastic reply. "Now drive on."

Boles took more than $400 from Wells Fargo and the mail. Waltrip continued on to Ukiah, where he reported the holdup to Sheriff Jim Moore. A journalist who interviewed the jehu wrote, "Waltrip says the opening at the end of that gun looked 'terrible big.' He would like to see it again, to note its dimensions, but 'not in the same way.'"[13]

Charley lost no time in making tracks out of Mendocino County. He knew that officers would probably watch the train depot in Cloverdale, so he decided to trudge past Clear Lake and cross the Coast Range, where he could board a railroad train in the Sacramento Valley. From the holdup scene, he hiked south to Eel River, then followed the stream east to Bucknell Creek. He crossed a hilly divide to McCreary Glade, home to an isolated sheep ranch in the hills west of Potter Valley. That afternoon, Charley spotted the lonely McCreary cabin and walked up with his bedroll slung over his shoulder and his shotgun safely concealed inside. The only folks at home were the rancher's wife, Salina McCreary, and her alert and observant eighteen-year-old daughter, Donna. Boles stepped forward and greeted Donna McCreary.

"I'm headed for Lakeport," Charley told her. "I'll have to ask you to show me the way. And how about some dinner?"

As Donna recalled, "The dinner things had been put away, but my mother got them out again and brought food from the pantry. That was nothing unusual in those hospitable days; my mother took no notice at all of the stranger. But visitors were an event in my life, and I was always quick to notice. It struck me immediately that this man was out of the ordinary—above the ordinary, in fact. He chatted to me as he ate, and his speech had a certain individuality, a poetic flavor. He made whimsical rhymes. I noticed that his clothing fitted him well. Moreover, when he washed his hands I saw he had lost one cufflink, and that made me notice the style of the one that remained. Presently he pulled out a very fine gold watch—I had never seen such a handsome watch—and said, 'Can you tell me the time? My watch has stopped.'

"I told him the time and he carefully set the watch. Immediately after he had dined he left, saying again that he was going to Lakeport. We pointed out the road and he departed, walking fast."[14]

By this time, Sheriff Moore was busy hunting the bandit. After the first robbery, he rode north to the holdup scene, where he found the empty express box, the mailbags, and an old axe. But he could not track the road agent because his boots had been muffled with cloth. Moore returned to Ukiah, only to learn that the same robber had held up a second stage. Jim Hume soon arrived from San Francisco, for he had received a wire after the first robbery. He suspected that the lone highwayman was Black Bart. In Ukiah, the Wells Fargo detective quickly engaged a twenty-two-year-old mountaineer and hunter named Buck Montgomery to hunt the stage robber. Montgomery rode to the first holdup site, while Hume and Sheriff Moore mounted up and went through Potter Valley to the scene of the last robbery. By then, Charley had probably removed his boot wrappings, for the two lawmen managed to cut his sign and trail him to McCreary Glade.[15]

As they rode up to the cabin, Sheriff Moore called out to Salina McCreary. "Did a stranger come this way? We picked up his trail and it seemed to lead here."

Mrs. McCreary told Moore about the visitor, but she scoffed at any suggestion that he could be a bandit. She insisted that he was a "gentleman tourist" but admitted that she had paid little attention to him. Her daughter, however, proved a gold mine of information. Hume later described the interview to his future wife, Lida Munson, who wrote that Donna McCreary "was so timid and shy of strangers that Mr. Hume had great difficulty in getting her to talk. But when he finally succeeded in overcoming her diffidence and inducing her to talk to him, he obtained a minutely detailed description of the 'gentlemanly tourist' such as could have been given only by one particularly observant and unaccustomed to meeting strangers.

"The girl had watched him with such interest and curiosity that nothing in his features, figure, manners, or clothing escaped her notice. She described him with the utmost detail—a broken watch chain mended with a leather string; a sleeve of his coat that had been ripped and mended with coarse white thread; shoes split across the ball of his foot to give more room in walking. He eagerly read a newspaper, holding it at arm's length as if in need of glasses.

"She described his slender hands which showed no evidence of labor; said he did not look like a drinking man, and did not use tobacco."

As Lida explained, "When Special Officer Hume left that Eel River Ranch, he had in his possession that which he long had sought—an accurate detailed description of Black Bart." The next day, Hume issued a reward notice for the wanted man: "An American over 50 years of age, 5 feet, 8 or 9 inches in height, weight about 155 pounds, high forehead with points running well up into the hair, cheek bones prominent; light eyes, deep set; heavy eye brows, hair gray, heavy mustache and chin whiskers well mixed with gray; two or more front teeth missing; long slender hands that do not show work; wears a No. 6 or 7 boot;

reads without glasses, holding the paper at arm's length; showed no signs of being addicted to the use of liquor or tobacco."

Lida concluded, "Following the distribution of this circular, and in spite of the fact that this description was in the hands of every sheriff in the state, hardly a week passed in which Mr. Hume did not receive a wire from a sheriff somewhere, saying he had arrested a suspicious character believed to be Black Bart. Mr. Hume's reply invariably was the same: 'Does he answer the description in my circular of October, 1878? If not, I don't want him.' Mr. Hume's confidence in the young McCreary girl's description of Bart was so great that his replies to these messages were invariably the same."[16]

Jim Hume, after interviewing Donna McCreary, rode into Potter Valley, hired a posse of five local men to hunt the bandit, and then returned to Ukiah. There he wrote to Lida, then his fiancée, "Some fellow, I think Black Bart the Po8, robbed the stage between here and Cahto on Wednesday forenoon, and Thursday forenoon, thirty miles from here, on the road to Covelo. Yesterday evening I got track of him on Eel River and during the night I started out five discreet men in pursuit from Potter Valley... It is a terribly rough country and I didn't want any of it in mine, so returned here to spend the Sabbath and await a report from my outfit. I feel certain they will get him in a few days."[17]

But Hume's efforts to capture the elusive highwayman failed. Boles, after leaving the McCreary ranch, walked south to Clear Lake, the second largest in California, besides Lake Tahoe. Charley skirted Clear Lake, then crossed the Coast Range into the Sacramento Valley. Hume's posse from Potter Valley trailed Boles toward the rail town of Williams, where they concluded that he had boarded a train. Buck Montgomery, however, found and followed the tracks of a man on foot south to Suisun Bay, at the upper reaches of San Francisco Bay, before losing the trail. Whether Bart escaped by train or on foot was never established, but once again he had vanished. Montgomery would go on to become a well-known and very popular Wells Fargo shotgun messenger.[18]

In Mendocino County, Charley Boles, for the first time in his stage robbery career, had narrowly escaped capture. And he knew that young Donna McCreary had almost done him in. "I always was afraid of that little girl," he later said. "She looked at me too closely. I was afraid of her from the first."[19]

8

Wells Fargo Detective

Jim Hume nervously fingered the lever of his Henry rifle. It was a warm August night, and a cool breeze drifted down the valley from Lake Tahoe. The sky was moonless, but a blanket of stars lit up the high mountain road before him. From his position next to the tollhouse on the Upper Truckee River, Hume strained to get a good look at three shadowy forms riding toward him in the starlit blackness. He was barely able to make out the horsemen, each carrying a rifle slung across his saddle.

For several days, Hume and his four-man posse had been hunting a trio of elusive road agents. Their leader was a thirty-seven-year-old Frenchman who called himself Hugh De Tell. He was a dangerous robber and burglar who had served three terms in California's state prison at San Quentin. De Tell's companions were Walter Sinclair, who had been released from San Quentin only a few months before, and a German desperado known only as Faust.[1]

Hume, as undersheriff of El Dorado County, had received

reports that the three outlaws rode out of Sacramento toward Placerville, burglarizing houses along the way. From Placerville, they continued up the stage road toward the summit of the Sierra Nevada, holding up travelers and looting cabins as they went. This was the same route used five years earlier by the short-lived Pony Express. Undersheriff Hume quickly raised a small posse in Placerville and galloped toward the summit, hoping to cut off the bandits before they reached Lake Tahoe or Nevada. Jim and his men crossed the Sierra Nevada without encountering the desperadoes, then raced down Meyers Grade into the Lake Tahoe basin. They set up an ambush at the Osgood Toll House, situated at the foot of Meyers Grade, where the modern-day Highway 50 bridge crosses the Upper Truckee River, eight miles south of Lake Tahoe. Any riders approaching would have to cross the river on the bridge next to the tollhouse.[2]

It was eleven o'clock on the night of August 2, 1867, when Hume and his men heard the hoofbeats of approaching horses. As the riders got closer, Hume shouted at them, "I am the sheriff. Surrender!"

Hugh De Tell did not hesitate. He swung up his rifle and fired, and a heavy ball ripped into Hume's right arm. Fortunately for the officer, it was only a flesh wound. Jim managed to raise his Henry rifle and yell, "Fire!"

He and his possemen, who were armed with pistols and shotguns, opened up a terrific barrage. Two slugs ripped into Faust's breast, tearing him from the saddle. The German outlaw was dead when he hit the ground. The posse's gunfire unhorsed De Tell and Sinclair. Sinclair cowered in the dust as their terrified horses raced away. De Tell dropped his rifle, then jumped off the bridge into the river. The possemen captured Sinclair and at daybreak began tracking De Tell. One of them sent a telegraph message to other law officers, advising that De Tell "started back towards Placerville, but as we have so good a description of him and Hume is on his track, no doubt he too will throw up the sponge."[3]

His prediction proved correct. Two of Hume's men captured De Tell near what is now Pollock Pines, where a bridge crossed the South Fork of the American River. De Tell and Sinclair were both lodged in the El Dorado County jail in Placerville. Sinclair told his captors that he was only twenty-one and had served in the US Army in Arizona Territory. In fact, he was several years older, and his main service had been two previous terms in San Quentin. Both men were convicted of highway robbery and sentenced to eight years each in state prison. Jim Hume quickly recovered from his wound, and two years later, the grateful citizens elected him sheriff of El Dorado County.[4]

Hume had much in common with Charley Boles. Jim was almost three years older and spent his early boyhood on a farm in the Catskill Mountains of New York. When he was ten, his father moved the family to northern Indiana, where he broke ground on a new farm. Like Boles, Jim performed well in school, became a voracious reader, and detested farming. "I never had a holiday," he once said. "It was work, work, work; plowing and grubbing from six o'clock a.m. until dark. When the ground was too wet to plow, we had to build fences or haul wood, or hull corn, or clean the barn—never an idle moment." In 1850, he and one of his brothers joined the gold rush to California. Hume settled in Placerville, and like Boles, he failed as a gold miner. He opened a general store but truly found his calling when the town's voters elected him marshal, or police chief, in 1862.[5]

Jim developed into a popular and highly capable officer. His gunfight at the Osgood Toll House was not the first time he had shown courage under fire. In 1864, soon after he became undersheriff, Hume led a small posse that tracked down the gang of Ike McCollum, a notorious highwayman. After a pitched gun battle in which one of Jim's possemen was wounded, McCollum escaped, only to be accidentally shot and killed by one of his own gang a few weeks later. Soon after, a band of Confederate guerillas known as Captain Ingram's Partisan Rangers robbed two stagecoaches east of Placerville. The outlaws then shot and killed a pursuing deputy sheriff, one of Hume's best friends. Though overwhelmed with anger and grief, Jim helped lead a massive manhunt that ended with the killing or capture of most of the gang.

In 1872, after serving one term as sheriff of El Dorado County, he was appointed warden of the Nevada State Prison near Carson City. As a result of political infighting, he resigned the next year. Soon afterward, Wells Fargo officials hired Hume as the company's chief special officer, thus beginning a thirty-one-year career that would make him America's most celebrated express

JOHN BOESSENECKER COLLECTION.

James B. Hume, chief special officer for Wells Fargo, as he looked in 1879. He was the West's most famous express detective.

detective. But contrary to myth, he was not the first Wells Fargo detective. That honor fell to Henry Johnson, a San Francisco police detective who worked as the express company's part-time sleuth from 1857 to 1871. Johnson handled everything from stage holdups to embezzlements by dishonest employees. During that period, several other lawmen also worked for Wells Fargo on a case-by-case basis. Jim Hume, however, became the company's first full-time permanent detective, and eventually supervised a small force of special officers who operated throughout the American West.[6]

His first major case for Wells Fargo began in July 1873, when a band of highwaymen robbed a stagecoach between Colfax and Grass Valley in the Northern Mines. They blew open the Wells Fargo strongbox, took out $7,000 in gold coin, and escaped. The holdup resulted in one of the most dramatic incidents in the annals of frontier banditry. One passenger aboard the coach was Eleanor Berry, a young mail-order bride. She was en route to Grass Valley to marry Lewis Dreibelbis, with whom she had corresponded but never met. During the robbery, she noticed that the masked bandit leader had a distinctive jagged scar on the back of one hand.

When she reached the rooming house occupied by Dreibelbis, the landlady explained that he was out of town but would soon return. Eleanor, still rattled by the holdup, was determined to marry. She donned her wedding dress and waited nervously for the groom. When finally the landlady announced that he was back, Eleanor stepped into the parlor room and found Dreibelbis, with a minister and a witness. Instantly she had second thoughts. Instead of a young man, he was grizzled and almost sixty. And his rough clothes seemed to belie his letters that boasted of financial success. But she made no objection, and the clergyman began the ceremony. As Dreibelbis recited the wedding vows, Eleanor thought that his voice sounded strangely familiar. Within moments, the ceremony was completed, and the newlyweds stepped to a table to sign the marriage license. As Lewis reached forward, Eleanor noticed on his hand a long, jagged scar. It was the same scar that she had seen on the highwayman's hand.

The young bride unleashed a bloodcurdling scream and fled from the room. Moments later, Dreibelbis strode quickly outside and vanished. Eleanor, shaken and humiliated beyond measure, left town the next day without revealing the reason. Jim Hume, unaware of the aborted wedding, worked hard to identify the stage robbers. Two weeks after the holdup, he got word that a stranger had appeared in Coloma, eight miles northwest of Placerville. The man drank heavily, spent freely, and deposited $1,000 in gold coin and a small bar of bullion with a local hotelkeeper. Hume went to the Coloma hotel and examined the gold coins and bar, which matched those stolen in the robbery. He arrested the stranger and brought him to jail in Placerville.

As the Wells Fargo detective later recalled, "I told him I thought I had a strong case against him, that the condition of his coin clearly indicated the effects of the giant powder [dynamite] explosion of the Grass Valley treasure box." The prisoner demanded a promise of immunity from punishment, but this the detective refused to give. However, Hume explained that the courts would deal leniently with a man who turned state's evidence, and the prisoner finally broke down and made a complete confession. He admitted that he was Lewis Dreibelbis and that he was an ex-convict. He confessed to both the Grass Valley robbery and the June holdup of a stage near Downieville. This led to the capture of the whole gang, four of whom were convicted and sent to San Quentin. In exchange, Dreibelbis was released without charge. He said nothing to Hume about his ill-fated marriage to Eleanor, no doubt because his first wife was alive and well in Iowa. Lewis Dreibelbis never saw Eleanor Berry again. She returned to her home south of San Jose, but was so distraught she tried to kill herself with chloroform.

A doctor rushed to her home and revived her. In the end, El-eanor's ultimate fate is unknown.[7]

Hume soon established a reputation as a pioneer in forensic detective work. In an 1878 stage holdup in the Klamath Moun-tains of Northern California, a Wells Fargo messenger shot and killed one of the bandits. The other two road agents opened fire with a shotgun and a Winchester rifle, but they only managed to kill one of the stage horses. Hume quickly responded. He inspected the dead horse, had all the buckshot removed, and kept it as evidence. Then he led a four-day manhunt that ended with the capture of two ex-convicts in their isolated mountain camp. The pair claimed innocence and were tried separately. Hume took the witness stand and showed the jury the buckshot from the dead stage horse. He then compared it to the lead shot found in the shells loaded in the ex-convict's shotgun. They were identical. That fact, coupled with other evidence, spurred the jurors to convict the man in just five minutes. His partner then pleaded guilty, and both were sent to San Quentin. This was one of the first cases in the West in which primitive bal-listics had been employed by a detective.[8]

But none of Hume's skill or persistence brought him any closer to finding Black Bart. Following the two holdups north of Ukiah, Hume and Jim Moore, sheriff of Mendocino County, became convinced that Black Bart was an ex-convict named Frank Fox. A one-eyed native of Ohio, Fox had been convicted of robbing a fruit peddler at gunpoint on a road near the coastal hamlet of Point Arena in 1871. He was convicted in Ukiah and handed an eleven-year jolt in San Quentin prison. In 1875, a fel-low prisoner who resembled Fox, and was also blind in one eye, confessed to the crime, and the California governor issued Fox a full pardon. Apparently Fox returned to Mendocino County, for Sheriff Moore picked up enough information about the ex-convict to persuade Hume that he was Black Bart.[9]

On January 20, 1879, Hume issued a Wells Fargo reward

notice for Fox. Contrary to depictions in countless Hollywood films, there were very few, if any, wanted posters tacked onto building walls in the Old West. In reality, reward flyers were mailed to law officers and frequently contained the admonishment, "Do not post." That is why Hume's wanted notice for Fox was prefaced, "For sheriffs and police officers only." The detective's circular advised, "From information in my possession, I am pretty thoroughly satisfied that one Frank Fox committed the following robberies, at two of which he left with the express box some doggerel signed 'Black Bart, the Po8.'" Hume then listed Bart's five stage holdups of 1877 and 1878 and concluded, "Please arrest the said Frank Fox and telegraph the undersigned at Sacramento, and sheriff at Ukiah. Any old convict who was serving at the same time with Fox will know him."[10]

But Frank Fox disappeared, and fortunately for the sake of justice, Hume never found him. By this time, lawmen all over Northern California were eager to capture Black Bart and earn the reward. One of them was Dan Haskell, chief of police of San Jose. Haskell enjoyed a long career as a highly capable lawman, but he could be as wrong as Hume. On April 15, 1879, he arrested Samuel Madison, who matched the description of Black Bart. Haskell kept the arrest quiet, notifying only Captain Appleton W. Stone of the San Francisco police.

Many San Francisco police detectives of that era performed private investigation work while they were on duty. Captain Stone did the same for Wells Fargo, and he went to the San Jose jail, took a long look at Madison, and agreed that he looked like Black Bart. He sent a telegram to Hume, who was busy handling cases as far away as Utah and Arizona. As a result, Samuel Madison, whom a San Jose reporter called "a worthless fellow," spent two weeks in the city jail. Finally Hume arrived and quickly concluded that Madison was not Black Bart. Haskell freed the prisoner, and Jim offered him $10 in exchange for a signed release of liability. Most working men earned no

FOR SHERIFFS AND POLICE OFFICERS ONLY.

From information in my possession, I am pretty thoroughly satisfied that one FRANK FOX committed the following robberies, at two of which he left with the express box some doggerel signed "BLACK BART, the P O 8:"

Aug. 3d, 1877, stage between Fort Ross and Russian River.

July 25th, 1878, stage between Quincy, (Plumas County), and Oroville, (Butte County).

July 30th, 1878, stage between La Porte and Oroville.

Oct. 2d, 1878, stage between Cahto and Ukiah, (Mendocino County).

Oct. 3d, 1878, stage between Cavelo and Ukiah, (Mendocino County).

The following is from the Register of the California State Prison:

Received Dec. 8th, 1871; Commitment No. 5059; Frank Fox, Native of Ohio; Crime, Robbery; Term, 11 years; from Mendocino County; age 27, (now 35 or 36); Laborer; Height, 5 feet 8¾ inches; Light Complexion; Gray Eyes; Light Hair; pardoned and restored by Gov. Booth, Feb. 11th, 1875.

DESCRIPTION—Left eye blind, (sometimes uses a glass eye); scar on left eye; U. S. on left forearm; two scars on base left thumb; stout built.

Please arrest the said FRANK FOX, and telegraph the undersigned at Sacramento, and Sheriff at Ukiah. Any old convict who was serving at same time with Fox will know him.

J. B. HUME,
Special Officer Wells, Fargo & Co.

Sacramento, Jan. 20th, 1879.

CALIFORNIA STATE LIBRARY.

Jim Hume's wanted notice for Black Bart, whom he mistakenly believed was Frank Fox.

more than $30 a month, so Madison eagerly took the money. He signed the document, agreeing to give up his right to sue for false imprisonment.

Jim Hume had acted shrewdly, for Haskell's political enemies soon heard about the arrest. They persuaded Madison to engage an attorney, who filed a $10,000 lawsuit against the chief. Madison, in his greed, neglected to tell his lawyer that he had signed a full release. When the case came up in court a few months later, Chief Haskell produced the signed agreement. Madison's attorney, thoroughly embarrassed, immediately dismissed the case. A grateful Dan Haskell became friends with Jim Hume. In 1882, he repaid Wells Fargo by capturing the notorious stage robber Dick Fellows, and the company later hired him as a shotgun messenger. Haskell served Wells Fargo faithfully for many years. Then, in 1905, bandits attacked his horse-drawn stage outside of Redding. In the ensuing gunfight, Dan Haskell died from two bullet wounds.[11]

While Hume ran down fruitless leads about Black Bart, he little suspected that the elusive highwayman was resting comfortably in his boardinghouse just a few city blocks from Jim's San Francisco office. Charley's favorite lodging place was the Webb House, situated at 37 Second Street, half a block south of Market Street. It was a spacious, three-story brick building with forty-five furnished rooms. One woman who lived there recalled that Boles was its "star boarder" because of his neat and gentlemanly demeanor. He especially enjoyed playing cards with Captain Russell White and his wife, who lived at the Webb House. White was head of the Underwriters Fire Patrol, a private fire department funded by several San Francisco insurance companies.[12]

It was probably through Captain White that Charley met Dave Scannell, the city's famed fire chief. Scannell was one of the best known men in San Francisco. A burly, adventurous native of New York City, he served as a volunteer fireman in New York during the 1840s before becoming an army captain in the Mexican War. Scannell then joined the gold rush and arrived in San Francisco in 1851, where he served as undersheriff and then was elected sheriff in 1855. By that time a political machine, created by Tammany Hall politicians from New York, controlled San Francisco's elections and its courts. Political ruffians, or shoulder strikers, stuffed ballot boxes, herded voters to the polls, and frightened off opposition voters. In 1856, extensive ballot fraud, municipal corruption, and the cold-blooded murder of a crusading newspaper editor who opposed the machine suddenly triggered a popular uprising. Six thousand citizens joined the newly organized San Francisco Committee of Vigilance, the largest vigilante movement in American history.

The vigilantes took over the city and removed two murderers from Sheriff Scannell's jail. They executed both men, then
hanged two more accused killers and rounded up the city's worst
political ruffians. The vigilantes banished thirty-eight criminals and shoulder strikers from California. Most were placed on
outgoing ships, while others fled to avoid capture. Dave Scannell opposed the Committee of Vigilance. Charley's Civil War
commander William T. Sherman, who at that time was a San
Francisco banker during a hiatus from his army career, accused
Scannell of being a New York shoulder striker. Nonetheless,
the vigilantes did not target Scannell, and he remained hugely
popular in the city. He served as chief of San Francisco's fire
department for most of the period from 1860 until his death in
1893. Charley Boles spent time with Scannell, got to know him
well, and later called him "a devilish nice fellow."[13]

JOHN BOESSENECKER COLLECTION.

*Dave Scannell, San Francisco's famed fire chief, who unwittingly befriended Charley
Boles.*

Charley did not always stay in the Webb House. Occasionally he boarded at the sumptuous Russ House, one of the most popular hotels in the city. It was a massive building at 219 Montgomery Street, occupying the entire block between Bush and Pine. The ground floor hosted retail businesses, and 342 hotel rooms filled the second and third floors. The site is occupied today by the Russ Building. Montgomery Street, and nearby Pauper Alley, were exactly where Charley wanted to be, central to his act as a successful mining man. From time to time, he also roomed in a smaller boardinghouse at 35 Montgomery Street, which had shops and offices on the ground floor and furnished rooms upstairs. Ironically, one of his fellow lodgers there was Miers F. Truett, a prominent merchant who had been a leader of the 1856 Committee of Vigilance.[14]

Hubert Howe Bancroft, California's leading historian of that era, aptly described Truett. "He was afraid of nothing; a man of iron, morally and physically. Two heavy muscular teamsters were one day fighting on the street, when Truett came along and seizing each by the collar held them off at arm's length, as the school-master separates pugilistic pupils." The ex-vigilante had no patience for criminals, let alone stage robbers. In 1871, Truett was a passenger aboard a coach in Sonoma County when it was stopped by the notorious John Houx gang. A blistering shootout erupted between the outlaws and stage passengers. Truett shoved his shotgun out the window and fired both barrels into an outlaw known as "Rattle Jack." The bloodied stagecoach escaped, with the driver and one passenger wounded and another passenger dead. Later Rattle Jack's buckshot-riddled corpse was found in the Russian River. One can only imagine Truett's consternation had he discovered that his congenial and gentlemanly fellow lodger was the much-wanted Black Bart.[15]

Charley's favorite boardinghouses were a stone's throw from Detective Hume's headquarters in the Wells Fargo building at the corner of California and Sansome Streets. No doubt Boles thought it a good joke on the wealthy express company. He spent the winter of 1878 to 1879 living comfortably on the money he had stolen in the two Mendocino holdups. Then, in June 1879, Boles bid his San Francisco friends goodbye, telling them that he had to visit his mines. Once again he returned to familiar territory, this time the stage road between La Porte and Oroville. On June 21, at a spot three miles west of Forbestown, he halted a stage driven by Dave Quadlin. The veteran reinsman later said that the road agent was "completely disguised with rags muffled about his head, hands, and feet, standing in the middle of the road." There was one passenger aboard, a woman, and Quadlin later said that she was "quite badly frightened." The Wells Fargo express box held only $50 and a silver watch. The jehu quickly complied with Charley's demand that he toss down the strongbox and the mail. Quadlin asked him to return the waybills and the mail, but Boles refused and ordered, "Pass on." The whip obeyed, and Boles kept him covered with his gun until the stage hove out of sight.[16]

While the Butte County sheriff made a fruitless search for the bandit, Charley slipped back to San Francisco. But his loot supported him for only three months. In October, he headed north by train for the railhead in Redding, seat of Shasta County, a prosperous mining region. He walked up the Siskiyou Trail to the top of Bass Hill, twelve miles north of Redding, and took up a position at a sharp bend in the wagon road. The Siskiyou Trail was the main stage route between California and Oregon. At ten o'clock on the night of October 25, 1879, the southbound coach approached, carrying a lone woman passenger from Oregon. As Charley stepped into the beams of the stage lanterns, the horses spooked and began to wheel off to the side of the road. The whip, Jimmy Smithson, quickly reined them in and halted his coach.

PHOTO BY DON GORDON.

The old stage route, now called Lower Forbestown Road, site of Black Bart's robbery of the coach from Forbestown to Oroville on June 21, 1879.

"Hold up your hands!" Boles demanded. "Throw out the mail sacks and the box!"

"The express box is locked fast to the stage," responded Smithson.

"We want the mail bags," Charley insisted, implying that he had confederates. The reinsman threw down five sacks of mail. Then Boles handed him an axe and said, "Cut the box open."

Smithson reached under his seat, where the express box was chained to the floor of the front boot. Wells Fargo had been robbed so often that its agents began attaching a chain from the iron handles of the strongbox to the frame of the coach. Smithson struck the wood-and-iron box several blows with the axe, but Charley was impatient.

"Hit it harder, or you'll never get it opened at that rate," he insisted.

The driver then told Boles to do it himself. Charley stepped forward, took the axe, and ordered, "Get out and hold the lead horses."

Boles instructed the woman passenger to exit the stage and take a seat on top where he could keep an eye on her. Next he climbed onto the front boot and chopped a hole in the strongbox, but found little of value inside. Then, while Smithson and the woman looked on, Charley slashed and emptied the mailbags. Finally he allowed the stage to continue its trip toward Redding. A local journalist reported, "It is not known how much the robber got, but there was little or nothing in the box when it left Yreka, though there may have been something put in at the way stations below. There was in all probability considerable money in the registered mail matter, as it was collected from the various offices along the route between Portland and where the stage was robbed." Another newspaperman reported that $1,400 had been looted from the mail.[17]

The next morning, Smithson returned to the robbery scene from Redding with his brother-in-law, Wells Fargo shotgun messenger John Reynolds. In a nearby gulch, they found the mail scattered about. Reynolds, an expert man hunter, cut the bandit's sign and followed it north a few miles. But Charley was too smart for him, and Reynolds lost the trail. Boles doubled back and hiked twenty-five miles east through the mountains to a point on the stage road that went from Redding to the remote town of Alturas in Modoc County, situated in the northeast corner of California. The spot he had picked was extremely isolated, twelve miles northeast of the settlement of Millville. Charley obviously knew the stage roads well.

On October 27, just two days after the Bass Hill holdup, driver Ed Payne was bringing his Redding-bound stage through a narrow, winding canyon. He had no passengers, and his Wells Fargo box was almost empty. However, the registered mail contained about $1,300 in cash. Charley stepped into the roadway and halted the stage. It was his eleventh holdup, and he wasted little time in taking the box and the mail. Then he ordered Payne to drive on, and the reinsman raced into Millville, where he raised the alarm. A message was sent to Redding, and soon John Reynolds of Wells Fargo started out at the head of a five-man posse that included a Native American tracker. They rode to the scene of the robbery, arriving the next morning. The posse-men found the shattered express box fifty feet from the road, and the Indian trailer quickly cut the bandit's sign. Reynolds and his men tracked the bandit south. One of the posse later re-called that the robber "hardly ever stepped on the ground; he stepped on the rocks and backtracked a lot." They encountered a boy who said he had met a stranger a mile from the holdup site. The man was undoubtedly the robber, for he had asked a lot of questions about the local country and distances to places and towns. But even the Indian tracker could not catch Char-ley Boles. The posse managed to follow the trail twenty-five miles south to Jelly's Ferry on the Sacramento River, where they lost the scent.[18]

In the two Shasta County holdups, Boles had reaped his big-gest harvest yet: $2,700. Jim Hume rushed to Redding and

Black Bart's favorite target, the Wells Fargo strongbox, carried under the stage driver's seat.

soon issued reward notices offering $1,300 for the stage rob-
ber. He wrote a letter to his fiancée correctly identifying the
stage robber as Black Bart but still insisting that he was Frank
Fox. Although Black Bart was now well-known to the police
and sheriffs of California, his name had not yet become common knowledge. It was left to the *Yreka Journal*, published in the
small mining town just south of the Oregon state line, to print
what may have been the first newspaper story about Black Bart.
Its report appeared in November 1879, not long after the two
Shasta County robberies.[19]

"The highwayman who stopped the California and Oregon
stage and Alturas stage a couple of weeks ago is believed to be
the well known scoundrel who signs his name 'Black Bart, the
Po8,' and is given to the habit of writing doggerel, or burlesque
rhyme," declared the *Journal*'s editor. "He is a shrewd and desperate customer to deal with, and so completely covered his
trail from the places of robbery that [he left] no trace on the
Sacramento River or Alturas roads or the country in the vicinity. He has evidently escaped through the stunted oak forests
at the head of the Sacramento Valley, north of Shasta, towards
Honey Lake Valley. A man has been sent to Susanville to hunt
for him and endeavor to get a description, so that he may be
captured, a standing reward of $1,300 being offered for his ar-
rest and conviction."[20]

But once again, Boles eluded pursuers and slipped quietly
back to San Francisco. It may have been during his flight from
Shasta County that lawmen almost captured him. Charley later
described the incident, which featured an encounter with a
skunk, to a newspaperman. As the journalist explained, "He
had not been walking very long when he heard voices behind
him, and looking down the mountain side, could see several
horsemen and footmen coming in his direction at a lively gait.
They were gaining on him very fast, and he was compelled
to do something very suddenly or be captured, and his only

chance for escape was to secrete himself before they caught sight of him. He began looking about him, and noticed a large, hollow fir log which lay on the ground. Plunging into it head first just before the vigilantes came in sight, he crawled to the farthest end of the hole, but he discovered to his horror that he had company, which by the peculiar odor emitted he concluded was a polecat—in fact, he knew it was. It was a time for tears but not for retreat, and he lay there in mortal agony and heard his pursuers come up and sit down on the log, while their dog tried to make the acquaintance of the fragrant occupant of the hole in the log. The smell finally drove them away, and Bart crawled hurriedly out, not only sick at heart and with the world, but terribly sick at the stomach. He declares that he did not get over the effects of his experience in the log for three months afterward, and that it nearly cured him of his propensity for robbing stages."[21]

9

The Gentleman Bandit

Charley Boles lived the high life in San Francisco. Though certainly not a member of upper-crust Nob Hill society, he nonetheless associated with reputable merchants, mining men, storekeepers, and even some of the city's ace police detectives. They all knew him under his principal alias, Charles Bolton. He wore expensive clothing, speculated in mining stocks, and enjoyed dining with friends and attending the city's racetracks. Declared a San Francisco journalist who later interviewed some of his acquaintances, "Mr. Bolton while in this city lived in luxury and never was known to perform a day's work."[1]

Charley later insisted that he was not a gambler, but he admitted betting on horses. As he once told a newspaperman, "It is very likely you have seen me with the sports [gamblers] of San Francisco. I am acquainted with quite a number of them. But I never gambled to the extent of a ten cent piece, except on horse races. I never visited a faro game or any other low place, except that I once went to the Bella Union, and that was from curiosity. I defy any man to say that I ever visited a place of ill fame in San Francisco." In the parlance of that era, a house of ill fame was a brothel, and the Bella Union, then a popular theater, had once been San Francisco's most famous gambling hall. Yet he did not wear those fine clothes purely to impress other mining men. Some years later, a San Francisco journalist who interviewed Charley's friends wrote, "It is known that he had a mistress somewhere in this city." Her name, however, is lost to history.[2]

Charley Boles was totally unlike the typical stage robbing ruffian who freely spent his loot in saloons, card parlors, and brothels, leaving a trail of cash for lawmen to follow. Prostitutes frequently informed on criminals, but because Boles was unknown in the red-light districts of San Francisco and Sacramento, the police never received any such tips about him. And he had no confederates in crime who could turn him in for the reward money. As a result, Jim Hume and his fellow detectives lacked the usual sources that led them to the lairs of highway robbers.

One of Charley's closest comrades in the city was Jacob M. Pike, a colorful ex-sailor who had arrived in San Francisco in 1850 at the height of the gold rush. Pike owned Charley's two favorite eating places. One was the United States Restaurant at the corner of Montgomery and Clay streets, which Pike advertised as the "largest, cheapest, and best restaurant in San Francisco," featuring a three-course meal for twenty-five cents. The other was the New York Bakery and Restaurant at 626 Kearny Street. Both were a stone's throw from San Francisco's city hall on Portsmouth Square, which then housed the police headquarters.[3]

Jacob Pike was no friend of highwaymen. After failing at gold mining, he ran a sawmill near Coulterville in the Tuolumne County foothills. In 1856, he joined a vigilante group and helped hang a Mexican bandit who had robbed several Chinese miners. Then Pike took over a general store on the Stanislaus River. "This location was a hard place for rough characters," he recalled. On one occasion in 1857, he attempted to disarm a pistol-wielding desperado but was too late. The ruffian shot and wounded one of the patrons in his store. The following year, Pike led a posse in pursuit of a band of Frenchmen who had slain two miners and wounded three more in a shootout over a gold mining claim. The murderers escaped after killing one member of Pike's posse. By 1861, he had married and moved nearby to the new copper mining town of Copperopolis in Calaveras County. With two of his brothers, Pike opened the town's first general store, and he soon became its first postmaster and Wells Fargo agent.[4]

During the Civil War, Copperopolis boomed because of the huge market for copper, essential in manufacturing cannons and shell casings. But with the end of the war, many of the mines closed down, and Pike gave up his store and moved with his wife and children to San Francisco. In 1871, he acquired the New York Bakery and Restaurant, one of the biggest and most popular eating places in the city, for the then-whopping sum of $10,000. Then, as Pike recalled, "The first of 1873 I bought a large restaurant called the United States Restaurant at the corner of Clay and Montgomery, and ran them both. My profits that year were sixty thousand dollars. The business in both restaurants was enormous. Used to give out in both restaurants about five thousand meals a day."[5]

Boles became a regular customer of the two dining halls, and he and Pike established a close friendship. Charley loved telling of his exploits in the war, and Jacob Pike was also a raconteur. The two would often sit together for long talks about mining, the stock market, and horse racing. Because of their proximity to police headquarters, a number of detectives frequented Pike's restaurants. "I have dined frequently with them," Charley later recalled. Several of the sleuths became—most unwittingly—friends of Black Bart.[6]

COURTESY OF PETER PIKE JR.

Jacob M. Pike, the colorful pioneer who became one of Charley's closest friends in San Francisco.

That camaraderie was all the more remarkable given that San Francisco's police department employed some of the most astute and experienced detectives in the American West. The San Francisco police of the nineteenth century were, by the standards of that era, extremely professional and well organized. At that time, the spoils system held sway, and most American police departments consisted of political appointees who were regularly replaced by successive administrations. Because an entire force would often be fired every few years to be supplanted by supporters of the new political party in power, few officers could gain experience. In San Francisco, however, the Committee of Vigilance of 1856 initiated reforms that helped remove its police department from political patronage and allowed dedicated officers to serve in long careers.

The result was a well-regulated force that numbered about

four hundred in 1880. Uniformed patrolmen, trained and supervised, were everywhere. By regulation, their short-barreled .38-caliber revolvers were kept out of sight, worn underneath blue knee-length tunics. Officers who were caught drinking, gambling, or sleeping on duty were routinely disciplined or fired. As early as 1857, the force initiated one of the first police rogues galleries in the nation, using newly available photography to take images of anyone arrested for a serious offense. Detailed records were kept of every arrest. Instead of modern facial recognition technology, the department employed Sergeant Tim Bainbridge as its identification officer. He had a photographic memory for faces, names, and details. Arrested crooks were brought before Bainbridge, who would invariably recognize them and provide their true identities and criminal histories.[7]

For five decades, the city's chief of detectives was Captain Isaiah W. Lees. Largely forgotten today, he was one of the most remarkable sleuths in American history. William Pinkerton of the famed Pinkerton Detective Agency called him "the greatest criminal catcher the West ever knew." Lees opposed corrupt politicians and played a major role in every major criminal case in San Francisco from 1853 to his retirement as police chief in 1900. He also trained a cadre of highly skilled detectives. Very little escaped their attention—from business affairs and politics to vice and crime. Captain Lees's men knew personally every thief, burglar, robber, and fence in the city, and they regularly visited pawn shops and secondhand dealers to identify and recover stolen property. They also checked hotel registers daily to keep tabs on new arrivals in the city, who were then "piped," or shadowed, to make sure they were not criminals. Their surveillance was so thorough that on one occasion in 1881, detectives spotted a suspicious stranger named John Curtin after he checked into a downtown hotel. They tailed Curtin for a week before Lees discovered that he was a former Pinkerton man from New York who had come to the city to work on a case. Captain Lees called off his men. Such incidents made it all the more remarkable that his detectives never suspected Charley Boles.[8]

Charley often socialized with several of Lees's men at the United States Restaurant and the New York Bakery. A journalist who later interviewed patrons of the New York Bakery wrote that Boles "would eat at the same table with a detective, preferring, so it seemed, their company to any other who happened to be there." One was Chris Cox, who spoke Chinese and was assigned to the Chinatown squad. An expert at murder investigations, he always carried a pistol and a silver-sheathed bowie knife in his hip pockets. The two became friends, and even discussed the mysterious lone bandit Black Bart. Cox served for twenty years before he was fired, along with fourteen other officers, on suspicion of corruption in 1894. Another chum of Boles was William S. "Billy" Jones, one of Captain Lees's favorite assistants. Jones, after pounding a beat for ten years, won appointment as a detective in 1878. But in 1885, Jones suffered, according to the official record, "softening of the brain" and was admitted to the state insane asylum in Napa, where he died the following year.[9]

Boles also knew Detectives Dan Coffee and Ed Byram. Coffee, who became a city policeman in 1869, made detective nine years later. Though he specialized in arresting pickpockets, he handled everything from murders to train robberies. Coffee was still serving as a highly respected detective in 1894 when, suffering from ill health and financial woes, he shot himself to death in his San Francisco home. Ed Byram, Coffee's partner, was the nephew of police chief Henry H. Ellis. Byram enjoyed a long and successful career, from 1876 to 1908. Perhaps his most notable exploit was the daring capture of Missouri train robber and outlaw leader Marion Hedgepeth in 1892. But despite the skill and experience of these crack sleuths, not one of them suspected that their genial, well-dressed companion was the West's most wanted stage robber. Charley was later asked if

JOHN BOESSENECKER COLLECTION.

Charley's comrade San Francisco police detective Ed Byram. When Charley's overcoat was stolen in 1879, Byram recovered it, never suspecting that his friend was Black Bart.

he feared that his detective friends might discover him. "No, they didn't know who I was," he responded. "I never associated with any but good people, and they never dreamed what my business was."[10]

In late 1879, Boles took up lodgings at the Commercial Hotel, situated near his two favorite restaurants, at the corner of Kearny Street and present-day Columbus Avenue. He was out on the town on December 16 when a sneak thief entered his room and stole his new overcoat. In that era, clothing was handmade, valuable, and therefore a frequent target of burglars and sneak thieves. Charley did not report the theft and instead just bought a new and expensive chinchilla fur coat. The next day he was in the hotel's reading room when he stepped outside briefly, leaving his coat inside. Someone, probably the same prowler, slipped inside and made off with it. Boles later said that "some thief stole the new garment" and he became "determined to have that thief punished."

He walked a few blocks to police headquarters at Portsmouth Square and reported the crime. Ed Byram and Billy Jones were assigned the case, and Byram quickly found the missing coat for sale in a secondhand clothing shop. "They brought the property back within an hour," Boles later explained. Detective Byram, who kept a highly detailed daily journal, recorded the incident two days later. "I recovered a black chinchilla overcoat from H. Isaac's, 239 Third St. Stolen from the reading room of the Commercial Hotel yesterday. It belonged to C.E. Bolton." In that era, police officers were not prohibited from accepting tips, and Charley said later that he "paid them for their trouble."[11]

Boles, when not bamboozling detectives, enjoyed a life of leisure in San Francisco. He was fascinated by life in the big city. His favorite pastime was loitering in front of the Bush Street Theater, situated at 325 Bush Street, between Montgomery and Kearny. The Bush Street Theater was one of the most popular entertainment places in the city and featured minstrel shows, plays, musicals, and variety acts. The playhouse was a substantial brick building, three stories high, with seats for one thousand four hundred patrons, and the ground floor featured several shops and businesses. One of them was Chris Buckley's Alhambra Saloon. Buckley, notorious as the "Blind Boss," ran Democratic politics in San Francisco during the 1880s until his 1891 indictment for bribery. In 1882, one of the ushers at the Bush Street Theater was sixteen-year-old David Warfield, who got acquainted with the natty Mr. Bolton. Two decades later, Warfield would become one of the most famous stage actors in America, and after that, co-owner of a national chain of movie theaters. A journalist who interviewed Warfield in 1923 wrote, "Black Bart became one of the sidewalk fixtures in front of the playhouse. He would stand for hours in one position watching the actors as they passed in and out of Chris Buckley's saloon."[12]

Directly across the street from the theater, at 316 Bush, was a tobacco shop and laundry agency owned by Frank Muncey. He and Charley became bosom friends, and Muncey, who knew him as Bolton, thought highly of the Civil War veteran. A newspaperman who later spoke with Muncey wrote, "Bolton was one of his patrons, and a frequent visitor at the establishment. He was an intelligent and companionable man, and fond of recounting his experience in the army, having been a Union soldier, and present during the siege of Vicksburg and in other military operations in the Southwest. Bolton then represented himself as a mining man, and such he was supposed to be. He was generous, and frequently lent a helping hand to impecunious miners who found themselves stranded at the Bay City."[13]

The Bush Street Theater is the large building on the left. Charley's favorite pastime in San Francisco was loitering on the sidewalk in front of the theater.

Boles, when not betting on the horses or loitering on Bush Street, surely also spent time and money on his mistress, whoever she was. But by mid-July of 1880, after six months of San Francisco leisure, he again found himself short of cash. Charley wasted no time in returning to the stage routes of Sonoma County on the North Coast, probably traveling by train to Duncans Mills on the Russian River. But this time he avoided the coastal road where, three years before, he had robbed Ash Wilkinson's stage and left his first poem at Shotgun Point in Timber Gulch. Instead, Charley walked north on the Meyers Grade, an inland stage road that led north through the rugged coastal hills to Fort Ross and Mendocino. He found a good spot on the road about four miles south of modern-day Seaview. At nine o'clock on the morning of July 22, masked and wielding a shotgun, he stepped in front of the southbound coach driven by Martin McClennan. The stage carried three passengers, two men and a woman.

Boles demanded the Wells Fargo box, but McClennan told him, "It is chained and locked to the bottom of the stage."

Charley had learned his lesson about a chained strongbox during his last holdup. Because he could not keep an eye on the driver and passengers while he worked on the box, he made no effort to break it open. Instead, he demanded, "Hand out the US mail."

McClennan tossed down six mailbags, and Boles ordered him to drive on. The jehu rushed into Duncans Mills and gave the alarm. McClennan and his passengers were so shocked they thought that they had been stopped by three masked robbers. Oddly, they also reported that the trio was armed with a single shotgun. A telegram was sent to Santa Rosa, the county seat, and soon the Sonoma County sheriff and two deputies were on their way in a buggy. They searched the holdup site and found five rifled sacks of mail but no trace of the highwayman.[14]

Three days later, McClennan drove his stage back north

on the return trip. At a spot near the robbery scene, he came
upon a man walking up the road. McClennan thought that
he recognized him as the robber who had wielded the shotgun. The reinsman, thinking quickly, offered him a ride, and
the man climbed aboard. McClennan struck up a conversation
and learned that the man's name was Lane Nelson, and that he
lived a few miles away. The driver dropped Nelson off at the
next stop. Then McClennan reported the holdup to the local
postmaster, who promptly went to a justice of the peace and
swore out an arrest warrant. The sheriff arrested Nelson and
several of his comrades. However, there was no evidence against
Nelson's friends, so the lawman soon released them. He then
brought Nelson to Santa Rosa and lodged him in the Sonoma
County jail. Although a judge found that there was probable
cause to hold Nelson for trial, he soon proved his innocence,
and the charges were dropped. Two months later, when another stage was robbed at the same spot, Wells Fargo detectives
hired Nelson and a number of other local men to hunt for the
stolen strongbox. They could not find it, but they did discover
a packet of San Francisco bank checks that Boles had discarded
after the July holdup.[15]

By that time, Charley had gone north, returning to Redding
in Shasta County. He apparently did not get much of a haul in
the Meyers Grade robbery, for he was already planning a new
series of holdups. From Redding he walked eleven miles up the
wagon road that led west through the mountains to the mining
town of Weaverville. At two the afternoon of September 1, 1880,
he heard the Weaverville stage approaching. Stepping into the
road, Boles aimed his shotgun at the driver, Charley Creamer,
and barked, "Drop that box!"

The reinsman had but one passenger, Mathilde Eliasen, the
thirty-six-year-old wife of a local miner. They were startled at
the apparition before them. The road agent had covered his head
in a flour sack with eye holes and a linen duster that concealed

his clothing. Like the victims of the Meyers Grade holdup, the pair was so rattled they thought that there were at least two bandits.

Creamer quickly threw out the Wells Fargo box, and Boles then ordered him to hand over the mailbags. The driver tossed out one sack from the front boot and climbed down and pulled two more bags from the rear boot. Eager to leave, Creamer swung back into his seat, but Charley asked if the stage had a second strongbox.

The driver answered in the affirmative, adding, "It is an iron box fastened securely to the stage."

"Get down and hold the leaders," Boles ordered, and then said to Mrs. Eliasen, "Get on top of the stage."

She asked if she could stand in the roadway, saying she feared that "the horses might start."

"Very well," Charley responded. "Suit yourself."

He then stepped to the side of the road and pulled out an old axe that he had buried in a pile of leaves. Climbing into the rear boot, he found an iron pony safe chained to its floor. He chopped the box loose from the wood flooring and shoved it to the ground. Charley then sliced open the mailbags with a knife and waved the stage on. Creamer laid down the lash and raced into Redding. There he and Mrs. Eliasen gave a detailed account to a local journalist. "He was as polite a man as ever cut a throat or scuttled a ship, and his politeness was only exceeded in his facetiousness, for during the robbery he entertained the only passenger, Mrs. Eliasen of Douglas City, with his witticisms," wrote the reporter. "After taking both boxes and going through the mail he departed, requesting the driver to go on as fast as he could and hurry the 'hounds' [lawmen] up, as he was quite lonesome in the mountains."[16]

For his efforts, Charley got only $108 from Wells Fargo and very little from the mail. Despite his goading the officers, he had no intention of waiting for a posse to arrive. Boles hiked

The iron "pony safe" that Black Bart chopped loose from the Weaverville stage in 1880. It is displayed in the Jake Jackson Museum in Weaverville, CA.

south a dozen miles through the rugged Klamath Mountains to Eagle Creek. On the morning of September 3, two days after the holdup, he walked up to the isolated ranch house of John T. Adkins, a cattle raiser. Adkins was out searching for stray stock, but his wife, Celia, greeted the stranger. He carried a three-foot-long blanket roll strapped across his back, fastened with straps, his shotgun hidden inside. Mrs. Adkins later said that the man asked "if he could get some breakfast, at the same time saying that he was able and willing to pay for it."

She agreed, and while she was cooking the meal, Charley picked up her one-year-old boy, bounced him on one knee, and let him play with his watch and chain. She served him breakfast with coffee, and recalled that "he took five full cups, apologizing that he liked strong coffee and had not had any for some time." When he was done, Celia Adkins gave him a sack lunch, and he thanked her and started east toward the railroad line. Charley may have planned to board a train, for the next day a railroad section boss spotted him walking along the tracks three miles south of Redding. Instead he hiked one hundred twenty miles north toward the Oregon state line, camping along the way. Boles passed Coles Station, where he had robbed his third stage in 1876, then crossed into Oregon. Two weeks had passed since he had robbed Creamer's stage, and Black Bart was ready to strike again.[17]

At eleven o'clock on the night of September 16, George Chase was urging his horses up the grade to Siskiyou Summit, six miles north of the state line. His coach, headed south to California, carried a woman passenger and $1,000 cash in the Wells Fargo box. The strongbox was chained to the floor of the driver's box. Charley stopped the stage, ordered Chase to get down at gunpoint, and then climbed onto the driver's seat. Pulling out a small axe, he chopped a hole in one end of the wooden box and removed the contents. Then, after taking the mail sacks, Boles ordered Chase, "Travel on."

The woman passenger was so frightened that although she only saw one bandit, she was sure she had heard others talking in the darkness. Chase drove thirty miles to Yreka and reported the holdup. A wire was sent to Redding, and John Reynolds, Wells Fargo's shotgun messenger, rode to the scene. He found the rifled mail sacks but no sign of the highwayman. Boles, after robbing the stage, had walked thirty miles north to Jacksonville, Oregon. He spent a day there, unsuspected, then headed back south into the Siskiyou Mountains. On the night of September 23, a week after robbing Chase's stage, he stopped the California-bound coach driven by Nort Eddings. The holdup site was near the spot where he had pulled his prior robbery. Charley first demanded the mail sacks, then used his axe to smash open the chained-down strongbox. This time his labors were well rewarded, for the box held $1,000 in gold dust. Then Boles waved on Eddings and his lone woman passenger.[18]

Charley's timing had been impeccable. Had he waited just three days, he would have encountered a Concord coach occupied by his old commander, William T. Sherman, and President Rutherford B. Hayes. President Hayes was on a tour of the American West, only the second US president to travel west of

the Rocky Mountains. (President U. S. Grant had visited Utah
five years earlier.) His visit was so unique that enthusiastic crowds
gathered at every place he stopped. Hayes and his wife had come
to California with General Sherman on the transcontinental
railroad. They traveled north by train to Redding, and then
continued on to Oregon by stage. Their coach passed along the
very road where Charley had just pulled his last two holdups.
And Boles was more than fortunate, for a detachment of US
cavalrymen accompanied the president's stagecoach. Surely they
would have made short work of any highwayman who pointed
a shotgun at the President of the United States.[19]

Wells Fargo officials sent their new detective, Charles Aull,
to investigate the Oregon robberies. Aull, a close friend of Jim
Hume, had been undersheriff of Stanislaus County, then spent
five years as a captain of guards at San Quentin prison. He
had only recently lost his prison job due to political turnover,
and Hume then hired him as a special officer. But Aull had no
better luck finding Black Bart than had his boss. Meanwhile,
Boles, following his usual custom, walked south from the Siskiyou Mountains, avoiding people whenever possible. In seven
days, he hiked almost two hundred miles to Paskenta, a small
settlement in the Coast Range of California. There he spent the
night of September 30 in the village hotel, telling folks that his
name was Harry Barton. He signed the hotel register in flow-
ing script, "H. Barton."

The next day, Charley walked south another twenty-five miles
to Elk Creek, another isolated settlement in the Coast Range.
There he had his closest call yet when he encountered a pair
of traveling salesmen, Floyd Vickers and B. F. White. Vickers,
who had been town clerk of nearby Red Bluff, was a handsome,
thirty-two-year-old womanizer. He had recently been fined
for assaulting a Red Bluff newspaper editor. That was the era
of rough-and-tumble journalism, and the editor rebuked Vickers in print, calling him a "pompous, short-winded, pugilistic,

artistic, crane-necked, sandy headed, stuffed shanked, traveling perfumery shop and slop bucket." A chastened Vickers left town, and with White traveled the rural countryside, selling life insurance. Vickers and White encountered Boles in Elk Creek, and for unclear reasons, they made a citizen's arrest. They certainly did not know that he was Black Bart, and probably arrested him as a vagrant or suspicious person. After Charley convinced them that he was Harry Barton, an honest and reputable man, they let him go.

A few weeks later, an exasperated Jim Hume heard about the arrest and quickly issued a wanted notice offering an $800 reward for "Harry Barton." Detective Hume gave only a few details about the incident. "On the evening of October 1st he was arrested by B.F. White and Floyd Vickers, at Elk Creek Station, in Tehama County; they released him after detaining him a short time. The robber was then going towards Lake or Sonoma County." However, Hume was able to provide a detailed description of the wanted man. "When last seen, October 1, 1880, was dressed in steel-mixed [gray] coat and vest, checked wool shirt, blue overalls outside and red duck pants underneath; kip boots badly worn and run over on inside; dirty light-colored felt hat; silver watch and heavy link silver chain. While traveling was seen to carry bundle or roll two and a half or three feet long, fastened with blanket straps, supposed to have an unbreeched shotgun inside."[20]

Charley, despite his narrow escape, was not dissuaded. He needed more money to support himself through the winter. Perhaps he did go south to Lake or Sonoma counties, or perhaps he walked to Sacramento. Either way, Boles stayed out of sight for six weeks. Then he reappeared on the ice-cold evening of November 20, 1880. Charley chose the same holdup spot where he had pulled his third stage robbery in 1876, just south of Coles Station on the Oregon state line. This time he trained his shotgun on Joe Mason, driver of a northbound coach headed toward

Jacksonville. Mason reined up and exclaimed, "It is the other stage coming from Jacksonville that you want."

"I guess not," Charley responded calmly. "Hand out the mail and the express box."

Mason tossed out one mailbag, then asked the robber for help with the strongbox. "Take the box out," the reinsman demanded. "It is too hard to pull out from under the seat."

Boles climbed up on the wheel, holding his shotgun with one hand, barrels pointed in the air. As he reached forward to seize the strongbox, Mason grabbed a hatchet from his seat and swung it up to cleave the road agent's skull. But Charley was too quick, and leaped to the ground. Boles had never fired his shotgun in a robbery and he refrained now. Mason whipped up his team and the coach rumbled off, quickly disappearing in the darkness. Charley, shaken by his close call, hurriedly opened the mail sack and removed a few letters. But in his haste to flee, he overlooked the registered mail packages. Meanwhile, Mason encountered the southbound stage and warned its jehu, Ab Giddings, about the robber. When Giddings reached the holdup

Stagecoaches lined up in front of Coles Station, just south of the California-Oregon state line. Charley Boles robbed two stages near this spot.

site, he found the opened mailbag and some letters strewn about the roadway.

A Yreka journalist reported, "The robber evidently became frightened at something when he cut open the sack, and made tracks to escape." Most likely Boles had heard Ab Giddings's stagecoach approaching. The reporter concluded that the highwayman "was evidently a green hand, probably a tramp."[21]

Given that it was Black Bart's sixteenth stage holdup, he could not have been more wrong.

10

The Chances I Have to Take

Hannibal, Missouri, was a far cry from the bright lights, expansive buildings, and crowded cobblestone streets of San Francisco. When Mary Boles moved there with her three teenage daughters in 1874, the town boasted dirt streets, board sidewalks, and wood-frame buildings, with a handful of modern brick and stone structures. Nestled along the surging Mississippi, Hannibal was sandwiched between two promontories, Lovers Leap and Cardiff Hill. Soon it would achieve lasting fame as the boyhood home of Mark Twain and the setting for his novels *The Adventures of Tom Sawyer* and *Adventures of Huckleberry Finn*.

In 1875 Twain vividly described Hannibal as "the white town drowsing in the sunshine of a summer's morning; the streets empty, or pretty nearly so; one or two clerks sitting in front of the Water Street stores, with their splint-bottomed chairs tilted back against the wall, chins on breasts, hats slouched over their faces, asleep—with shingle-shavings enough around to show what broke them down; a sow and a litter of pigs loafing along the sidewalk, doing a good business in water-melon rinds and seeds; two or three lonely little freight piles scattered about the levee; a pile of 'skids' on the slope of the stone-paved wharf, and the fragrant town drunkard asleep in the shadow of them." Then, at the sound of an approaching riverboat, everything changed instantly. "The town drunkard stirs, the clerks wake up, a furious clatter of drays follows, every house and store pours out a human contribution, and all in a twinkling the dead town is alive and moving. Drays, carts, men, boys, all go hurrying from many quarters to a common centre, the wharf. Assembled there, the people fasten their eyes upon the coming boat as upon a wonder they are seeing for the first time."[1]

Since the author's years in Hannibal during the 1840s and '50s, the town had grown into a bustling river port and commercial center of ten thousand people. It was serviced by three railroads and even boasted a newly built train bridge across the Mississippi River. In Hannibal, Mary struggled to support herself and her daughters. Although she had convinced herself that Charley had been captured or killed, Mary still held out hope that he was alive and would someday return to her. As her nephew Charles E. Booth recalled, "She always talked a great deal about him and would go miles to see any person who had recently returned from Montana to ascertain if he had met any person answering his description. She met a young man in 1875 who was confident he had seen her husband and she became nearly crazy in her anxiety."[2]

Mary used the money from the sale of her Iowa home to buy a house in Hannibal with her brother Henry Johnson and his wife. She later claimed that her sister-in-law swindled her out of her ownership interest in the property. Jim Hume added that Mary used some of the Iowa money to pay for a fruitless search for her errant husband. Hume said that she "sacrificed her little home to raise money to locate his whereabouts, and afterward, pinched by poverty and distress, turned to manual labor to support herself and her deserted children." As the detective declared,

"While he dwelt in idleness and comfort upon the proceeds of his crimes, she was left in poverty to endure all the misery of hope deferred and heart-breaking uncertainty; striving continually to obtain some trace of him living or dead, traveling for miles to see anyone coming from Montana in the vain hope that they might know something of the wanderer."[3]

Mary found employment as a dressmaker and taught her daughters the value of hard work. On their arrival in Hannibal in 1874, the eldest, Ida, was seventeen, Eva fifteen, and Lillie thirteen. Neighbors later described Mary as "a very estimable woman" and her daughters as "bright and unusually pretty." Despite their poor financial straits, Mary and the girls were highly respectable and regularly attended church. Ida and Eva enrolled in Hannibal's public high school, and the town newspaper even mentioned Eva as one of its top students. Ida became a maid for the family of a prosperous grocery store owner, and Lillie worked as a clerk in a hat shop. In 1880, Eva married Oscar James, a locomotive engineer on the Missouri Pacific Railroad. Oscar later purchased a lodging house in Hannibal, and provided one of the rooms for Mary to live in.[4]

By the time of Eva's wedding, Mary seems to have given up any hope of seeing Charley again. In 1881, she listed herself as a widow in the Hannibal city directory. But her husband was alive and well, enjoying his opulent lifestyle in San Francisco. His holdup spree in 1880 had netted enough money to support him comfortably for ten months. During at least some of that time, he lodged at the lavish Russ House on Montgomery Street. During those months, lawmen heard nothing from the elusive lone bandit. However, by late August 1881, Charley was running out of cash. Once again he boarded a train for Redding, then walked north on the stage road ten miles past Yreka. Boles made camp next to the road, twenty miles south of Siskiyou Summit, the scene of two of his 1880 holdups.[5]

On the night of August 30, 1881, John Sullaway was at the reins of the coach en route from Roseburg, Oregon, to Redding. His stage carried nine mail sacks and a Wells Fargo box, but no passengers. After passing into California, he continued south, crossed the Klamath River by ferry, and then urged his horses up a long, steep grade. Sullaway was hungry, and with one hand he ate a snack while controlling his team with the other. At 1:30 in the morning, he spotted a campfire ahead. Fearing that the flames would spook his horses, he quickly slipped on his gloves and took a strong grasp of the reins. Suddenly a figure in a white linen duster appeared out of the darkness, illuminated by the fire.

"Halt!" Boles ordered, his shotgun only a few feet from Sullaway's head.

BRUCE LEVENE COLLECTION.

John Sullaway, right, and a fellow stage driver pose with their whips and winter clothing in the 1870s. Sullaway was held up by Black Bart in 1881.

The driver reined up and responded with alacrity, "Put down your gun and help yourself."

"I would not hurt you for a thousand dollars," Charley declared, "but I mean business. Get down and go ahead of your team."

Sullaway obeyed and took hold of his lead horses. Then Boles clambered into the driver's box, threw out the mailbags, and began chopping at the strongbox with an axe.

"I don't have very good tools for this business," he wise-cracked to the jehu. Then, after opening the box, he told Sullaway, "Drive on. I guess I've made a water haul."[6]

The express box had been empty, for the slang term "water haul" meant a fruitless effort, derived from a fisherman's net that caught nothing but water. Sullaway raced into Redding, and soon a posse was on its way to the robbery site. As usual, they found little except the looted mail sacks. Charley had no trouble eluding the lawmen, and he stayed out of sight for five weeks, probably making camp in the Siskiyou Mountains. He reappeared late on the moonlit night of October 8 at the top of Bass Hill, twelve miles north of Redding. It was the same spot where he had stopped Jimmy Smithson's stage two years earlier. This time Horace Williams was in the driver's box of the Oregon coach, on its way down the Siskiyou Trail to the rail-head in Redding.

"I had three passengers riding inside and, with fresh horses, was making fine time," Williams later said. "About three minutes after we reached the top of the hill I saw what I thought was an animal running down the hill toward me, but when he straightened up and raised his gun, I knew what was up and halted at his command."

Boles called out, "I want the treasure box of Wells Fargo & Company and the US mail sacks."

"The express box is locked to the stage," Williams responded.

Charley asked how many passengers the coach carried, then ordered, "Make them get out and walk down the road."

The passengers obeyed, as Williams recalled. "As they went down past the team he came toward the stage, and when they had gone about three hundred feet away he told me to get down and hold my leaders. I did so and he stood up on the front wheel and broke the box open with a small axe he carried under his belt, putting everything into a white sack he carried, and also threw out the mail sacks to be opened after I had driven on."

Charley found only about $60 in the strongbox. He climbed down and ordered Williams to get back onto the box. As the driver settled in his seat, he asked Boles, "How did you make it?"

"Not very well for the chances I have to take," was the rueful reply. Charley was right, for he had made another water haul. The six mail sacks held no registered letters and therefore little of value. Once again, Boles vanished on foot. Two local officers and an Indian trailer could not find him. Three days later, he struck again. Charley retraced his steps following his 1879 holdup on Bass Hill, hiking east through mountainous country to the stage road that ran from Alturas, Modoc County, to Redding. On the afternoon of October 11, he encountered the westbound stage, with one elderly passenger, near the settlement of Montgomery Creek, thirty-five miles northeast of Redding. The driver, Louis Brewster, had stopped to repair his brakes when a figure suddenly emerged from the roadside brush. Brewster saw that he wore a long linen duster buttoned up to his neck to conceal his clothes. A flour sack mask covered his head, and his boots were wrapped in burlap sacks. Brewster mostly noticed the double-barrel shotgun pointed at his head.

"You have found me, have you?" Charley asked sarcastically.

"It looks like it," the reinsman replied.

"Well, throw out the bags."

Brewster moved very slowly, and Boles lost his temper.

"I have called on you again," he said, referring to his last holdup on that route. "Don't make any trouble or I'll blow your damned head off."[7]

It was only the second time he had uttered an oath in any of his holdups. Charley ordered the driver to get down and hold the lead horses so he could attack the strongbox. The passenger gave a humorous account of what happened next. "The robber spoke sharply, and you bet the driver moved lively then because he seemed to recognize his man and he knew if it was Black Bart, he meant business and no foolishness. Well, when the driver went to his leaders' heads to hold them so that they wouldn't run away, while the highwayman was opening Wells Fargo's box, he kind a looked into the stage and saw me there. 'Git out of that,' said he, and it was said in such a commanding tone that although I was lame and weak, I got out just like a boy. 'Now, walk on ahead and don't you look back.' You ought to have seen me move off on the double quick. Why, I felt like a sixteen-year-old boy, and I walked too, almost run in fact, nor I didn't look back either."[8]

Charley then ordered the jehu to drive on. Brewster proceeded to the next stage stop, then returned to the scene with several armed men. Boles had vanished, but a mounted posse soon began tracking him south toward the Sacramento River. Jim Hume quickly responded with fellow Wells Fargo detective John Thacker. The latter, a former Nevada sheriff, had worked part-time for the company since 1875, and had been hired as a full-time detective just five months earlier. Hume had his hands full with cases in California, Oregon, Idaho, Nevada, and Arizona. He desperately needed the help of John Thacker and Charles Aull. Thacker and Hume became good friends and worked closely together for more than twenty years. The two Wells Fargo men began their own hunt for the lone highwayman. They identified the bandit as Black Bart and found that he had walked to Jelly's Ferry on the Sacramento River, stopping

BRUCE LEVENE COLLECTION

An old engraving shows Black Bart holding up a stagecoach.

for food at remote farmhouses. This was the identical route Boles had taken after his 1879 robbery of the same stage.[9]

Hume wrote to the Wells Fargo agent in Redding, advising that "a suspicious looking individual took breakfast at Jelly's Ferry, just below Ball's Ferry, and he left his carpet sack in the brush a short distance from the house until after his meal. He remarked that he had come from Puget Sound to see a friend, only to find that his friend had died." A Redding journalist remarked, "The old scoundrel is a sharp 'un and if Hume catches him it will be quite a feather in his cap." But once again, Charley managed to elude Wells Fargo's chief sleuth.[10]

Meanwhile, other lawmen were busy arresting suspected Black Barts. Two officers in Oroville, seventy-five miles south of Jelly's Ferry, collared a man named Joseph Eldridge who they thought matched the bandit's description. He had recently traded a double-barrel shotgun for a rifle, and the shotgun turned out to be stolen. There was no evidence to connect him with the stage holdup, so Eldridge was convicted of petty theft and given sixty days in jail. Two weeks later, the city marshal of Red Bluff picked up a tattered vagrant who met Black Bart's description. He claimed to be Sam Haslett, well known to western newspapermen as "Pilgrim, the tramp printer." Haslett was part of a community of itinerant typesetters who drifted from town to town, printing local newspapers. During his long career, he traveled on foot three times from New York City to San Francisco.

Haslett's arrest created an uproar among newspaper editors. Declared the *Sacramento Union*, "If it is Haslett discharge him at once! True, he is an incorrigible tramp, but he is not the stuff of which highwaymen are made. He might surreptitiously snatch something to eat, and would certainly take unlawful possession of a bottle of whiskey if the opportunity was favorable, but that is the extent of harm there is in the Pilgrim." A Red Bluff newspaperman visited the prisoner and immediately recognized him as "Pilgrim, the old pioneer and hero of the Pacific Coast." In purple prose, he proclaimed that Haslett was "well and favorably known from the Gulf of Georgia, Strait of San Juan de Fuca and Alaska on the north, to Mexico on the south" and possessed "a character as spotless as the perpetual snow drifted on the lofty peaks of the Sierra Nevada Mountains." The embarrassed city marshal promptly released Haslett. The Pilgrim later described the affair to the editor of the *Sacramento Union*, who wrote, "He says his arrest in Tehama county, on suspicion of being Black Bart, a notorious highwayman, was a case of mistaken identity, and was duly apologized for by the officer who committed the blunder."[11]

The *Sacramento Union*'s account, published in November 1881, was one of the earliest to identify Black Bart as a noted stage robber. Prior to that, he had been notorious only to lawmen and detectives who received the Wells Fargo reward circulars that described his methods. Newspapers had reported his many holdups but, in the main, had not identified him as the culprit. There were many bandits then operating in California, but none were as active as Black Bart, or as elusive. During the next year, newspapermen would become increasingly aware of the mysterious highwayman, and would devote more and more ink to his exploits.

Charley Boles always spent the winter months in San Francisco. However, his pickings from the last three holdups were so slim, he must have believed that stage robbing was added to his long list of failures. As a result, for the first time since 1875, he made a robbery expedition into the Sierra Nevada in the dead of winter. By this time, he had found a suitable high-country hideout: the Mountain House, located at seven-thousand-foot-high Henness Pass at the crest of the Sierra. The Henness Pass Road, today largely unpaved and infrequently used, was then the principal wagon trail from Marysville across the mountains to Reno, Nevada. It was known as the Northern Route because it was north of the competing wagon road that ran from Sacramento through Donner Pass and along the Truckee River to Reno, which roughly followed modern-day Interstate 80.

Charley stopped often at the Mountain House, where he became friends with its owner, Daniel T. Cole. The latter had come to California in 1852 at age twenty and built the Mountain House in 1860. His spacious building boasted two stories, sixteen lodging rooms, a dining hall, a saloon, and a post office. Cole later opened a stage line between Nevada City and Downieville, with the Mountain House a principal stop on the route. He knew Boles as Charley Bolton and believed he was a gentleman. A Nevada City journalist later reported that Cole "is an intimate friend of Bolton" whose visits to the Mountain House lasted "two or three weeks at a time." No doubt Charley picked up information about Wells Fargo shipments when he stayed there.[12]

On a freezing December 16, 1881, Boles appeared on the wagon road about four miles east of Dobbins, a stage stop in the Sierra foothills sixty miles west of the Mountain House. This spot, near the present-day junction of Marysville Road and Oregon Hill Road, was a long upgrade, ideal for a holdup. Charley, cold and hungry, was also frustrated and angry at his lack of success in the last three robberies. But now he hoped for a full

The Mountain House at Henness Pass in heavy winter snow, high in the Sierra Nevada mountains. It was one of Charley Boles's favorite hideouts.

Wells Fargo box on the approaching stage from Camptonville to Marysville. Later that day, the whip, George Sharpe, gave a Marysville journalist a vivid account of the holdup.

"I was driving slowly up a bit of rising ground when suddenly a man jumped out from behind a tree by the side of the road and yelled, 'Hold on there, you son of a bitch.' I pulled up the horses pretty quick and set the brake. Then I sat still and looked at the man. I had never been stopped on the road before, and was surprised like. The man was about my size, pretty stoutly built and about five feet ten inches high. His face was covered with white cotton cloth, but one corner of the cloth was torn so that I could see that his eyes were blue. He had on a long linen duster and a pair of blue overalls. On his head was a little whitish felt hat, with some light colored hair sticking out through the crown. That's about all I remember of his looks. He spoke in a clear, ringing voice, without any brogue or foreign accent. There was a double-barreled muzzle-loading shotgun in his hands. I could see the caps on the nipples. I saw all these things in a good deal less time than it takes to tell about them.

"As soon as I stopped the horses the robber got back behind the tree, so as to keep out of range of any guns that the passengers

might have. He kept his shotgun bearing on me from the word
'Hold.' 'Throw out that box,' was his next order. I supposed he
meant the Wells Fargo box, but I didn't stop to make particular inquiries, and I threw it out on the side of the road towards
him. 'Now throw out the other box and be quick, damn you,'
he said. 'There isn't any other box, boss,' I said. 'This line packs
only one Wells Fargo box.' 'Well, then, throw out them mail
bags, you son of a bitch,' was his answer. There was a through
mail sack from Camptonville, and some little bags with mail for
way stations. I searched around among the bags under my feet,
and getting hold of the Oregon House bag, I threw that out.
'Throw out the rest of them, God damn you,' he said. 'That's
all there is,' I said, thinking it a matter of principle to lie, under
the circumstances.

"Then he gave his gun a flourish, squinted along the top of
the barrels at me, and yelled out, 'None of your damned funny
business. Sling out that mail quick, or I'll blow the top of your
damned head off, you son of a bitch, you.' It seemed the proper
thing to throw out the rest of the mail, and I did so. 'Now drive
on, you son of a bitch,' he said. I drove on. He kept me covered
with the shotgun until the corner of the coach shut me out of
range, and then he brought the gun to bear on the passengers
inside. There were five of them, all Chinamen. I never heard
such a pow-wow as those Chinamen made when they saw the
gun pointed at them. There was a white boy on the box seat
with me. He was badly scared. After I had driven on a piece, he
said to me, 'I'm glad that robber didn't get my parcel,' showing
a little package wrapped up in a newspaper. 'What have you got
in that?' I asked him. 'I've got my lunch in it,' he said. And that
was all the poor little cuss did have in it."[13]

Once again Charley had made a water haul. The Wells Fargo
box was empty, and the mail contained little of value. The violent language he used on George Sharpe was out of character and
showed how frustrated he had become as a result of his bad luck.

Boles immediately set out to stop another stage. Five miles due south of Dobbins, on the wagon road between the mining town of North San Juan and Marysville, was the Bridgeport covered bridge across the South Yuba River. The bridge, built in 1862 and still standing, is more than two hundred feet in length and remains the world's longest single-span wood-covered bridge. Just a few hundred yards south of the bridge is a long, winding upgrade, an ideal spot for a stage holdup.

To get there, Charley made a lengthy detour around the deep Yuba River canyon, walking twenty-five miles through North San Juan to Bridgeport. He spent the Christmas season near the bridge, observing triweekly stagecoaches rumble down the wagon road. On December 27, just eleven days after holding up George Sharpe's coach, he took up a position on the grade just south of Bridgeport and waited for the down stage from North San Juan. The lumbering coach, horses straining to climb the long hill, soon approached. Luther Sherman was at the reins, and he carried no passengers. Charley leaped out in front of the lead horses and covered Sherman with his shotgun.

"Stop!" he yelled. "Throw out the treasure box and mail!"

Years later, when Sherman was an elderly man, he claimed that he had outwitted Black Bart and foiled the robbery. That was hardly true. According to the local newspaper, Sherman "promptly obeyed" the highwayman's order.

"Drive on," Boles instructed, and once again Sherman complied. The entire holdup took only a few minutes. As the stage pulled out of sight, Charley slashed open the mailbags and rifled the Wells Fargo box. But once again he got nothing for his efforts. The jehu rushed eleven miles to Smartsville and raised the alarm. A three-man posse galloped to the holdup site but found nothing but the shattered express box and emptied mailbags lying by the roadside.[14]

Jim Hume was then in no position to investigate the crime. On December 14, two days before the Bridgeport holdup, he had received a report of a brazen train robbery near El Paso, Texas. Two masked cattle rustlers had entered the express car, over-

The long grade just south of the historic Bridgeport covered bridge, where Black Bart robbed his twenty-first stage on December 27, 1881.

powered the Wells Fargo messenger, and looted $1,500 from the safe. Hume rushed by train to the border city. After a thorough investigation, he arrested the real thief. The messenger admitted that he had embezzled the money and then dreamed up the robbery to cover his theft. With the crooked Wells Fargo man behind bars, Jim boarded a return train to California. At a railroad stop in Arizona, he got a wire advising that one day earlier, bandits had attacked a stagecoach from Tombstone to Bisbee, riddled it with gunfire, and forced the Wells Fargo messenger to hand over $6,500.

The road agents turned out to be members of the Cowboys, the Wild West's biggest outlaw gang. In the previous few years, they had robbed, raided, and smuggled with impunity, killing at least thirty-five men along the Mexican border. In Tombstone, they had tangled with Wyatt Earp, his brothers, and Doc

Holliday. Two months earlier, three of the Cowboys died in the so-called Gunfight at the O.K. Corral. Jim Hume knew the Earp brothers well; Wyatt and Morgan had both served as Wells Fargo shotgun messengers in Tombstone. On January 7, 1882, Hume got off his train at Benson and boarded a stage for Tombstone to investigate the stage holdup. The coach carried nine passengers, one on the box with the driver and eight, including Hume, on the seats inside.

As darkness fell, the fifty-four-year-old detective, exhausted from his long trip, fell sound asleep. At 1:00 a.m., the stage was crossing an arroyo six miles from Tombstone when two masked holdup men stepped into the road and shouted, "Halt!"

Jim, startled, opened his eyes, only to see the gaping twin barrels of a shotgun pointed at his stagecoach window. The Cowboys demanded the Wells Fargo box, but the driver did not have one on board. Hume saw just two bandits, but he thought there were two more in the blackness. The bandits then ordered everyone out of the stage, lined them up, and went through their pockets. They took from Hume an ornate pair of silver-plated Smith & Wesson six-guns, each mounted with a four carat diamond. From the other passengers, they got a pistol and $75 in coin.

"What kind of a layout is this?" one of the Cowboys complained. "It's the poorest crowd I ever struck."

Unknown to the bandits, the passengers were experienced frontier travelers, and they had hidden more than $1,200 in cash before climbing out of the coach. The Cowboys, not thinking to search inside the stage, waved the driver on. Upon arriving in town, Jim explained the affair to the *Tombstone Epitaph*. Its editor reported, "Mr. Hume states that to attempt to use his revolvers under the circumstances—and being also under the impression that there were four robbers—would inevitably involve a sacrifice of the lives of several of the passengers, and as there was none of his employers' treasure on board, he considered he would be acting the part of wisdom to refrain from violent measures." The news of Wells Fargo's chief detective being robbed by highwaymen quickly hit the wire services, and he was widely criticized. In one example, a San Francisco newspaper declared that "a man of Hume's reputation and supposed 'sand,' armed to the teeth as he was, should have been able to take care of the two highwaymen." Either way, it had been the most humiliating experience of his professional life.[15]

Jim Hume was unable to capture the Tombstone stage robbers, and on January 19, 1882, he arrived back at the Wells Fargo office in Sacramento. One week later, Black Bart struck again. By this time Boles had gone westward, probably on foot, and crossed the Sacramento Valley and the Coast Range to Mendocino County on the North Coast. At a spot six miles north of Cloverdale, on the wagon road that followed the course of the Russian River, he waited for the southbound coach from Ukiah. The place he chose was near the spot where Cummiskey Creek flows into the Russian River. At three o'clock on the afternoon of January 26, the stagecoach approached, with Harry Forse at the ribbons. He carried two Wells Fargo boxes and three mail pouches, but no passengers. Forse suddenly spotted a masked, shotgun-wielding highwayman in the middle of the road. At the robber's command, the reinsman tossed out the boxes and the mail. Forse later said jokingly that the road agent then ordered him to "git" and he "got."[16]

The whip raced a half mile to a toll station, where he shouted that his stage had been robbed. One of the men at the tollhouse later explained, "When Forse gave the alarm, another man and myself took the best guns in the house, his being a six-shooter and mine a shotgun, and ran to the place where the stage was robbed. We then saw tracks going up the bank which we followed to a point just inside a picket fence, where we found the express boxes and mailbags opened and letters scattered about, but no robber in sight. I threw the bags and letters over the fence and we then started on the robber's track, which led over open ground for about two hundred yards, where he crossed the branch [Cummiskey Creek] at a very rough place and took to the timber, in which it would be difficult to see a man. I crossed over the branch, leaving my companion, and went up on the side where we had first seen the tracks. I soon found tracks on my side of the creek and called to my companion to come to me. The ground was such that we soon lost the track again, and being unable to find it, returned to the place where we had found the mails and express boxes and took them to the toll house."[17]

A few days later, Jim Hume was at the scene. With local officers, he made an extensive hunt for the bandit. Hume concluded that once again his quarry had hiked east, skirted Clear Lake, and crossed the Coast Range into the Sacramento Valley. There he could have boarded a railroad train for Sacramento or San Francisco. Despite an $800 reward offered by Wells Fargo, lawmen had no luck in finding the slippery bandit. Charley Boles, on the other hand, had finally struck pay dirt. The Wells Fargo strongbox held more than $400. Though far from a fortune, it was enough to support him for four salubrious months in springtime San Francisco.[18]

11

Buckshot for Black Bart

Perhaps it was inevitable, but Black Bart soon inspired a youthful copycat. He first appeared on May 24, 1882, when the unlucky Horace Williams was at the reins of his stage climbing Bass Hill, north of Redding. A young girl rode on the seat next to Williams, and two passengers relaxed inside. Just as they reached the summit, the girl spotted a masked man with a rifle and cried, "Oh!"

"Halt!" the bandit yelled as he stepped in front of the lead horses. "Throw down that box!"

Williams reined up, then calmly told the road agent that the strongbox was bolted to the stage.

"No, 'taint," the robber replied. "Throw it out."

The highwayman had done his homework. Williams tossed down the unchained Wells Fargo box and three mail sacks. When one curious passenger poked his head out the stage door, the robber snapped an order to get back inside. Then the bandit took cover behind a tree as the stage rumbled down Bass Hill. He got only a small amount of cash from the Wells Fargo box. The jehu was convinced that he had been robbed a second time by Black Bart. In Redding, Williams described the affair to a newspaperman, who wrote, "Horace thinks the robber is the same fellow who did the deed before, as his voice sounded the same. He was dressed in a blue jumper and overalls, with the legs of the latter in his boots; had on a wide brimmed hat, dirty boots, and looked like a sheepherder. For a mask he had a cotton, polka-dot, red and white handkerchief with eyes cut out."

Three days later, a ragged young stranger appeared in the settlement of Anderson, just south of Redding. He was bearded, six feet tall, two hundred pounds, and roughly dressed. The man made camp outside of Anderson, then walked into town and bought a pair of new boots. He pulled out a roll of greenbacks and paid the storekeeper with a $20 bill. Such currency—about $500 in modern money—was a rarity, and raised eyebrows among the townsfolk. The stranger stepped across the street to a saloon, where he played cards with several local men, who jokingly accused him of being the stage robber.

"Oh, that's too thin," he replied with a laugh. But the alert town constable heard about the stranger and followed him to his camp. Waiting for the man to leave, the officer searched the camp and found a rifle and a polka-dot handkerchief with eye holes. Even more damning, he discovered a diary with a description of Black Bart and copies of his two poems. The journal included a note to his sweetheart: "I am robbing for a living now, and doing pretty well." It also contained a scrap of Bart-inspired rhyme:

O, it may be for sorrow
Or for worse.
But money in that box tomorrow
is money in my purse.
I have long strove for great riches
And now I have them, you bet.

The constable arrested the stranger, who turned out to be John Lee Ragsdale, an eighteen-year-old sheepherder from Southern Oregon. Ragsdale was lodged in jail in Redding, where he pleaded guilty to robbery in exchange for a four-year jolt in San Quentin. A Redding journalist wisecracked, "Black Bart, the stage robber, would feel insulted if he knew what a miserable looking tramp was captured under suspicion of being him."[1]

But that was not the last heard from Black Bart's imitator. In 1883, Ragsdale tried to escape from San Quentin, thus losing a full year of credits that he had earned for good behavior. Upon his release, he ran up a criminal record in Oregon. Ragsdale apparently settled down by 1900, when he married and began raising a family of seven children near Jacksonville. However, in 1917, Ragsdale, then fifty-four, was arrested for raping his eighteen-year-old stepdaughter. His wife promptly filed for di-

John Lee Ragsdale, the Black Bart copycat.

vorce, and an outraged jury sentenced him to twenty years in the
Oregon state prison. But before Ragsdale could be transported
to the penitentiary, he seized an iron bar and beat his jailer to
death. Then he took one hostage and the jailer's Smith & Wesson revolver and fled, with a Jacksonville posse in pursuit. When
Ragsdale found himself surrounded by possemen and a detachment of state militia, he pressed the pistol barrel to his left temple and blew out his brains.[2]

Meanwhile the real Black Bart, after spending the spring of
1882 in San Francisco, again found himself short of cash. Because
his last holdup just north of Cloverdale had proved a success,
Charley returned to the same stage route. This time he walked
north past Ukiah to a spot on the road about five and a half miles
south of the town of Willits. The place he chose was five miles
north of Black Bart Rock, where he had robbed Alex Fowler's
coach in 1878. At three o'clock in the morning of June 14, 1882,
Boles stopped the stage driven by nineteen-year-old Tom Forse.
The young whip was a nephew of Charley's last victim, Harry
Forse. That was no happenstance, for Tom's father owned the
stage line. Young Forse carried two passengers, a Chinese man
and Hiram Willits, a pioneer for whom the settlement of Willits was named. He was also the town's postmaster.

Boles stepped in front of the rumbling stage and shouted,
"Halt! Throw out the box and mail sack!"

At that, Forse called into the coach, "Mr. Willits, shall I
throw it out?"

But the postmaster was too terrified to utter a word in response. Forse tossed down the Wells Fargo box and two mail
pouches. Then, as he drove off, Forse watched the road agent
light a candle and begin breaking open the box, which proved
to be empty. The jehu whipped up his team and rushed to
Ukiah. There Forse sought out the county sheriff, and the pair
returned to the holdup site. As usual, they found nothing but
the rifled express box and the opened mailbags. A wire was

sent to Jim Hume, who arrived in Ukiah the next day. A local newspaperman interviewed the detective and reported, "Wells Fargo & Co. not having lost a dollar, he returns to the city, leaving Uncle Sam to follow and catch the man that robbed his mail—if he can."[3]

But Federal authorities rarely investigated mail robberies in California, and this holdup was no exception. Charley walked east to the Sierra Nevada, where he probably stayed at the Mountain House at Henness Pass for a few weeks. Through the proprietor, Dan Cole, he had become well acquainted with a pioneer named Norval Douglass. Their friendship proved even more remarkable than Charley's camaraderie with San Francisco police detectives, for Douglass was a Wells Fargo shotgun messenger. Like Boles, Douglass had led an eventful life. After joining the gold rush, he served as a deputy US Marshal for Northern California in 1851 and then became a soldier of fortune. In 1853, he joined William Walker's controversial and ill-fated filibustering expedition into Mexico. In the parlance of that era, filibusters were mercenaries who invaded Mexico and Central America and tried to set up their own governments. When one of Douglass's fellow filibusters stole a sack of corn, he yanked a revolver and shot the man dead. Douglass returned to California, bought a farm near Merced in the San Joaquin Valley, and dabbled in local politics. When his farm failed due to drought, in 1877 he moved to Colfax in the Sierra Nevada Mountains, fifty miles up the Central Pacific Railroad from Sacramento.[4]

Within a couple of years, Douglass became a shotgun messenger on the stage roads in Placer County. At fifty-seven, he was certainly one of the oldest Wells Fargo guards, and was even four years senior to Jim Hume. His principal route was the wagon road between the Colfax train depot and Downieville. Dan Cole's Mountain House was one of the stage stops, and there Charley first met him. A few years later, Douglass recalled to a journalist that he became "well acquainted with the man Bolton" and explained that he "rode with Bolton on the same stage at different times and always regarded him as an honest man." No doubt Boles, on those stagecoach rides, picked up pointers on Wells Fargo's operations from the unsuspecting Douglass. Yet his fellowship with the shotgun messenger also explains why Black Bart never pulled a stage holdup in Placer County.[5]

Charley was determined to make a big score, and the stage-coaches carrying gold shipments out of the mining region held the most promise. So he walked north to his old stomping ground, the stage road from La Porte to Oroville. At daybreak on July 13, 1882, a coach rumbled out of La Porte with James H. "Hank" Helm at the ribbons. The Wells Fargo box held a shipment of gold bullion, worth about $500,000 today, and guarded by George Hackett. He had been a Wells Fargo shotgun mes-

COURTESY OF MARY GILL SMITH.

Norval Douglass, the Wells Fargo shotgun messenger who unwittingly befriended Black Bart.

senger for seven years and, in his long career with the company, never lost a cent. Later that evening, Helm gave a Marysville journalist a gripping account of their encounter with Black Bart.

"I was driving three horses, with George M. Hackett, Wells Fargo's messenger, on the box beside me. There were no passengers. We had $18,000 in bullion aboard. The stage was stopped about seven o'clock [a.m.] about five miles this side of La Porte and a mile and a half beyond Diamond Springs. The road at that point is level and the horses were trotting along quietly. Nobody would expect to find a robber in such a place. Hackett was sitting sideways in the seat, talking to me, when a man ran out from the left side of the road and tried to catch hold of the leading horse... He wore a linen duster and his face was covered with a big white mask.

"As soon as I saw him I whooped up the horses, with a view to get past him. But the lead horse was frightened and swung off to the right side of the road and against the side of the hill, stopping the team. The man carried a double barreled shotgun. He didn't say a word, and didn't raise his gun, but carried it in one hand hanging by his side. As soon as Hackett could get his gun ready he fired. The gun was loaded with buckshot. The robber then made a motion as if to shoot, but didn't seem able to get his gun to his shoulder. He then ran around to the other side of the leader and I yelled to Hackett to 'sock it to him.'

"Hackett then fired over the heads of the horses the contents of his second barrel. The robber then took to his heels. He ran down the hill, straight away from the road. Hackett jumped down and ran after him a short distance. Hackett had a buttoned glove on his left hand and had his cartridges in his left pocket so that he couldn't reload his gun in time to get another shot at the robber. When he saw that pursuit was hopeless he came back to the stage. We picked up the robber's hat in the road. It was a soft hat, of black felt, very old and weather beaten and full of ragged rents. It had four fresh buckshot holes in it, with hair sticking to some of them. The man's hair was light in color, streaked with gray. As he ran down the hill he tore off his mask, and I noticed that he had a bald spot on the top of his head. Hackett had no pistol with him. If he had had a pistol, he could have dropped the robber easily. He can drop a rabbit at a hundred yards with the big pistol he generally carries."

Hackett did not try to track the fleeing bandit, said Helm. "It wasn't Hackett's business to follow the robber; he had to come back and take care of the treasure. Put-up jobs have been made before now for the robber to get the messenger out of the way while another one would come up and go through the stage." Charley Boles had made the near-fatal error of tangling with a Wells Fargo shotgun messenger. Never before, in twenty-three holdups, had he tried to stop a stage with a guard on board. Instead he had assiduously avoided them. The fact that he did so now showed how desperate he had become. Two pieces of Hackett's buckshot had creased his scalp, one leaving a four-inch scar on his forehead. It was his closest brush with death since the Civil War.[6]

The Wells Fargo messenger quickly searched the roadside brush and found two pairs of opera glasses hidden behind a log. Charley had evidently used them to watch oncoming stages. Hackett then swung aboard the coach, and Helm rushed his team nine miles down the road to Strawberry Valley. A telephone line had been installed there two years before, with connections to La Porte and Oroville. Now they used it to make one of the first telephone reports of a stage holdup in the Old West. While a posse saddled up in La Porte, Helm continued on fourteen miles to the stage stop at Forbestown. Hackett climbed down and switched the heavy Wells Fargo shipment onto a waiting Oroville-bound stage driven by Frank Morse. The coach rolled out of Forbestown at 1:00 p.m. and headed down the foothills toward Oroville. They had gone eight miles when the sharp-eyed Hackett suddenly exclaimed, "There's a fellow after us!"

Just ahead was a masked road agent, partly concealed behind an oak tree, his shotgun trained on the stagecoach. Hackett reacted instantly and fired one barrel of his shotgun. The outlaw returned fire immediately, and two buckshot balls tore into the messenger's face. One ball ripped though Hackett's lip, breaking two teeth, and another pierced his cheek. Ignoring the bloody wounds, Hackett jumped down from the driver's box and took dead aim at the fleeing bandit. He pulled the trigger but, much to his consternation, the shotgun misfired. Hackett, bleeding profusely, was forced to give up the chase. Morse drove him into Oroville, where a doctor dressed his wounds and pronounced them not serious.[7]

An Oroville journalist interviewed Hackett and wrote, "He says that this last man was not at all like the one that attacked them this morning. The man who made the last attack was of medium size, and had on a linen duster. The other was tall, with a dirty duster." This was the only time in the Old West in which a Wells Fargo shotgun messenger had foiled two different stage holdups on the same day. The company's grateful officials presented him with a gold pocket watch, inscribed, "Presented to George M. Hackett, guard, for protecting express on La Porte stage against two attacks by highwaymen, July 13, 1882." The second bandit was certainly not Black Bart. The two holdup sites were sixteen miles apart, and Boles, after being wounded in the first attempt, could not have traveled that distance on foot in time to attack the other stage. Of the second bandit, Hackett later said, "I could never find out who this party was."[8]

Charley Boles disappeared for two months while his head wound healed. By this time he had become well aware of Jim Hume's attentions. The San Francisco and Sacramento dailies ran regular stories about Wells Fargo's chief detective and his manhunts for and arrests of express robbers. Several smaller rural newspapers carried accounts of Hume investigating Black Bart's holdups. As an inveterate newspaper reader, Boles learned that

George Hackett, the Wells Fargo shotgun messenger who shot and wounded Black Bart in 1882.

one of the West's most capable sleuths was hunting him. But that did nothing to dissuade Black Bart, who was unfazed by his close call with George Hackett's shotgun.

That fall he returned to his old stomping grounds on Bass Hill, north of Redding. At one in the morning of September 17, 1882, he stopped the coach of the much-robbed Horace Williams. This was the fourth time in less than a year that Williams had been held up on Bass Hill. Boles had robbed him at the same place almost a year before, then John Ragsdale held him up, and five weeks after that, another highwayman stopped his coach.

Williams had two passengers on the seat next to him when Charley appeared in front of him and sang out, "Throw out that box!"

"I can't do it," the whip replied, explaining that it was chained to the stage. Boles ordered the passengers to get down and walk up the road. Then he told Williams, "Get out in front of your team and hold them."

This time Charley was not concerned about the driver and passengers. He pulled out a short-handled axe that dangled from his belt, hacked open the strongbox, and then used a knife to slice a *T* in the mailbags. When he was done, Williams climbed back into the driver's seat.

"Drive on," Boles ordered the reinsman.

"They'll catch you one of these days," an irritated Williams declared.

"Perhaps," Charley responded. "But in the meantime, give my regards to J.B. Hume, will you?"

But the joke was on Black Bart, for the Wells Fargo box held just thirty-five cents. Williams later said that he was carrying $250 in gold coin as a favor for a friend, stowed away behind the driver's seat. He slipped the packet of coins into his pocket, with the bandit never the wiser. Williams whipped up his team and headed for Redding, now bearing the dubious distinction as the only man stopped twice by Black Bart.[9]

Jim Hume rushed to Redding, arriving the next day. He quickly concluded that the job was the work of Black Bart, and he surely was unhappy with the bandit's taunt. Hume could find no trace of the highwayman, and he soon returned to San Francisco. However, a few days after the holdup, Shasta County Undersheriff Robert Kennedy and fellow officers collared a suspicious character whom they had tracked south from Redding. Kennedy told a reporter that he "is confident that the man is the famous Black Bart." But the Wells Fargo agent in Redding wired Hume, "Kennedy and others arrested a man for the stage robber. Kennedy says he has the right man but he is not Bart." The suspect turned out to be a notorious confidence man. When he proved an alibi, the undersheriff was forced to drop the charges.[10]

Once again, Charley vanished for two months. He needed enough money to last through the winter, so he returned to the railhead at Cloverdale in Sonoma County. Boles then walked east on the wagon road that connected Cloverdale with Lake-

port. In those years, it was a private toll road that wended its
way from Clear Lake south through the Coast Range to Geysers Road and then proceeded west eight miles into Cloverdale. At the opposite end of Geysers Road, in the rugged hills
twenty miles east of Cloverdale, was the Geysers Resort, then
one of California's most popular tourist destinations. It featured
a luxurious hotel and hot springs that attracted everyone from
Ulysses S. Grant to Mark Twain.

But Boles had no interest in the stagecoaches crammed with
tourists that regularly journeyed between Cloverdale and the
Geysers. He knew that those stages did not carry Wells Fargo's
express or the mail, but the coaches from Lakeport did. Charley stationed himself at a bend in Geysers Road, five miles east
of Cloverdale. On the afternoon of November 24, 1882, he
stopped the stage driven by Dick Crawford. The reinsman had
a friend on the seat next to him, plus two men and two women
passengers inside. At the highwayman's command, Crawford's
comrade threw down the Wells Fargo box and the mail pouches.
Charley ordered the stage on, then broke open the box and removed $475. Boles was satisfied, for that was enough to last him
through the winter.[11]

Charles Cook, a Cloverdale constable, began hunting the
bandit. Two days later, he was joined by Charles Aull of Wells
Fargo. The express company's sleuth suspected that once again,
the bandit might flee across the Coast Range to the Sacramento Valley. He promptly reported to Wells Fargo headquarters in San Francisco, "The robber is without any doubt Black
Bart. The mail sacks are cut the same as all of the robberies he
has committed, 'T.' I start out this morning with the constable
and if we find any further trail will follow as long as there is a
hope of getting him. If either Hume or Thacker is in the city
I would advise they go up to Williams, Willows, and Orland,
in Colusa County, as I think he goes out through that country, and by notifying the ranchers right and left we might cut

off his retreat. Stony Creek in Colusa County is a tough place, and I have long thought that B.B. might live in that vicinity."

The next day, Aull tracked Black Bart to the Geysers, then lost the trail. He rode south through the mountainous country to Calistoga in Napa County, where he penned a second report to Wells Fargo officials. "The stage robber was tracked along top of [a] ridge near the Geysers. He came to scene of robbery and went the same route. I found on arrival here that Buck English was discharged last month from San Quentin. Buck has served two terms from Lake Co., once for robbery and once for larceny, last term eight years… He fills the modern rendition of the Jeffersonian test, 'He is capable, he is on it.' He lives at Middletown, Lake Co., 18 miles north of this place, and on direct line of route the stage robber went and came from scene of robbery. While all the ear marks are those of Black Bart, still Buck is bright enough to ape his style if he knew it."[12]

As former captain of guards at San Quentin prison, Aull knew Lawrence Buchanan "Buck" English well. He was a notorious

A contemporary illustration showing Black Bart holding up a stagecoach.

desperado who came from a very rough family. One of his brothers had been lynched in Idaho, another was shot dead in a feud, and a third died in a saloon gunfight. In 1875, Buck robbed a stagecoach near Middletown and then served two prison terms for larceny and highway robbery. Released in 1882, he ran up a hard record in California and Oregon. Following another stage holdup in 1895, lawmen shot and badly wounded him. He recovered and served a long term in San Quentin. But despite that extensive criminal career, Aull was wrong, for Buck English had nothing to do with the Cloverdale stage robbery. A frustrated Charles Aull returned to San Francisco empty-handed.[13]

The Wells Fargo man would have been shocked to discover that the mysterious poet-highwayman had slipped back to the bay city. He stayed at the Hancock House at 781 Mission Street, a short walk from the city's financial district. Its owner advertised the weekly rates: "single rooms, $6 to $10; board, $5 a week; tourists and transients solicited; Mission Street cars pass the house." There Charley registered as "E.C. Bolton" and gave his occupation as "speculator." He liked the easy access to streetcars, for a short ride down Mission Street brought him to Woodward's Gardens. It was the city's most popular amusement park, filling two city blocks and featuring botanical gardens plus a zoo, art museum, music hall, and outdoor theater. Other streetcars connected with the Bay District Race Track, a one-mile-long course situated in San Francisco's Richmond District. Charley loved betting on the horses, and the Bay District Race Track was the city's biggest and most popular.[14]

He was free, with no responsibilities. His hands were soft and smooth, his rough calluses from farming and mining long gone. He carried a gold cane in place of a shovel. He slept in soft beds in fashionable hotels and lodging houses. Instead of subsisting on bacon and hardtack, he dined on fine food in popular restaurants. To his San Francisco friends, he was a prosperous mine owner and stock speculator. Charley Boles was living the life he had always wanted.

12

Throw Down the Box

Charley Boles, before he abandoned his family and turned outlaw, had always been close to his younger sister, Maria. She had lived with their parents on the family homestead in New York until 1855, when she was twenty-two. Maria then married Thomas P. Bradshaw, the son of a farmer who lived very close to the Boles place. The young couple moved to Ontario, Canada, where Bradshaw became a Methodist clergyman. They raised four children, and in the early 1870s moved back to New York State. Ten years later, they traveled west on the transcontinental railroad and settled in Reno, Nevada, where Thomas Bradshaw became minister of the town's Methodist church.

Charley, while he was posing as a mining man in San Francisco, apparently began corresponding with his sister. It would have been a simple matter for him to contact Reverend Bradshaw through the Methodist church in New York. Although his letters are long lost, Maria must have been shocked to hear from him, as the Boles family all thought he was dead. After all, their father's will had listed him as deceased in 1872. What false stories Charley told Maria can only be imagined, but somehow he convinced her not to tell his wife that he was alive. Most likely Boles persuaded his sister that Mary had obtained a divorce and wanted nothing to do with him. The result was that Charley reconnected with Maria and began making occasional visits to the Bradshaws in Reno. Needless to say, Maria and her family had no idea that Charley was a notorious stage robber. Thomas Bradshaw must have been very impressed by his brother-in-law, who he thought was a well-to-do mining man, because a few years later, he left his ministry and became a mine owner himself, albeit a real one.[1]

Boles, when not visiting his sister in Reno, passed the winter of 1882 to 1883 in San Francisco. He continued to spend much of his free time in front of the Bush Street Theater and across the street at Frank Muncey's cigar shop and laundry agency. Though Charley did not smoke cigars, he would drop off and pick up his clothing at the tobacco store. Muncey would send the clothes for cleaning at the Ferguson & Biggy California Laundry a few blocks away. In 1882, Muncey sold his business to Thomas C. Ware, a forty-one-year-old Kentuckian and former sailor. Ware later said that he had first met Charley in 1876, and the two became close friends. Boles enjoyed socializing at the tobacco shop. "He used to sit on the railing around the cellarway in front of Ware's cigar store and talk with men who patronized the place and with acquaintances who happened by," recalled a San Francisco fireman who knew Charley. "He never stayed long, perhaps a half hour or so. I met him there and talked with him several times. He was neatly but not flashily dressed, well spoken."[2]

Meanwhile, Jim Hume had worked tirelessly throughout 1882 to identify and capture Black Bart. At year's end, the Wells Fargo detective issued a highly detailed, three-page wanted notice offering an $800 reward for the elusive lone highwayman. The

circular provided every pertinent fact that he had been able to
glean about Black Bart. Hume listed sixteen stage holdups that
he had connected with Bart and even included reproductions
of his two handwritten poems. Based on Hume's painstaking
detective work, the wanted flyer also provided a comprehensive
word portrait of the mysterious bandit.

"He is generally masked with a flour sack over his face, and
an old long linen duster to cover his person," Hume wrote. "In
attacking a stage he usually jumps out in front of the team, in
a stooping posture, and seeks to shield himself in front of the
lead horses. He is always armed with a double-barreled shotgun,
which he unbreeches, and rolls in his blankets, as soon as he is
safe from immediate pursuit; always brings an old axe to the
scene of the robbery, which he uses to open the box, and leaves
in vicinity of robbery. In opening the mail sacks, he cuts them
with a sharp knife; thus, 'T' on top of the sack, near the lock.

"He has never manifested any viciousness, and there is reason to believe that he is averse to taking human life. He is polite to all passengers, and especially so to ladies. He comes and
goes from the scene of robbery on foot; seems to be a thorough
mountaineer and a good walker, as he sometimes covers long
distances in a day, getting food from houses in out-of-the-way
places, but has never been known to remain over night in a
house that is occupied; never allows himself to be seen in the
vicinity of robbery, and never shows up for food until twelve
or fifteen miles away.

"The only baggage visible when traveling is a roll of blankets, generally tied with bale ropes at the ends, although at one
time he had a long valise. Four times he has attacked two lines
of stages terminating at the same point, with but a day or two
interval. All of the robberies are confined to the counties of
Mendocino, Sonoma, Yuba, Sierra, Butte, Plumas, Shasta, and
Trinity. None have occurred below Sacramento, which indicates
that his home was within the scope of the counties mentioned,

as he seems to be most familiar with that country. There have been several other 'one-man robberies' during the time specified, which have not been investigated, the loss being nominal, which may have been committed by this facetious individual signing himself 'Black Bart.'

"From the various places where he has obtained food, and from persons who have seen him while traveling through the country, the following description has been obtained, which is believed to be correct: An American; age over 50 years; height, 5 feet 9 to 11 inches; rather slender build; weight, about 155 pounds; high forehead, points running well up into hair; cheek bones prominent; lower part of face thin and rather long; light eyes, deep set; heavy eyebrows; hair gray; heavy mustache and chin whiskers, well mixed with gray; two or more front teeth missing; long, slender hands that do not show work. He sometimes complains of throat disease; he seems to be educated and is well informed on current topics. The manner of leaving the doggerel verse with express box after robbery and the postscript to first verse would indicate there was a vein of humor or waggery in his composition. It is not believed that he is addicted to the use of liquor and tobacco; is a great lover of coffee; wears about a No. 8 boot; is a great reader, and when reading without glasses holds his paper off at full arm's length. At no place where he has stopped for food has he been looked upon as suspicious in deportment or appearance, and it is most probable that he is considered entirely respectable wherever he may reside."[3]

The reward notice fully demonstrated Jim Hume's thoroughness. Though he had never laid eyes on Black Bart, his description—much of which came from young Donna McCreary—fit Charley Boles to a T. Hume's only errors were his belief that the bandit lived in one of the rural counties and that he never robbed a stage south of Sacramento. In fact, Bart's first holdup, at Funk Hill, took place well to the south of the capital city. But despite Hume's exertions, he could not lay a glove on Black Bart.

In the spring of 1883, Boles hit the road again. He returned almost to the very spot of his last robbery, on Geysers Road, four miles east of Cloverdale. At eleven thirty on the night of April 12, 1883, he lay in wait for the stage from Lakeport to Cloverdale as its whip, Will Krumdick, was urging his team up Chicken Hill. His load was light, for the coach held no passengers. Charley suddenly appeared in the glare of the headlamps with a white sack mask and a double-barreled shotgun. Boles yelled, "Halt!" but Krumdick did not hear him and failed to stop. Charley then shouldered the shotgun and shouted twice more, and finally the reinsman pulled up.

Black Bart's holdups had become so routine that he simply called out, "Express box," and Krumdick tossed it down. Then Boles ordered, "Mail," and the whip threw out one sack. But Charley knew there were others, and at his demand, Krumdick tossed down five more mailbags. Then Boles ordered the jehu to drive on. He found a meager $32 in the Wells Fargo box, and nothing in the mail. In frantic desperation, he tore open every letter and scattered them across the roadway.

Wells Fargo officials quickly hired two local men to hunt the road agent, and they tracked him east toward the Geysers. The company's agent in Cloverdale reported, "No doubt but it is Black Bart as he opened the box and mail sacks in his old style— and answers to his description." When the two man hunters returned to town empty-handed, the Wells Fargo agent sent in a second report. "They found no trace whatsoever. They traced a man to Napa but found they were on the wrong track. Went all over the county from Geysers to Calistoga." Once again, Black Bart had vanished.[4]

Charley returned to San Francisco, where he obtained a room at the Webb House on Second Street, just south of Market Street. Its new manager was Emily Burling, tall and attractive, the forty-one-year-old wife of a bookkeeper. Boles stayed there for two months and became friendly with his landlady, though there is

The Webb House is the large three-story building on the right. It was one of Charley's favorite lodging places in San Francisco.

no evidence of any deeper relationship. But he soon ran out of money. Charley then decided that the Sierra mining region had better prospects than the North Coast, so for the first time, he ventured into Amador County. Its county seat, Jackson, was a busy gold mining town fifty miles southeast of Sacramento. On June 22, 1883, Boles broke into a cabin near Ione, eleven miles west of Jackson, and stole a tattered blue coat and a ragged pair of trousers. That night, a few people noticed the nondescript traveler as he walked through the foothills to the Morrow grade, four miles west of Jackson. He was wearing the pilfered clothing. On the way, Boles slipped onto the nearby Morrow farm where he stole an old axe. Then he made camp in the brush and waited for daylight.[5]

At 9:00 a.m., the stage from Jackson, headed toward Ione, rattled into sight and started up the grade. An experienced jehu, Clint Radcliff, was at the ribbons, and he carried but one passenger. Suddenly the masked road agent, wielding a shotgun, burst out of the roadside bushes and ordered Radcliff to halt and throw down the box. The holdup only took a moment, as Radcliff quickly threw down two Wells Fargo strongboxes and four bags of mail. Then he whipped up his team and started off. He had not gone far when he heard a loud gunshot. The bandit was not shooting at him. As a Jackson newspaperman who interviewed Radcliff wrote, "After the stage had gone a little distance the highwayman fired off one barrel of his gun, it is presumed accidentally."

The whip raced seven miles into Ione, where he raised the alarm. A posse quickly mounted up and galloped to the holdup site. They found only the rifled boxes and mail pouches, along with the bandit's discarded old clothing, hat, and mask. This time Charley did not make a water haul. The Wells Fargo boxes had held $574, and the registered mail provided another $165 in cash. Word was sent to Jim Hume and John Thacker, and they arrived in Jackson the following evening. Hume told a reporter that "the mysterious person calling himself Black Bart is answerable for the deed," and added, "A standing reward of $800 is offered by Wells Fargo for the capture of Black Bart." The two detectives spent a week in Amador County, searching for the road agent and running down clues, but as usual, they came up empty.[6]

Jim Hume was so frustrated that he persuaded Wells Fargo officials to hire a private detective, Harry N. Morse, to work full-time on the Black Bart case. Morse was the most famous lawman on the Pacific Coast, and his exploits were the stuff of legend. As a fourteen-year-old seaman from New York, he joined the gold rush in 1849, then worked at everything from gold mining to driving a wagon to running a hotel. During the Civil War, Morse became captain of an Oakland militia unit, and in 1863, he won election as sheriff of Alameda County, across the bay from San Francisco. At first the twenty-eight-year-old rookie sheriff was decidedly ineffective, but he rapidly gained skill as a horseman, tracker, and gunfighter.

In 1866, Morse began tracking down the most dangerous outlaws in the state, routinely leaving his bailiwick on extended manhunts. On one occasion, he trailed a murderer for twelve hundred miles before capturing him near Los Angeles. He took part in several hair-raising gun battles, wounding one notori-

ous desperado and killing another. Then, in 1871, he trailed
the bandit chieftain Juan Soto to his hideout high in the Coast
Range and, in a close-quarters gun duel, shot him dead. It was
the most famous outlaw-lawman shootout of the California frontier. Three years later, the state governor appointed him head
of a special posse to track down Tiburcio Vasquez, the most
notorious California outlaw since the gold rush. Morse and his
possemen tracked Vasquez for sixty-one days and two thousand
seven hundred miles until they finally located him in what is
now West Hollywood. Los Angeles lawmen used Morse's information to raid Vasquez's hideout, where they shot and captured
him. In 1875, the bandit leader was convicted of participating in
a triple murder-robbery and hanged on the gallows in San Jose.

Three years later, Morse retired as sheriff and opened a private detective agency in San Francisco. He quickly became California's preeminent private investigator and cracked two of San
Francisco's most serious cases of municipal corruption. In the
Dupont Street Frauds case of 1879, Morse exposed the city's
bribe-taking mayor. Then he took on a smuggling organization known as the Harkins Opium Ring, which resulted in the
prosecution of a corrupt federal magistrate in 1883. But despite
many years of success, Harry Morse would have his hands full
trying to capture Black Bart.[7]

He first went to the scene of the holdup near Ione and began
interviewing witnesses and local officers. "I spent three or four
days there making investigations and came back and reported to
the company my idea about the matter," Morse later explained,
saying that he worked closely with Hume and Thacker. "We
often consulted and compared notes and at length concluded that
we would have to wait until another robbery had been committed by him, and then with any clue we might obtain, act
quickly." He added, "Once we thought we had a clue to him
but it proved to be a mistake."[8]

Morse got that clue in September 1883, when he, with Jim

JOHN BOESSENECKER COLLECTION.

Harry Morse, the famed California lawman.

Hume and Charles Aull, went to Napa to interrogate yet another suspected Black Bart. Soon after the robbery of Will Krumdick's stage from Lakeport to Cloverdale, a drifter had shown up at a remote ranch north of Napa. For the previous eight years, the man had made periodic visits to the ranch, giving his name as Nelson Barber. He always traveled on foot and claimed to be a livestock dealer. Each time Barber would beg a free meal and then disappear for months at a time. The rancher became convinced that he was Black Bart. Barber was well-read, well-dressed, and matched the highwayman's description. Eager to claim the $800 reward, the rancher kept an eye out for Barber, and when the drifter returned to his ranch, Napa county lawmen arrested him.

They jailed Barber in Napa, where he was questioned closely by the three Wells Fargo sleuths. Morse and his fellow detectives then brought the prisoner to San Francisco, where they continued their investigation. Within a few days, a Napa journalist reported, "A letter received from San Francisco Monday evening from Detective Aull states that the detectives are clearly of the opinion that the man Barber arrested last week is not Black Bart the highwayman, although a first-class counterfeit of him. They took the pains to verify many of Barber's statements and found them all straight, hence they consider there is no further reason for his detention. Barber was paid by the officers for all the trouble he had been put to and sent on his way rejoicing."[9]

By this time, Boles was on one of his frequent visits to Sacramento. In mid-August 1883, he arrived in the state capital and checked into a lodging house on Fourth Street. According to a Sacramento reporter who later interviewed some of Charley's acquaintances, "For the first time, as recorded in his long career, [Boles] was 'captured,' and became a slave to the charms of a woman, the object of his heart's idol being the temporarily engaged chambermaid of his lodging house, a woman well known on the streets of this city." The reporter provided only the paramour's first name, Mollie, and said that she had another lover, a Sacramento fireman. "The Po8 spent the greater part of his time in his room writing and whispering words of love and devotion into the ear of his 'Mollie darling.' Cruel fate in this, as in many other love affairs, had placed an obstacle in the way of the entire twenty-four hours being passed in love's embrace, as at night the lovely maid had to hie herself away to the abode of her other admirer."

In early September, the capital city was agog at the arrival of a circus, the only one to tour California that year. It featured five elephants, camels, and other exotic animals, as well as numerous female acrobats and high-wire performers. Charley got tickets and took Mollie and two of her friends, one a tall woman identified only as Susan, to the circus. "On another occasion," wrote the Sacramento reporter, "he took his adored to a shoe store on J street, where he had her tiny feet fitted with the best the establishment afforded, urging her not to think of price at all but to please her taste." Boles left town for a few days, then returned on September 6 and checked into the International Hotel on K Street, two blocks from the train depot. Mollie, Susan, and their friend came to visit, the journalist said. "At a seasonable hour, two of the females withdrew after having given the Po8 and his 'Mollie darling' their blessing for the night."[10]

Charley stored his valise in the hotel's baggage room, then returned to San Francisco, where he checked into the Webb House at 37 Second Street. There he carefully began planning his twenty-ninth, and most ambitious, holdup. In an effort to disguise himself, he grew a full gray beard. Then, in early October, he told his landlady, Emily Burling, and several friends that he had to leave town to check on his mines. He packed his things in his trunk and left it in the baggage room of the Webb House. Crossing San Francisco Bay by ferry, he took a train to the depot at Milton, terminus of the busy stage line to Sonora. This was the same route where he had held up his first stage, at Funk Hill, eight years before. But this time Charley left nothing to chance. He spent the next few weeks reconnoitering in the foothills and visited Tuttletown, on the Sonora stage road. There he learned that large shipments of gold bullion from the nearby Patterson Mine were regularly sent by stagecoach to the Milton depot.

Boles then walked to a lumber camp a few miles away. When no one was there, he crept in and stole a sledgehammer, a crowbar, an iron wedge, two picks, and an axe. It took him several days, and a number of trips, to lug the heavy load to the top of Funk Hill. There he made camp under a large rock outcropping at the summit. Once again, Boles had prepared well, for he had learned that Wells Fargo shipped its treasure from Sonora in an iron box bolted to the floor of the coach. He was now well equipped to break open the safe.

On October 25, he walked into Angels Camp, where he paid a storekeeper a dollar for a bag of crackers and twenty-five cents for a cup of sugar in a paper bag. He also obtained an empty flour sack that he intended to use as a mask. The next day, he was spotted walking along the stage road by sixty-year-old Thomas P. Martin, who had a log cabin a mile from Funk Hill. One of Martin's friends later said of him, "He had a small garden, a few head of stock and did a little mining in the gulches for his living. He was a fine hunter and a well educated man—very shrewd and a close observer. He was also known to be strictly honest and afraid of nothing."

Martin subsequently described his encounter with Black Bart. "I saw a man in the woods, well dressed, in a white shirt, collar and cuffs. On seeing me he ducked out of sight as quickly as possible and I immediately became suspicious of him. I made up my mind if I ever saw that man again he wouldn't get away from me." Four days later, on October 30, Martin was out hunting when he spotted the stranger walking toward him on the road. Martin quickly hid behind a tree, and when the man got close he stepped out and said, "Hello, stranger, what are you looking for way up here in these mountains?"

"I am trying to locate a quartz lead I found here several years ago," Boles replied.

"Oh, well, if you will stay with me for a few days I'll help you locate it," Martin offered.

"I haven't time on this trip, but I'll come back some time again."

Martin then asked him where he was going. "I have been over to Chinese Camp and to Jamestown to see a party on business," Charley answered. "I am now on my way to Jackson, where I live."

"Are you acquainted in Jamestown and in Chinese?" Martin queried. Boles answered that he was, but Martin later said that when asked, the stranger "could not recognize the names of citizens there." Boles walked off, and Martin would soon have good reason to remember him.[11]

Within a day or two, Charley appeared at Reynolds Ferry on the Stanislaus River, about three winding miles from Funk Hill. The ferry was operated by eighteen-year-old Jimmy Rolleri. His father ran a nearby mining claim, and his mother, Olivia, was in charge of their large house by the river. Many years later, she became a much beloved and hospitable figure, widely known as Grandma Rolleri. But at that time, she was only thirty-nine. The Rolleri house served as a stage stop and home to their ten children, five boys and five girls. Jimmy, the second eldest, hunted for deer in his spare time to provide food for the family. The older girls helped their mother with household chores. Decades later, daughter Louise Rolleri, who was eight in 1883, vividly described their home, as well as their visit from Black Bart.

"The house was very old fashioned," she said. "There was a porch that ran all along the front of it and along the side—that was the side by the river. Coming in from the front, you went into a very large room. At one time it had been a barroom. Well,

Reynolds Ferry on the Stanislaus River, operated in 1883 by Jimmy Rolleri.

the bar ran along one side of the big room. And at the end of the bar there were steps and they went up into the dining room."

Louise explained that the house had three bedrooms upstairs where her five brothers slept, and four more downstairs for their mother and the girls. "At the end of the little hall was a great big back parlor. And then, beyond that, was a bedroom. And that's where Black Bart spent that night. We didn't exactly run a hotel. But sometimes travelers would want to stay overnight, as well as eat a meal or two. So we used that back bedroom for them. He came there before supper and asked for a room to stay all night. He was on foot. And I remember distinctly that when Mama showed him the spare bedroom he was to sleep in, he asked her for a key to the door. It seemed so funny to us girls. Nobody had ever asked for a key before. That seemed to us like a very peculiar thing to do. I remember I couldn't understand that. Nobody ever locked their doors in those days.

"He ate supper with us that night in the big dining room. We had a great big long table. And I remember another thing we talked about afterward, a thing that seemed so peculiar to us girls especially. He didn't seem to want to sit around after supper and talk with the family. That's the way everybody else did who ever stayed there in those days. They'd sit around after supper and we'd get acquainted. But he went right to his room and stayed there." Louise concluded, "He was up and gone long before any of the family got up the next morning. He only stayed that one night and in the morning he was gone."[12]

Charley returned to his camp on Funk Hill. At just over one thousand seven hundred feet in elevation, Funk Hill is actually a mountain, covered with long grass and studded with chaparral and scrub oak. Though its height is just average for the Sierra Nevada foothills, it took three miles of winding stage road from Reynolds Ferry to reach the summit. The Milton-bound coaches first crossed the ferry, climbed out of the Stanislaus River canyon and circled around the south side of Funk Hill, then turned west and proceeded another three miles to Copperopolis. The crest of the hill is a large outcropping of rock, about two hundred feet above the stage road. Charley's camp was at the base of the outcropping. He used a pile of wild grass for a bed and made a small campfire that could not be seen from a distance. He walked a mile down the hill to a ravine to get water. Using a pair of field glasses, Boles was able to watch the stagecoach road for half a mile before it reached the summit. Just below his camp was a large flat boulder situated about fifty feet from the road. It made an ideal hiding place for a highwayman to surprise and stop a reinsman and his coach.

On the morning of October 31, Boles was scanning the road with his field glasses when he spotted the stage approaching, slowly climbing the hill. Suddenly, in the distance below him, a man with a handkerchief masking his face emerged from the roadside brush. As Charley later recalled, he thought, "Well, here's a go. This fellow is going to take in the stage. Here's another agent in the business." Boles said that he "made up his mind he would let him capture the stage, and after he had got the plunder he would capture him and take the booty from him." He added that "it would be a good joke if the man should be captured and sent to San Quentin, while [I] had got away with the plunder. Nobody would believe that he had been robbed. No story of that kind told by him would be credited, or if the fellow should not get much from the stage, I could have turned him over to Wells Fargo & Co. and got the reward." But Charley's imaginings were just that, for the man was an innocent traveler, not a stage robber.[13]

Two days later, Boles appeared at the Patterson Mine in Tuttletown. According to an early-day account, "He represented himself as a mining man. His affable manner and pleasing ways soon won the good graces of the mining officials, and he was shown every courtesy. He was taken through the mine mill and even into the assay office, where he saw a bar of bullion valued at $4,800, just melted. He was told that the bar would be taken to Sonora that afternoon and shipped next morning by express over the Sonora and Milton stage line to San Francisco." That was exactly the information that Boles needed, and he returned to his camp on Funk Hill.[14]

Charley awoke before dawn the following morning, November 3, 1883. After building a small fire to warm himself from the cold night, he downed a breakfast of crackers and coffee. Then, using his field glasses, he watched for the daily stage. Boles said later that as he surveyed the road far below, he muttered to himself, "This is where I committed my first robbery. I wonder if this will be my last?"[15]

13

Fiasco at Funk Hill

"I watched through my glass from my lookout the stage slowly ascend the hill," Charley recalled. "I noticed two men on the seat, one with a gun. The stage went out of sight for a minute, going around a bend of the road, and when it came in view again I noticed that one man had left the seat. That alarmed me some. I supposed they had seen me, and that this fellow had got off with his gun in the hope of catching me. I had a flour sack over my face with holes for my eyes, and a pair of overalls that I had picked up in an old cabin.

"As the driver came up close to the bush I stepped out in front of the team and asked the driver who that man was that he had on the seat with him with a gun. The driver said it was a boy hunting stock, and that he had got off below to go around the mountain. I then told the driver to get down and unhitch his team. I helped him with one hand, while with the other I kept my gun up, ready for use. When I jumped out from behind the bush I got right in front of the horses' heads in a crouching position, with my gun pointed so that if anyone in the stage should attempt to fire at me he would hit the horses, and if any-one on the seat wanted to do anything I could knock him off with my gun.

"The driver took the horses over the hill out of sight. Then I got my tools, a sledge hammer, big crow bar, an old wedge that had been used for splitting wood, a couple of picks, and an axe. I got into the stage, the iron box being screwed to the bottom. I hit the door in the middle with the sledge, which caused the corners to raise. I then drove the axe and wedge into the crack, and forced the door. It took me about half an hour to get the box open. Meantime the boy had walked around and came in sight of the driver. By the time I got the box open I was so completely exhausted that a ten-year-old boy could have captured me.

"As I got out of the stage with my booty the driver and the boy hove in sight, and fired at me. I started to run toward the rock where I had left my hat, but they shot at me twice before I got to the rock, and, as it was getting so hot for me, I left my things by the rock and took another direction around the moun-tain side. I did not know how many were after me. I was so tired that I could only run at a dog trot, carrying my burden of treasure, which weighed about sixteen pounds. After running about a mile I made up my mind I would take a good rest, as I was too tired to go further. I threw the sack containing the gold into the end of a hollow log and covered it up with dirt, and then started down into the ravine and brought up on the other side. I then buried my gun in a hollow tree and threw away ev-erything else that I could get along without."[1]

Charley's account was the most detailed he ever gave to a journalist about the holdup. Other witnesses later provided more details. Wells Fargo's agent in Sonora was Julius M. Alexander, the twenty-six-year-old, college-educated son of a pioneer Cali-fornia family. Years later, Alexander fondly recalled the mining town as "Sonora with its stores of iron doors and its streets of gold." He described what had happened at noon the day before

An old engraving shows Black Bart breaking open the iron Wells Fargo safe after he robbed Reason McConnell's stage.

the robbery. "There came a rap at the back door of my office. It was the superintendent and foreman of the Tuttletown mine, about eight miles distant from Sonora, and they had with them about $2,500 in amalgam wrapped in an old gunny sack. I carefully unwrapped the gold, weighed it on the scales and gave them a receipt for the exact amount, as the scales weighed to the fraction of an ounce, and Sonora gold was valued at $16 an ounce. Stage robbers were plentiful in the mountains those days and I was instructed to send out a shotgun man for guard whenever I thought necessary. This time I could not find my trusted man, so took the chances, and the chances happened to be against the express company this time. But this was not a large shipment, much below the average from the Southern Mines. Morning came, and in the starlight, for the stage started at 3:30 a.m., I wedged the gold into the iron box bolted to the bottom of the stage and the four horses were off."[2]

At the reins was Reason E. McConnell, one of the best-known jehus in the Sierra gold region. McConnell had seen many adventures on the frontier. In 1864, at age twenty, he and his family had accompanied a wagon train west on the Overland Trail, fighting off attacks by Plains Indians. After arriving in California, he worked as a ranch hand and then became a stagecoach driver. By 1883, he had been a whip for thirteen years and had been held up four times by stage robbers. After one incident, Wells Fargo officials presented him with a gold pocket watch for his heroism. He proudly carried it the rest of his life.

On November 3, 1883, McConnell readied his team, loaded the stage, and pulled out of Sonora at four in the morning. He had no passengers, but the iron Wells Fargo safe, underneath the middle seat, held almost sixteen pounds of gold worth $4,100,

DON GORDON COLLECTION.

Stage driver Reason McConnell, who was held up by Black Bart on Funk Hill in 1883.

much of it from the Patterson Mine, plus another $600 in gold coin and dust. Boles was more than fortunate that no shotgun messenger was on board. McConnell proceeded west seven miles through Tuttletown and then continued another four miles to Reynolds Ferry, arriving at 6:00 a.m. He stopped at the Rolleri house, where he ate breakfast, then left with Jimmy Rolleri for the nearby ferry on the bank of the Stanislaus River.[3]

Jimmy's sister Louise later recounted a conversation between the reinsman and her brother during McConnell's last trip a day or two earlier. "Mr. McConnell," she said, "had told Jimmy that he often saw deer near the road up on Funk Hill, up above Angels Creek. He saw them almost every morning after he left the ferry, he said. And he told Jimmy he ought to ride up with him one morning and get us some deer meat. But Jimmy told Mr. McConnell that he didn't have any shells for his rifle and so he couldn't go with him. And Mr. McConnell, he said that he would get some for Jimmy and bring them along with him on his next trip."

Louise explained that when the jehu returned the fateful morning, "He said he had got Jimmy's shells and he gave them to him. And Jimmy went and got his rifle and some money to pay for the shells and he got up on the driver's seat with Mr. McConnell and they started off. Well, as luck would have it, they didn't see a single deer that morning and, by the time they had nearly reached the top of Funk Hill, Jimmy began to think he had gone about far enough. So he asked Mr. McConnell to stop and let him down. He said it would make a long enough hunt for him if he got off there and hunted all the way down the hill, home. So he got off the stage and Mr. McConnell started up the horses and drove on and Jimmy started working his way down the hill."[4]

McConnell later described what happened next. "The road was a gradual uphill grade and from the summit the stage could be plainly seen winding its way up the mountain for half a mile or more. I was within a few yards of the top of the mountain, known as Funk Hill, when my lead horses stopped suddenly, and throwing their ears forward, looked toward a big rock. I looked and in the brush could see a pair of legs wrapped in gunnysacks. As I drove up he stepped boldly out with a double barrel shotgun leveled at me. He had a white flour sack over his head, with two holes cut out for eyes, and a slouch hat over it on his head. My team shied at this weird spectacle and I had trouble holding them. As he stepped out I asked him what he wanted, but without replying, he stepped sideways to the opposite side of the road, keeping his gun [ready]. He didn't seem to be looking at me, but for the boy."

McConnell, despite the fact that he was staring down the barrel of the bandit's shotgun, demanded, "What in the hell are you looking for?"

"Where is that man you had on with you?" Boles retorted. "Is he inside?"

"No, he was only a boy looking for deer and has gone back to the ferry," the driver answered.

"If that's the case, get down and unhitch your team."

"Let me drive up on level ground," responded McConnell. "I can't unhitch here. The stage will run down hill."

"Put your brake on," Charley demanded, "and wrap your lines around it and get down."

The jehu demurred. "It's a spring brake and won't hold. If you want me to unhitch here, put a rock behind the back wheel and I'll do it if no other spot will suit you."

"You get down from there and do it damn quick," Charley snapped. "Get that team off and no more back talk."

McConnell later explained, "And from the tone of his voice I knew he meant business and I had better obey. I got down off the stage, put a rock behind the wheel, and began to unhitch and put the traces [harness straps] up in place."

PHOTO BY DON GORDON.

The old stage road near the top of Funk Hill. The large boulder that concealed Black Bart is on the far left and today is mounted with a plaque that commemorates the holdup.

At that, Boles barked, "Never mind putting up those traces. Hurry up and get that team out of the way."

McConnell complied and unhitched the team. He then walked around his horses to get a better look at the highwayman.

"If you would keep your eyes on your work more and not as much at me, we'll get along better," Charley told him dryly.

McConnell recalled that his horses spooked after he unhitched them from the coach. "I had just gotten the lead bars unhooked from the pole when the robber tore off one of the side curtains of the stage, frightening my team, and they made a bound to get away. I was between the leaders and the wheeler in a very dangerous place. I quickly grabbed the lead lines with one hand and the wheel horses with the other, and as they started, the lines slipped off the brake and the wheeler's trace caught in the gooseneck on the end of the pole and held them. I hung to the lead lines and they dragged me for about ten feet before I got them stopped."

Boles, alarmed by the commotion, ran toward McConnell and shouted, "What in the hell are you trying to do?"

"Can't you see what I'm trying to do?" the exasperated jehu exclaimed. "I am trying to hold my horses. If you didn't make quite so much noise down there I might be able to do it."

McConnell then walked his team up the slight grade until he was out of sight of the stage. As he tied the horses to a tree, he spotted Jimmy Rolleri on the hillside below, trying to get a clear shot at some deer with his lever-action Henry rifle. "At this moment," he recalled, "the robber began hammering on the steel box, making such a resounding noise it frightened the deer away, and the boy turned and looked in my direction. Of course, I didn't dare call to him, so I frantically waved my hat and motioned for him to come to me. It was the best I could do and was glad to see him started toward me. As he came close he could see that I had the horses some distance away from the stage and knew at once that I had been held up.

"While waiting for the boy I crept a short distance from my team toward the stage and could see the robber standing with one foot on the brake block and the other on the wheel, and pounding the box with all of his might. The box was securely bolted to the bottom of the stage under the middle seat and it was a difficult task to get to and break open. I went to meet the boy and just as I reached for his gun the hammering ceased. Now that the robber had succeeded in reaching the treasure and the noise had ceased, I was a little leery, as he had the advantage over me.

"I decided to take a chance because I had a rifle and he had a shotgun. At any rate I would try to get in the first shot and try to keep out of the range of his shotgun for I knew he would shoot to kill. I crept to within one hundred fifty yards of the

The stagecoach robbed by Black Bart on Funk Hill as it looked in a photo taken about 1910.

stage and saw the robber just coming out of it with his gun under one arm and the bag of gold under the other. I took careful aim and pulled the trigger and the gun snapped. I tried again and it fired. I saw where the bullet struck and knew it must have shot a hole through his clothes or the sack of coin under his arm. He looked around and saw me throw in another shell, but instead of stopping to shoot back, he ran straight from me."[5]

The reinsman added, "I got in four shots before he was out of sight and decided I didn't care for the job of following him any further."

But the account that Jimmy Rolleri gave his family was a little different. "Mr. McConnell took Jimmy's rifle and shot," Louise Rolleri explained. "I don't know how many times he shot. But Jimmy told us it didn't look to him like any of the shots hit the man. Then Jimmy reached out and took hold of his rifle and said to Mr. McConnell, 'Give me the rifle. I'll hit him and I won't kill him, either.'"

Louise added that her brother was an expert hunter and marksman. "Most boys his age in the mountains are awful good shots. So Jimmy shot and he told us he was sure he hit the man's hand, for he jerked the hand back and dropped some things that were in it and picked them up again and started running away from the stage, up toward the ridge. He didn't go near the big outcropping of rock near the road but took out through the brush. There was a lot of young scrub oak growing there then and the man dodged and ran through the thickets of scrub oak and disappeared." Louise's account was confirmed by the local newspaper a few days after the holdup, but the reporter claimed that Jimmy's shot missed its mark: "McConnell fired two shots at him without effect; the boy then took a shot at him with no better results."[6]

McConnell and young Rolleri then walked the horses back to the stage. The reinsman recalled, "I hitched up my team, picked up the broken treasure box and some tools the robber had left behind, and lit out for Copperopolis, three miles away, as fast as I could go. While I was hitching up, the robber hove in sight and the boy saw something drop from the bundle he was carrying. I had driven about half a mile when I looked at my watch and it was 8:15 a.m. At Copperopolis I hired a buggy for the boy to take the express agent back to the scene of the holdup. Also [I] found a driver to take the stage on to Milton."[7]

A posse of young men accompanied Jimmy Rolleri and the town's Wells Fargo agent, William H. Case, to Funk Hill. As they searched the hillside for any other trace of the highwayman, Sheriff Ben Thorn rode up on horseback with Reason McConnell. Thorn had received a telegram from Copperopolis about the robbery. He helped the possemen scour the scene. They found a bloodstained waybill taken from the Wells Fargo safe, showing that the bandit had been injured, possibly by a bullet. Behind the large boulder near the stage road, they discovered a derby hat, two paper bags bearing the imprint of the store in Angels Camp, two flour sacks, an empty leather opera glass case, a magnifying glass, three detachable linen shirt cuffs, a razor, a belt, and some buckshot knotted up in a

Jimmy Rolleri, who fired at Black Bart with his rifle on Funk Hill.

silk handkerchief. Wells Fargo Agent Case gathered up all the items and took them to his office in Copperopolis while Sheriff Thorn and the rest searched for the bandit.

"Apparently a person had been lying at the base of the rock," Thorn recalled. "We tracked around all day. We came across a man named Martin who lived about three quarters of a mile from the scene of the robbery. Martin said he had met an elderly man with gray whiskers near his place in the woods and had a conversation with him. [Martin] asked the man where he was going, [and he] said he was going to Jackson where he lived." The sheriff concluded, "Martin said he would know him if he ever saw him again." Thorn then rode to Angels Camp, where he interviewed the storekeeper and several other townsfolk who had seen the stranger. He quickly concluded that the stage robber was Black Bart.[8]

A determined manhunt was now underway. Reason McCon-nell sent a telegram to Jim Hume and John Thacker in San Fran-cisco. He later explained, "Mr. Hume was out of town when the wire was received but Mr. Thacker got to Stockton as soon as possible." In Stockton, the local sheriff, Tom Cunningham, had a well-deserved reputation as one of the best peace officers on the Pacific Coast. He was a close friend of Hume, Thacker, Thorn, and Morse. In 1874, Cunningham had ridden with Harry Morse on the epic manhunt for the notorious Tiburcio Vasquez. He had tracked down countless dangerous outlaws without kill-ing any of them. Cunningham was then was out of town, so Detective Thacker got Orrin Langmaid, Stockton's former chief of police, to borrow the sheriff's man-hunting bloodhounds. Then they boarded a train for the depot in Milton, got a wagon and team, and rushed to Copperopolis, arriving at 2:30 in the morning after the holdup.[9]

They were met by Sheriff Thorn and Reason McConnell. At daybreak, the officers went to Agent Case's Wells Fargo office to view the items found at the scene. They carefully looked over the leather case, the cuffs, and the handkerchief that held the clump of buckshot. Sheriff Thorn recalled, "The handkerchief on one corner in small letters had the following characters, F.X.O.7., in capitals." He also said that it was Agent Case who first noticed the laundry mark. John Thacker, however, later claimed that it was he who had discovered the mark. In a letter to Orrin Lang-maid, he wrote, "Do you remember the conversation between Wells Fargo & Co. Agent [Case] and myself, when the handker-chief was handed to me with the buckshot in it? The agent said there is no marks on it, and I said never mind I will examine it for myself and I spread it out and found the mark on it and you took a memorandum of it. I said this is a laundry mark and will bet one thousand dollars it lands his boat."[10]

Then the small group of lawmen prepared to resume the manhunt. "After breakfast Thacker, Thorn, Langmaid, myself, and the bloodhounds started for Funk Hill," McConnell later explained. "After arriving at Funk Hill the dogs were given the scent of the hat, but I guess it was too old, for all they did was run around in all directions and yelp once in a while, and we couldn't follow them." Unable to track the bandit, the possemen returned to Copperopolis. There Thacker and Thorn gathered up the collection of personal items and drove to Milton, where they boarded a train for San Francisco to meet with Jim Hume. The two officers recognized the importance of the clues, and based on the descriptions provided by Martin and the Angels Camp storekeeper, they were certain that the stage robber was Black Bart.[11]

While the manhunt was going on, Boles made tracks out of Calaveras County. Though he hid his bag of loot in a hollow tree, he pocketed several hundred dollars in gold coin. Then he skirted to the west of Angels Camp and walked north toward Mokelumne Hill, avoiding anyone he came across. That night he stayed in an abandoned cabin, where he found an old hat to replace the derby he had lost. Charley then walked northwest out of the foothills to Brighton, on the outskirts of Sacramento, arriving on the night of November 5. He made the eighty-mile journey on foot in just two days. The next morning, he hiked into Sacramento and stopped by the International Hotel, where he retrieved the valise that he had stored there two months earlier. Then he got a bath and a shave, leaving only his luxuriant mustache and imperial. Boles then went to a tailor shop, where the owner took his measurements for an expensive $45 suit.[12]

He penned a letter to Emily Burling at the Webb House, saying that he would return in a few days and asking her to reserve a room for him. Charley also sent a note to his friend, tobacco store owner Thomas Ware, telling him that he was soon coming back to the city. Later that day, with the gold coin from the holdup, he bought a railroad ticket and entrained for Reno. There he registered as C. E. Bolton at the Palace Hotel and probably made a short visit to the home of his sister Maria and her minister husband. Two days later, Boles returned by rail to Sacramento, where he picked up his new suit. Apparently his paramour, Mollie, had returned to her fireman beau, for Charley went to the home of her tall friend, Susan. There, according to a local reporter, Susan "furnished consolation and food" to Boles during several "days of seclusion" before he boarded a return train for San Francisco.[13]

On the afternoon of November 10, Boles crossed San Francisco Bay by steamer and disembarked at the Ferry Building at the foot of Market Street. He walked six blocks up Market to Second Street, turned the corner to the Webb House, and checked into room 40. Charley had his trunks brought up from the baggage room and changed into a clean suit of clothes. He fastened a glittering diamond stud to his white shirtfront, slipped a large diamond ring onto one finger, and walked to his favorite eating place, the New York Bakery. There he was greeted by the owner, his friend Jacob M. Pike, and the pair chatted about the latest crop news and the recent decline of mining stock. Boles took a seat at a table across from a mirror, where he could admire his stylish attire. When one of Captain Lees's detectives passed by, the two exchanged pleasantries. After the meal, he returned to the Webb House, where he spent a quiet night. In the morning, he returned to the New York Bakery for breakfast. He and Pike spent a leisurely two hours discussing the latest racetrack news and a forthcoming match between two of the country's most famous wrestling champions, William Muldoon and Clarence Whistler.[14]

For Charley Boles, life couldn't be better. Once again he had outwitted the lawmen, and he must have been hugely relieved by his narrow escape from Funk Hill. The newspapers had given extensive coverage to the daring holdup and had blamed it on Black Bart. But much to his delight, they reported that the officers and their bloodhounds had given up the hunt. The gold shipment he had stolen was securely hidden in the hillside for-est. He would wait a few weeks until the heat died down, then return to Funk Hill and retrieve his largest bounty yet. The $4,000 in gold was enough to support him for years, especially if he could use it to make a killing in the stock market.

But Jim Hume and Harry Morse were working hard to spoil his plans.

14

Black Bart Throws Up the Sponge

Jim Hume and Harry Morse leaned over the desk in the Wells Fargo detective's San Francisco office. Before them lay Black Bart's derby hat, cuffs, opera glass case, and handkerchief. They had been brought in by John Thacker and Sheriff Thorn earlier that day. Morse looked carefully at the laundry mark on the handkerchief: F.X.O.7. "The first worthwhile clue we've uncovered yet," he remarked. "It won't be an easy job but maybe we'll get lucky." Morse recalled, "Hume took the hat and opera glass case to see if he could have them identified, placing the handkerchief in my hands, with instructions to find the owner of the mark, if possible." Meanwhile, as Thorn later explained, "Hume and myself spent considerable time in endeavoring to find where the field glasses had been bought." After three days of fruitless searching, Thorn gave up and returned to San Andreas.[1]

John Thacker later explained the meaning of the laundry mark. "The 'F' stood for the name of the driver of the laundry wagon, the 'X.O.' for the owner of the garment, and the figure 7 for the substation from which the packages were delivered." The detectives recognized that the mark would have been used in a city like San Francisco, Sacramento, or Stockton, for in a small town, a launderer would know everyone's clothing and would have no reason to mark it. San Francisco was therefore a good place to start the search. As Morse later explained, "I left all other business and devoted myself exclusively to this. I knew I had a job before me, as there were ninety-one laundries in the city." That same day, November 7, four days after the robbery, he began the painstaking legwork of visiting every laundry. Morse showed each proprietor the handkerchief and asked them to check their books for the mark. Finally, late in the afternoon of November 12, after six days of searching, he hit pay dirt. At the Ferguson & Biggy California Laundry, the co-owner, Phineas Ferguson, checked his records and found the telltale mark. Ferguson said that it belonged to a customer named C. E. Bolton. He added that Bolton's laundry was dropped off and picked up at the tobacco shop of their agent, Thomas C. Ware, at 316 Bush Street.

Morse wasted no time. He walked briskly from the California Laundry on Stevenson Street, crossed busy Market Street, and proceeded two blocks up Montgomery to Bush. Ware's shop on Bush Street was just a few doors west of Montgomery, where the garage entrance to the Russ Building now stands. Morse stepped inside and struck up a conversation with Ware, telling him that his name was Hamilton. "I made the most cautious inquiries at the laundry and found that he was well known there. The laundryman said Bolton was a mining man who often visited his mines, although he [Ware] did not know where they were situated. Sometimes he would be gone a week or two and sometimes a month. I assumed as a pretext that I wanted to consult with him on some mining matter, and not being certain that he was the Bolton I was looking for, I wished he could describe him. The laundryman did so and remarked that he had left the office but a few minutes before, and would be around again next morning if not that evening. I also learned that he roomed at No. 37 Second Street, room 40."[2]

Morse thanked Ware and left his shop. He immediately assigned one of his sleuths, John Curtin, to keep a close watch on the Webb House. Curtin was the same former Pinkerton detective who had been mistakenly shadowed by Captain Lees's men two years earlier. By that time it was five in the evening. Morse then walked back to the shop and resumed his chat with Ware on the sidewalk in front of the store. Suddenly Ware blurted out, "Why, here comes Bolton now. I'll introduce you to him."

Morse quickly looked Bolton over. "I knew at once from the descriptions I had received that he was the man. He was elegantly dressed and came sauntering along carrying a little cane. He wore a natty little derby hat, a diamond pin, a large diamond ring on his little finger, and a heavy gold watch and chain. He was about five feet, eight inches in height, straight as an arrow, broad shouldered, with deep sunken, bright blue eyes, high cheek bones, and a large, handsome grey mustache and imperial; the rest of his face was shaven clean. One would have taken him for a gentleman who had made a fortune and was enjoying it, rather than a highwayman. He looked anything but a stage robber. He was quick in his movements and had muscular and symmetrical lines."

Amid the clatter of wagons and buggies on the Bush Street cobblestones, Charley stepped jauntily up the sidewalk, swinging his cane. Across the street to his left was his favored haunt, the Bush Street Theater, and ahead of him stood Ware and a stranger. As Boles approached, Ware introduced Morse to him as Mr. Hamilton. "I shook hands with Bolton," recalled the detective, "and asked him if he was Mr. Bolton, the mining man. He said, 'Yes, I am.' I then told him that I had a matter of importance relating to some mines which I wished to consult him about, and asked him if he would spare a few minutes with me. He said 'Certainly,' and we walked together down Bush to Montgomery Street, then to California and Sansome, bringing up at Wells, Fargo & Co.'s office. We went upstairs to the

The Russ House at the corner of Bush Street, left, and Montgomery Street in the 1870s. Thomas Ware's tobacco shop was on Bush Street, to the left of the Russ House and just out of sight. Harry Morse arrested Black Bart on the Bush Street sidewalk, near the spot where the horse and wagon are.

superintendent's office. I introduced him to Mr. Hume, who requested him to be seated, saying that he wished to have a little talk with him. Mr. Hume commenced by inquiring about his business. Bolton said he was a mining man. Mr. Hume asked him where his mine was situated. He said in Nevada, on the California line. On being closely pressed, he was unable to give either the name of the mine or the exact locality. He then began to get a little excited, and great drops of perspiration stood out on his forehead and nose."

It was then nine o'clock, and Charley knew he was in big trouble. "I am a gentleman and don't know who you are," he declared. "I want to know what all this inquiry is about."

"You shall know presently," Hume responded. Then he came directly to the point. "Mr. Bolton, were you not in Calaveras County on November 3rd?"

"I was," Boles replied.

"What were you doing there?"

"That's none of your business," Charley snapped.

The questioning went on, but then, as Morse recalled, "I noticed that on Bolton's right hand there was a piece of skin knocked off, about the site of a ten-cent piece." Charley had either scraped his hand while breaking open the express box, or Jimmy Rolleri was correct that he had nicked the bandit.

"How did you get that?" Morse demanded as he pointed to the injury.

"If it is your business, I will tell you that I struck it on the car rail," Boles answered angrily, adding that it happened "while I was getting off the train at Truckee."

"No, you didn't," exclaimed Hume. "You got that when you broke open our box a little while ago."

Charley continued to proclaim his innocence as the interrogation went on for three hours. One of the detectives produced the derby hat found on Funk Hill and asked him to put it on. Boles complied, and remarked innocently, "Why gentlemen, it fits very well, doesn't it? And it is a very good hat. Perhaps you would allow me to buy it from you."[3]

Under further quizzing, Boles admitted that he was from Jefferson County, New York, and claimed that he was forty-seven, lopping seven years off his actual age. As Morse later explained, "He was asked a great many questions, many of which he could not, and others he would not, answer, and at length grew indignant. He said it was the first time in his life that his character had even been called into question; that he was a gentleman and that he would refuse to answer any more questions."

As Charley squirmed in his chair, Hume finally said, "If you will tell me where you were on the 1st, 2nd, 3rd, 4th, and 5th days of November, I'll keep the telegraph offices open all night in order to verify your statement and if you will not do that I am going to take you down and lock you up."

"Take me down and lock me up," was the defiant response.[4]

JOHN BOESSENECKER COLLECTION.

Wells Fargo headquarters at the corner of California and Sansome Streets in San Francisco. Here Hume and Morse interrogated Charley Boles.

The two detectives were hardly dissuaded. Hume immediately sent for Captain Appleton W. Stone of the San Francisco police. The fifty-six-year-old Stone was a close friend of Hume. He had arrived in California during the gold rush and joined the city police force in 1865. Like others in the department, he frequently performed private detective work, and during the previous eight years, he had assisted Hume in numerous Wells Fargo investigations. Stone was also a good friend of Harry Morse. In 1872, he had helped then-sheriff Morse capture Procopio Bustamante, nephew of the infamous gold rush bandit chieftain Joaquin Murrieta. Stone had been tipped, probably by a prostitute, that Procopio was holed up in a bordello on San Francisco's notorious Morton Street. Today, ironically enough, it is called Maiden Lane, and is lined with fashionable shops and galleries adjacent to Union Square. While Stone and two other officers guarded the brothel's front door, Morse slipped in the back. Ramming the barrel of his six-gun into the desperado's right ear, Morse said simply, "Put up your hands, Procopio. You're my man." The capture of the notorious bandido was quickly featured in newspapers across the country.[5]

It was 9:00 p.m. when Captain Stone, with Morse and Hume, bundled Boles into a hack and drove a few blocks to the Webb House. They were met by John Curtin, and all five climbed the stairs to room 40. "On arriving at the room, we immediately proceeded to search for evidence," explained Morse later. "We found a large trunk, two valises, three or four suits of clothes, among them a suit answering the description of that worn by the man who robbed the stage near Copperopolis. In one of the pockets I found another handkerchief bearing the same mark as that found at the scene of the robbery, and perfumed with evidently the same perfume. Upon opening the trunk we found a lot of shirts, cuffs, and collars, all having the same laundry mark, and also a letter, written by Bolton, the writing in which corresponded with the handwriting of the doggerel written by the robber on one of the express company's waybills and left on the treasure box, and would leave no doubt in the mind of anyone that they were written by the same person."[6]

The detectives then told Charley that a handkerchief with the same mark was found at the scene of the holdup. Boles declared, "I am not the only one whose things bear this mark. Others have their washing done at the same place. Somebody may have stolen the handkerchief from me, or I may have lost it and someone else found it."

Then, in what Morse described as an "air of offended dignity," Boles exclaimed, "Do you take me for a stage robber? I never harmed anybody in all my life, and this is the first time that my character has ever been brought into question."

Morse and Hume ignored his repeated protestations and kept

searching the room. They found the small pocket Bible that Mary had sent to him as a New Year's gift in 1865. Despite abandoning her and his family, to say nothing of his decidedly unchristian bandit career, Charley had kept it all those years. Hume, without showing the Bible to him, read the inscription: "This precious bible is presented to Charles E. Boles, First Sergeant, Company B, 116th Illinois Volunteer Infantry, by his wife as New Years gift."

Then he asked Boles, "You gave the name of Charles Bolton. That is not your true name. What is it?"

"T.Z. Spaulding," Boles snapped sarcastically.

"No, you're mistaken," the detective calmly replied. He held up the Bible and pointed to the inscription on the flyleaf. "That's your name."[7]

The detectives then walked Boles into the hallway and started for the stairs. They had made so much noise in ransacking the room that they awoke the landlady, Emily Burling. A journalist who interviewed Mrs. Burling the next day wrote, "She left her apartments to inquire into the matter, but was met on the stairs by Mr. Bolton, who, in a tremulous voice, the perspiration running down his furrowed cheeks, informed her that the four gentlemen by his side, in front and behind him, were friends of his who had come to see him on important business."[8]

The officers put Boles into a waiting hack and headed to the city prison. There he was searched, and in his pockets the detectives found $160 in gold coin and $10 in silver. Charley insisted that his name was Spaulding, and the booking officer registered him under that name. The detectives, hoping to keep the arrest quiet, did not provide his true name. Then Boles, for the first time in his life, spent the night behind bars. A worn-out Harry Morse boarded a ferry to his home in Oakland for some much-needed rest. In the morning, Hume and Captain Stone loaded Bart onto a bay steamer and met Morse and Thacker at the ferry landing near Oakland. Hume had business in Southern California, so Morse, Thacker, and Stone took their prisoner by train to Stockton. Meanwhile, Hume had wired Sheriff Thorn to meet them at the Stockton depot with the hunter, Thomas Martin.

By this time, police reporters had learned that Wells Fargo detectives had booked a mysterious suspect into the city prison. Using their sources in the jail, they quickly discovered that a suspected Black Bart had been arrested at the Webb House. One journalist talked to several police detectives, but probably on Captain Stone's orders, they refused to answer any questions, saying, "For the reason, sir, you know, we are not sure that we have the man."

The reporter hurried to the Webb House and looked up Emily Burling, whom he described as "a most affable and pleasing lady." When he told her that Mr. Bolton had been arrested on suspicion of being Black Bart, she exclaimed, "Oh, my! That man a stage robber! Who would have thought it? Why, he told me that he was a mining man, and has been living in this town for something like five years."

The journalist, writing in the third person, said, "At this juncture the reporter read the description of Black Bart to her, he being satisfied that Bolton and Bart were the same, and to all the little details, such as the color of the eyes, the missing front teeth, the prominent cheek bones, the gray hair, the high forehead, the long, slender hands, and affable and courteous manner in which he treated everybody, the lady answered 'yes' a dozen times and then suddenly relapsed into silence, as if she had been the means of his capture."[9]

Soon afterward another newspaperman arrived at the Webb House and found one of the housekeepers. The reporter asked her, "Does Mr. Bolton room here?"

"Yes, he does," she replied. "Can you tell me where he is? He went away very mysteriously last night."

The journalist wrote that he "informed her of who her boarder was, a piece of news that nearly caused her to faint. She too, like Ware, believed him to be a mining man and had often been told that his numerous absences were caused by business. He had roomed in the house while in the city for five years and was highly thought of by all who knew him, on account of his gentlemanly manners and pleasing address. She described him as Ware did, even to the missing front teeth and long slender hands. She found his room in a terrible state of disorder yesterday morning, but had no idea what caused it until told."[10]

Meanwhile Boles and his captors chatted amiably in their passenger car. Unknown to them, news of the arrest had been wired ahead to Stockton. As Harry Morse recalled, "Bart seemed full of fun all the way going up, and showed no desire to escape. He was not ironed, and his jaunty appearance warded off any suspicion of his identity." The detective continued, "When we got off the train at the Stockton depot and were met by Sheriff Thorn and Martin, the hunter, the latter's eyes fell immediately on Black Bart, and he exclaimed, even before he saw the officers, 'That's the man, that's him!' identifying him in a crowd of more than a hundred people who had gathered there to see the noted prisoner. Bart was at once taken to a photographer's to have his picture taken. At first he strongly objected, saying that we had no right to do it, and he had done nothing. But finally he submitted and sat quietly, and a good picture was obtained."

The photos were taken at the gallery of J. Pitcher Spooner. Spooner had him stand while he focused his camera, a huge accordion-like box with a lens that protruded like a small cannon. Charley put on a show of humor and quipped, "Will that thing go off?" Then he added with a laugh, "I would like to go off myself."

Spooner took several images of Black Bart, which have now become iconic. Two showed him standing, wearing an overcoat and derby hat and holding his gold cane. Sheriff Tom Cunningham joined them, and with Morse, Thacker, Stone, and Thorn, posed for a group photograph, which has also become a famous

Black Bart
Poe 5

One of the photos of Charley Boles taken in Stockton by J. Pitcher Spooner.

and widely published image of California's most notable pioneer lawmen. In the photo, three of the officers are holding celebratory cigars, and Thorn clutches a hatchet on top of an opened champagne box—probably a photographer's prop.[11]

The officers then walked Boles to a nearby restaurant for dinner. As Charley later said, "Fellows ran right into the restaurant where we were eating and wanted to know where that Black Bart fellow was. To get rid of them I had to say that he escaped from the train up the road. They seemed satisfied and left." Boles added, "They let me eat in peace." When they finished the meal, Sheriff Cunningham locked him up for the night in the county jail.[12]

By this time, San Francisco and Stockton newspapermen were all over the story. According to the *Stockton Evening Mail*, the detectives provided details of the arrest "in strict confidence, and with the understanding that no mention of the arrest should be made in the newspapers, as the case was being worked up quietly, and as there was no positive proof against the prisoner. The officers also promised that after the detectives had concluded their investigations and made a complaint against the prisoner, they would furnish the reporters with the full details, but that at the present time the publication of the matter would tend to defeat the ends of justice. The reporters gave the promise exacted of them, but the representative of one paper this morning saw fit to break his alleged word of honor and published the matter."[13]

According to the *Mail*, the offending newspaper was the *San Francisco Examiner*, owned by mining magnate and politician George Hearst. The *Examiner* was already well on its way toward creating yellow journalism, the sensationalist and exaggerated reporting that would be championed by its owner's son, William Randolph Hearst, after he took over the newspaper in 1887. In a headlong rush to "scoop" its competitors, the *Examiner* provided a quasi-factual front-page account of Black Bart's arrest. It also provided this glaring example of rank fiction: "It is said that during the year 1871 he plied the honest vocation of pedagogue in a country school in the northern portion of the state, but while in this position his proclivities for poker met with the serious disapproval of the moral sentiment of the community. In consequence, Black Bart was unceremoniously and bodily bounced from the position where the recommendations of a moral inculcator, as well as those of an intellectual teacher, were demanded. Whether this act of the school trustees served to lend additional impetus to his downward tendency can be only a matter of presumption. However, be this as it may, a few weeks after Black Bart had retired from the ranks of private life a stage was robbed in the vicinity. Circumstantial evidence fastened suspicion on the ex-teacher, who, strangely enough, disappeared just at the time he was most earnestly wanted."[14]

The *Examiner* had actually concocted this tale two months earlier, when Black Bart's identity was unknown. Charley soon read the story, which he found more than amusing. Yet the *Mail*'s charge that the *Examiner* violated its pledge of confidentiality was overly harsh. The other leading San Francisco dailies—the *Alta California*, the *Call*, the *Chronicle*, and the *Bulletin*—simultaneously gave detailed and reasonably accurate accounts of the arrest. They all got their information from Hume, Morse, and Stone. The newspapers also blamed Black Bart for only twenty-three stage robberies, because the actual number of twenty-nine was not yet known. The criticism of the *Examiner* was only the precursor to a coming journalistic conflict in which the San Francisco press engaged in a battle royal over Black Bart's story.[15]

That morning, November 14, Morse, Stone, and Thorn boarded a train at the Stockton depot and took Boles to the railhead in Milton. By prearrangement, Reason McConnell was waiting for them, as was a large crowd intent on seeing Black Bart, who was still immaculately attired and bejeweled. Said Morse, "Here we met the driver of the stage that was robbed on the 3rd. He came up and spoke to the prisoner but said he could not identify him, as the robber was disguised in flour sacks, but the voice was the same. Bart seemed unconcerned and kept up his jokes. The great crowd that had assembled attracted his attention and he said, 'The whole town has turned out to meet me. I guess they'll know me when they see me again.'

"At Milton we took a team and drove over to San Andreas—twenty-two miles. The whole population of the town—men, women, and children—had turned out, and it was amusing to hear the remarks as they mistook the natty looking prisoner for an officer and some one of us for the culprit. It was agreed that we would start the next morning for the scene of the robbery to look for further evidence, and that before we went we would have another interview with Bart. I was selected to interview him. At seven o'clock in the evening he was taken into the jailer's room and I was left alone with him. I had written down all the facts we had gathered in connection with the case.

JOHN BOESSENECKER COLLECTION.

Left to right: Sheriff Tom Cunningham, Captain Appleton W. Stone, Sheriff Ben Thorn, Wells Fargo detective John Thacker, and Harry Morse. They posed for this image in Spooner's photo gallery to celebrate the capture of Black Bart.

These I carefully read to him, examining what bearing they would have at the trial. He would often break off and go into other subjects. He would give graphic descriptions of his experience in battle and how he was wounded. Then he would branch off into Bible matters, in which he seemed well posted. He thought that Moses had a great deal of pluck to reprove the Lord for his harsh dealing with the children of Israel on different occasions. I would bring him back to the right subject again, and for five hours and a half I talked with him, ending the interview at 12:30 in the morning."

Finally Boles exclaimed, "I don't admit that I committed this robbery, but what benefit would it be to the man who did, to acknowledge it?"

Morse explained that if the case went to trial, the prosecutor would prove that he had committed numerous robberies. But if he pleaded guilty and returned the stolen gold, "It would save the county the great expense of a trial and would, no doubt, be taken into consideration by the court and effect a mitigation of his sentence."

At that, Charley declared, "Suppose the man that did commit the robbery should do this. Would it not be possible for him to get clear altogether?"

Morse responded that if he was convicted of all the stage robberies he would probably be sentenced to life imprisonment.

"I want you to understand that I'm not going to San Quentin. I'll die first!" Boles exclaimed. "These men may all come up and testify just as you say. Men are apt to commit perjury and courts are apt to be prejudiced, and whether a man is guilty or not, he has to suffer the consequences."

Charley then told Morse about a stage robbery in which a man was arrested, and witnesses all testified against him.

"I know of my own knowledge that he didn't do it. I wonder whatever became of him?" Boles muttered.

Charley was probably talking about one of the numerous suspects who had been jailed as Black Bart. But in his quest for Morse's sympathy, he exaggerated, for none of the men were wrongfully convicted of stage robbery. By then Morse knew that he had broken Black Bart. He called in Sheriff Thorn and Captain Stone, and after a few minutes of conversation about the stolen loot, Charley suddenly said, "Well, let us go after it."[16]

Yet Ben Thorn told the story a little differently. In his version it was he, not Morse, who obtained the confession. According to Thorn's account, "Harry Morse locked himself in the San Andreas jail with his prisoner and for five hours he pleaded with him to confess his many crimes and tell where he had secreted the proceeds of his last robbery. Bolton sturdily denied that he was Black Bart, and dared Morse to bring evidence before a jury that would convict him." Finally Sheriff Thorn and Captain Stone entered the cell and methodically presented all the evidence of his guilt. Bolton thought it over and said quietly, "Can you prove all that?"

"I can," answered Thorn.

"What became of the stolen money?" Stone asked.

"It lies concealed in a tree," Boles answered. "Take me to the place and I'll get the treasure for you."

"We'll start immediately, then," Thorn and Stone told him.

"All right, let's travel," Charley said, in a resigned tone.[17]

As Morse later explained, "We then got a team and at one o'clock started out of San Andreas. The night was cold and clear and the moon was shining brightly and we had a ride of twenty-four miles through the foothills and mountains, over deep gulches, canyons, etc. He told interesting stories all the way. He said it was a great relief to him, for there had been a great strain on his mind, and this was the first time he had had the opportunity to tell anybody about this thing." During the buggy ride to Funk Hill, Charley made a full confession, describing the stage robbery and his subsequent flight to Sacramento. "On the way Bart told me of his doings," recalled Morse. "He said that he had been about mills and stage offices, learning when bullion was to be shipped and when the stage was to carry money."

"I would have left a little poem at the scene," Boles told them, "but I had to leave too quick."

At daybreak, he led the officers to a gully three hundred yards below Funk Hill, where he pointed out a hollow tree stump.

"There is the tree in which the treasure lies," he said.

The officers reached into the stump, and from under a pile

of dirt and leaves they pulled out the sack with $4,000 in stolen gold.

"There it is, just as I put it there," Charley exclaimed. "That is the package."

He rubbed his hands together and almost squealed in delight. Boles fully understood that if he expected any mercy from the courts, he had to return the loot. Morse and his fellow lawmen lugged the sack back to the buggy and started for San Andreas. They did not retrieve the bandit's shotgun, which was found by a California Indian a few days later and turned over to Wells Fargo officials. They stopped in Copperopolis to eat breakfast. There his captors were surprised when he politely declined their offers of a drink and a cigar. Before returning Charley to his San Andreas jail cell, Morse stepped into the telegraph office in Copperopolis. He sent a brief wire to Wells Fargo headquarters in San Francisco, using a popular idiom for a pugilist who lost a bare-knuckle prizefight: "Black Bart throws up the sponge. Stone, Thorn, and myself have recovered all the stolen treasure."[18]

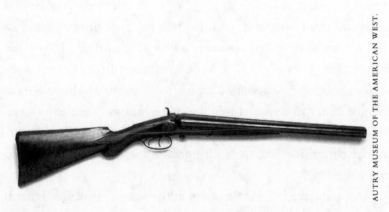

AUTRY MUSEUM OF THE AMERICAN WEST.

Black Bart's twelve-gauge shotgun, found on Funk Hill in 1883. Today it is on display in the Autry Museum of the American West in Los Angeles.

15

That Telltale Handkerchief

A small group of young female schoolteachers gathered at the entrance to the Calaveras County jail, situated at the rear of the courthouse in San Andreas. They had come to see the infamous Black Bart. Charley never shied from attractive women, and he stood in his cell, gazing at them intently through the bars of his door.

"Look at him!" one of the teachers whispered in admiration. "They say he is awful brave."

"Pooh!" exclaimed another of the women, glaring at Boles. "I had rather see a good looking fellow any day than to see him!"

Charley overheard the remark, which offended his dignity. As the gawkers pressed closer to get a good look at him, he turned his back and refused to acknowledge them. Pulling a chair up to his cell door, and with his back facing the women, he sat down and proceeded to read a Stockton newspaper account of his arrest. A local reporter who observed the encounter wrote, "All efforts to break his uncompromising silence failed signally, and the disappointed school-marms filed out into the jail yard with a look of hostile disgust."

The journalist, eager to get the first newspaper interview with Black Bart, stepped up to the grated door and asked him, "You have a good many visitors?"

"Oh, yes, and I like company, too," he answered politely. "I always did enjoy sociability. It was rather rough to turn my back on the ladies, but then they came through curiosity, and not from sympathy."

The newspaperman took a good look at Charley and was impressed by his appearance. "The prisoner was neatly dressed in a brown suit, spangled with red threads. On his scarf glistened a diamond pin, and on his hand a diamond ring flashed as he occasionally grasped a slat of the latticed door. His language is well chosen and grammatical, free from profanity, quiet, and of such an earnestness and naivete as to impress one that he is telling strictly the truth—an effect which is strengthened by his bold dodging or refusal to answer any disagreeable question."

In an effort to get him to open up, the reporter said hopefully, "The newspapers are attributing a good many crimes to you."

The approach worked, said the reporter. "The prisoner's blue eyes snapped, and his gray eyebrows lowered for an instant, while the creases in his face quivered from nervousness." Then Boles responded in a husky voice, "If all they say were true, I could not live long enough to get justice done me. I have learned twice as much about myself as I ever knew before."

"Then you did not commit twenty-three stage robberies?"

"No, sir, and if I were Black Bart—" He quickly caught himself. "Well, I have no desire for notoriety. When a man is successful in anything, other things are credited to him, and a good many more than he is entitled to, and it makes him notorious. But I don't know as I ought to talk."

"Go on," urged the reporter. "That's all right, we are talking only about the last stage robbery."

"Yes, that's what I was talking about," Boles replied cagily. "One case at a time is enough, God knows!"

"You appear to be pretty well educated."

"Oh, no. I never claimed that."

"You served in the Civil War, I believe?"

"Yes. I enlisted in 1862 under Sherman, and served with him up to the time of the grand reunion in Washington, in which I took part. Except at the times that I was in the hospital—for I was wounded three times—I fought in every battle under Sherman. I enlisted as a private and came out a first lieutenant of the—" Again he quickly checked himself. "Well, now, I don't want to disclose my identity. I have relatives living, and I would not want them to hear of this disgrace."

The journalist said that Boles described how he had first come to California in the gold rush, insisting that he had only associated with "honest and honorable men, men who did not dream that he was a successful stage robber, and who would not help him, now that they know it." Charley explained that San Francisco "has been not a home, exactly, but a stopping place, a headquarters." The newspaperman added that Boles held no grudge against the lawmen who arrested him. "The officers, especially Sheriff Thorn and Harry Morse, had treated him like a gentleman, and he had scarcely felt that he was a prisoner."

In response to questions about his friends in San Francisco, Charley said, "I am acquainted with several of the detectives and officers there, and I have dined frequently with them at the United States Restaurant. The only time that I ever hired one was about four years ago, when I lost an overcoat."

"And you had the cheek to employ a detective?"

"Oh, yes. I got Jones and I think Byram, too. They brought the property back within an hour."

The journalist said that Charley then told the story of the theft "with an air comical in its expression of injured innocence." After Boles finished, he declared, "There is not a man in San Francisco who can say that I owe him to the extent even of a five-cent piece."

That remark caused the newspaperman to break into a broad grin. Charley, chagrined, let out a chuckle and responded, "Of course you'll say it is easy to pay your bills with other people's money."

"Did you ever rob a passenger?"

"No, sir, no. I would rather go to San Quentin for life than to take a dime from a passenger, or to injure him in any way. One can rob men at any place."

"But your gun was loaded with buckshot, wasn't it?"

"Yes. Of course when a person goes into that line of business he must be prepared for emergencies. But I want to say here that I never harmed a single individual, and never committed any crime except against Wells, Fargo & Co. I have never laid myself liable before the courts even in a civil suit."

"How long had you been watching for the last robbery?"

"For about a month. I had business around there," he said with an ironic smile, "and I visited the scene of the halting early on that Saturday morning. I lay concealed behind a rock, whence I could see the stage through a pair of opera glasses."

Charley answered more questions about how he had held up the coach, and then declared, "If it had not been for that handkerchief, I'll bet a thousand dollars they never would have got me! A thousand dollars I say, but then that's just a way of speaking, you know. I have no money now. I never was much troubled with riches, and, on the other hand, I never was absolutely needy."

"Of course not," agreed the journalist. "How old are you, Mr. Bolton?"

"Nearly forty-eight years old," Charley lied.

"You appear to be fifty-eight."

"Well, I have had a rough life of it."

"I hope you will never be caught in stage robbing again."

"Oh, my God, no! Never! If I ever live my term out in San Quentin I'll never stop another stage, so help me God! I hate this robbery; I detest it as much as anyone. It is a despicable business. But there is not much use for me to live now."[1]

At that point, Sheriff Thorn and the local judge walked in and ended the interview. At six o'clock that evening, November 16, 1883, Thorn took his prisoner before a justice of the peace to be arraigned. The sheriff stepped to the witness stand and testified that Boles had confessed to the Funk Hill stage robbery and had led them to the hidden treasure. A reporter who watched Charley in court wrote, "He sat leaning back in an armchair with arms folded, now and then glancing coolly at the group which had gathered before the table." The justice explained to Boles that he had been charged with robbery, and asked, "Guilty or not guilty?"

JOHN BOESSENECKER COLLECTION.

Charles Boles in an engraving made from an 1883 photograph.

"I am guilty," Charley promptly responded. "I would merely say that I wish as little delay as possible."

The justice of the peace then held him to answer the charge, and bound him over for trial. Sheriff Thorn returned Charley to his jail cell, and the next day brought him before Judge Charles V. Gottschalk in the Calaveras County superior court. Once again Boles admitted to robbing the stage on Funk Hill, waived his right to a trial, and pleaded guilty. However, according to a journalist in the courtroom, "He denied being Black Bart and declared that this was his first, as it should be his last, offense against the law. He said that circumstances over which he had no control had urged him to the commission of the crime, and that he had yielded to temptation after severe struggles. He implored the mercy of the court." Another reporter remarked that Charley's speech "seemed to have no effect whatever upon the judge, and was considered rather weak by the lookers-on." Judge Gottschalk then intoned "that C.E. Bolton be punished by imprisonment in the state prison of the State of California for the term of six years."

Charley smiled, and one of the journalists observed that he "seemed rather pleased with the sentence." Neither the judge nor the prosecutor thought to seize his gold cane, pocket watch, or jewelry, all of which he had purchased with his ill-gotten gains. With credits for good behavior, he would be eligible for release in about four years.[2]

The next day, Sheriff Thorn bundled his notorious prisoner into a stagecoach bound for Milton. There were two other passengers aboard, a Chinese man and Mamie Bunt, the twenty-year-old daughter of a pioneer family. Many years later she described the stage ride. "It was generally known that Sheriff Thorn was to take the noted robber away. All were alert to catch a glimpse of him, both at San Andreas and all points or stations along the route. He was not handcuffed," she recalled. "He was a model prisoner all along the trip to Milton and gave no trouble to Thorn, who placed no restrictions upon his movements, but allowed him to leave the stage at the different stage stations where they stopped to water the horses or change them for fresh ones." Mamie Bunt remembered the trip fondly. "At one place he went into a store and bought a large bag of candy," she said, and handed it to her. "Of course, [I] accepted in the spirit in which it was given."[3]

The trip to San Francisco took two days by stage, train, and steamboat. Sheriff Thorn arrived with Boles at the San Francisco ferry landing late in the afternoon of November 19. Morse met them, and the trio proceeded to Jim Hume's office at California and Sansome streets. There Hume had a long discussion with the highwayman. "I told him," Hume said later, "that I had him in my book charged with twenty-one robberies. I asked him to tell me which he had committed in order that I might see if there were any other stage robbers to look for."

Boles thought it over and then asked, "You don't intend to use them against me?"

"No," said Hume. "We are done with you."[4]

As the detective later explained, "Then he confessed to the twenty-one robberies and seven more." The interview completed, all four repaired to Ned's, a fashionable restaurant where they spent two hours enjoying a lavish dinner. Wells Fargo footed the bill of $18.75, more than $500 in current money. Then they brought Boles to the city prison, situated in the basement of city hall on Portsmouth Square. By that time word had quickly spread, and an eager crowd jammed into the jail lobby to catch a glimpse of Black Bart. "If he had been Longfellow he could not have had more attention shown him," declared one of the newspapermen who had rushed to the lockup.

Prisoners whose cells faced the jail keeper's desk peered through their barred doors and called out, "Black Bart! That's him. Here he comes. That's Black Bart!"

As spectators crowded into the lobby, several gasped loudly. "That's the man! Why, I've seen him a thousand times."

A score of Charley's friends and acquaintances were in the throng, along with half a dozen police detectives who walked down from their offices upstairs. One detective, William Jones, who with Ed Byram had recovered Charley's stolen chinchilla coat, was too embarrassed to admit that he knew the road agent. After looking Boles over, Jones blurted out, "I don't know him. Never saw him before."

Ed Byram was also there, and just as humiliated. He stared at Black Bart for a full five minutes but did not speak to him. Detective Chris Cox, however, had no such scruples. Stepping forward and seizing the prisoner's hand, he exclaimed, "There's a man I've seen a thousand times!"

"You bet you have, old man," Boles responded warmly. "Oh, my old friend Chris. Just the same as you used to be. Well, I see you once more, don't I?"

Then Charley laughed gleefully as he reminded Cox of how many times they had dined together at the New York Bakery. Even though Cox had been thoroughly deceived, he held no ill will toward Black Bart. Then, almost as if on cue, Jacob Pike, the restaurant's owner, stepped up and greeted Boles warmly. Charley described the holdup to him and explained how he had been captured. He finished by saying, "Only for that laundry mark, Pike, and they would never have caught me. If I'd had time to clean up after me that time, I'd been eating at your place yet."

Pike was followed by Charley's friend Thomas Ware, who apologized profusely for spilling the beans to Harry Morse, saying that he had done so unintentionally.

"I know that, my dear fellow," Boles responded. "Don't talk about it any more."

A newspaperman who watched them wrote, "The two men shook hands cordially and held their hands locked for quite a

JOHN BOESSENECKER COLLECTION.

San Francisco police detective Chris Cox in 1903. He readily admitted that he had been deceived by his friend Black Bart.

long time. Ware congratulated him upon looking so well. Black Bart made no answer, but as he stood the tears came to his eyes."

Charley, humiliated that so many of his friends were seeing him behind bars, said to Ware in a breaking voice, "By God, I can't choke this thing down!"

When another man stepped forward to greet him, Boles exclaimed regretfully, "I cannot call you my friend now. After this I have no friends."[5]

At that point, two well-dressed, middle-aged women pushed their way through the crowd. The younger one was Emily Burling. Tall and beautiful and wearing a long sealskin coat, she wept uncontrollably.

"You here?" Charley said in amazement.

She pressed in close to him and seized his hand, at the same time dabbing her eyes with a handkerchief. The two stepped aside and exchanged earnest whispers. As they huddled together, a dozen voices in the crowd exclaimed, "That's his landlady."

A reporter for the *Alta California* watched the pair and suspected that she might be far more than that. He wrote that "the 'landlady' looked reproachfully at the worthy crowd" until they stepped back so she could finish her talk in private. But a journalist for the *San Francisco Call* observed, "Only the younger woman spoke to Black Bart, and she, nervously applying a small silk handkerchief to her eyes, was beseeching the man to permit a visit from another woman, probably his mistress."

Charley refused, saying, "It will do no good. I don't want to see her."

Finally, after whispering together for fifteen minutes, she said in a choking voice, "Good bye."

"The best of friends must part," the *Alta*'s man reported, "and so the stately 'landlady' shed a few more tears, pressed a long lingering press upon her robber friend's hand, and left, a dead and awful silence pervading the prison, only to be broken by the gatekeeper's quick and skillful turn of the lock, that in another moment separated her from Bart for three years and a half."[6]

Captain Stone then escorted Boles to a jail cell, but allowed the throng and several reporters to crowd into the narrow corridor. Charley suddenly turned toward the newspapermen and exclaimed, "I feel the degradation of this position keenly. I realize the enormity of my crime, and I know that the judge dealt with me as leniently as he could and do what was right, but I had rather sunk in the bay while we crossed tonight than meet the men I have since we arrived."

"Ain't you sorry for what you've done, Mr. Bart?" called out one of the group.

"I only wish that one of the balls fired after me from the Copperopolis stage had been well directed," Charley responded. "I laughed at them as they whistled by me then, but now I wish it had been an expert who pulled the trigger. No one knows how deeply I feel my disgrace. If the man with the gun had killed me I would have been buried there and the world would never have known who I was. I had a presentiment that I was going to danger when I saw that stage coming down the hill, but once in the road with my gun at my shoulder my curiosity overcame me, and I felt bound to see what was in that box. So I ordered the driver to throw it down, though I would not have harmed him if he had refused. I was exhausted when I got the box open and could not run very fast, so somehow in my haste to get out of range of the driver's rifle I dropped that telltale handkerchief. If I had had my usual time to clean up and cover my tracks they never would have caught me and they never would have found the stuff."

"Why did you confess?" asked one of the reporters.

"Because I was told they had overwhelming proofs of my guilt."

"What did they promise to do for you if you would confess?"

"Well, they all agreed they could get me a light sentence, but only on condition that I restored the stolen treasure as well."

When one newspaperman asked him if he was Black Bart, he said, "The officers say that I am Bart, but I say no. You can believe either that you like. It does not make any difference now who I am, at least for me."[7]

Responding to another journalist, Charley briefly described the Funk Hill robbery, and added, "It was the hardest job I ever had, though, to open that box."

"Why didn't you force the driver to open it?"

"Why, it would have taken him three weeks, and I was in a hurry just then," he replied with a grim smile. "There was no time to waste. As it was, I was surprised that I got through so quickly. I had a fine lot of tools—all that was needed, and I used them to the best advantage. When I got through I was so weak a child could have captured me, and after I got into the brush I could hardly walk. Still, I made these things," and he motioned toward his legs, "go along very lively. If there had been anyone behind that gun who knew how to use it, I would have been a dead man today."

For a moment Charley grew somber. "I do not care for the years of imprisonment, nor shoveling sand or whatever I will do at San Quentin. But the shame of my old friends finding me out hurts me more than all. There isn't a man in this city can say he ever saw me do wrong or ever met me in questionable places. I never drink, smoke or chew; all my friends are gentlemen, and I never associated with other than gentlemen."

Then his sense of humor quickly returned. "To be sure, I can't claim to be perfect. They do say I will rob a stage occasionally. But no one can say that I ever raised my hand to do anyone harm. I merely carried a gun to intimidate the driver. As for using it, why, for all the gold that road ever carried, I would not shoot a man. I could easily have killed that driver while he was popping at me. And it was a loud call—two bullets passing through my clothing."

When asked how the arresting officers treated him, he praised Sheriff Thorn and what he facetiously termed his "hotel"—the Calaveras County jail. "I never before took to men whose company was forced upon me. But Mr. Thorn, Mr. Stone and the gentlemen with them did everything in their power to make me comfortable. In fact, I grew so attached to them that I would not stay away from them. When I went to San Andreas I stopped at Mr. Thorn's hotel to be near him and because it is a temperance house; and I have never been in a better kept hotel. When I went to bed at night I never took the trouble to bolt the doors. I knew they would attend to all that."

He explained how Harry Morse had questioned him for almost six hours, and he had finally confessed to Sheriff Thorn and Captain Stone. "Besides all he told me," Boles said of Thorn, "I knew he could easily obtain more evidence, and I confessed. I was glad to do so, for I didn't want any more suspense. If I had made a fight, my sentence might have been twenty years, and

I would have come out of jail a broken-down old man. As it is, I will be less than fifty-two when I come out, and will have a chance to redeem myself."

In addition to lying about his age, Charley continued to insist that he was not Black Bart. "In every paper I pick up I see those big black headlines, Black Bart. Everywhere I go people crowd around to see Black Bart. Why, when I wake up in the morning I expect to see in big letters on the wall of my cell, Black Bart."[8]

The *Call* reporter was the last to interview him. In response to his questions, Boles declared, "I never was arrested before in my life, and no man can trace a dishonest act to me in this city."

"What prompted you to commit the stage robbery of which you pleaded guilty?" asked the journalist.

"That is hard to say," Charley answered. "There was a combination of circumstances that forced me to that act that only one person in the city other than myself understands, and I can't explain."

He was probably referring to his mistress, but the newspaperman did not press him on that point.

"Do you still insist that you are not Black Bart?"

"So I told the officers," he replied evasively.

"And you don't plead guilty to those Black Bart verses?"

"So I told the officers."

At that point a well-dressed man, another of Charley's friends, stepped into the cell, held out his hand, and said, "Well, old fellow, I'm sorry to see you here, but I'm glad to see you."

Boles was surprised, and replied regretfully, "I can't claim your friendship now, but I am glad to see you."

As his friend left the cell, Boles turned to the reporter. Referring to San Quentin prison, he said, "If you are ever over the bay there, look me up. I suppose I'll be wearing the zebra stripes and shoveling sand. Good bye."[9]

The next morning, an even larger crowd crammed into the jail, among them numerous police officers. To accommodate them, the jailers allowed him out of his cell and let him sit in a chair in the corridor. One visiting newspaperman wrote that he greeted his guests and "held quite a levee. He was still dressed in his stylish suit, wore his diamond ring, and toyed with his cane." The two who spoke with him the longest were the chief of police and Charley's friend Thomas Ware, who was so overwrought with guilt, he came a second time to the jail. Boles asked Ware to take charge of his trunk and return it to him on his release from prison.

The journalist talked with Boles, who complained about the newspaper reports that implied he had a romantic relationship with his landlady. "He said it is a shame that a 'gentleman' cannot receive a lady friend without some of the papers accusing her of being his mistress," wrote the reporter.

"Blamed if it isn't enough to aggravate someone," Charley added. When several women asked to meet him, Boles declined, saying, "Each and all of them would be thought my mistress, and might get their names in the paper."[10]

Another reporter asked Boles, "But do you now deny that you are Black Bart?"

"I don't think I want to say any more," was his curt response.[11]

That afternoon, several detectives escorted Boles to the Montgomery Street gallery of Isaiah W. Taber, one of San Francisco's best known photographers. One journalist said that the process "required some time, as the detectives desired that he should be taken in five or six different postures and from as many different views of his face." The resulting photographs, all bust images mounted on cardboard cabinet cards, have become famous. Two of them were profile views, showing the right and left sides of his face. Two more, almost identical, pictured him facing the camera, his head turned slightly to his right. The last photo was another bust image, with Boles wearing his derby hat.[12]

By the time Taber finished, it was too late in the day for the detectives to take Charley across the bay to San Quentin. They returned him to his cell in the city prison. There Jim Hume interviewed him at length, and he again confessed to twenty-eight stage robberies. As Hume explained, "Later, in San Quentin, he confessed to another one, making twenty-nine in all." The next day, Sheriff Thorn visited the jail, loaded Boles into a hack, and took him to the wharf. They then boarded a steamboat to the state prison, located on Point San Quentin at the upper end of San Francisco Bay.[13]

JOHN BOESSENECKER COLLECTION.

One of the images of Black Bart taken in San Francisco by photographer Isaiah W. Taber on November 20, 1883.

While Thorn and his prisoner were on their way to San Quentin, Isaiah Taber offered copies of the Black Bart photos for sale as souvenirs. He even put one of the images on display in his front window. Two days later, the *San Francisco Chronicle* reported, "His photograph in front of a Montgomery Street gallery is daily surrounded by an eager crowd, and nine out of every ten observers state that they have often seen him on the streets." Perhaps that was wishful thinking, but Black Bart was now well on his way into the halls of Old West legend.[14]

16

A War of Words

Newspapers across the nation featured stories on the sensational arrest of Black Bart. "TRACED BY HIS CUFF. BLACK BART, GENTLEMANLY STAGE ROBBER, CAPTURED," heralded the *Boston Globe*. "BLACK BART, THE PO8" was the headline in the *Philadelphia Times*. The *Omaha Bee* referenced a legendary seventeenth-century English highwayman when it titled its account, "THE POET ROBBER—THE MODERN CLAUDE DUVAL." But nowhere did journalists spill so much ink on the story as in San Francisco. And to sell newspapers, they stirred the embers of controversy in every aspect of their coverage.[1]

Charley's friends in California were shocked by the news. Dr. Joseph Hostetler, the regimental surgeon for the 116th Illinois, had settled in Napa, where he was interviewed by a local newspaperman, who wrote, "He was the last man whom he would ever suspect of being guilty of the least dishonest or disreputable act, nor is there a man for whom he would be willing to do more." The journalist also spoke with a San Francisco businessman, Andrew Johnson, who said he had known Boles for twelve years. "No finer gentleman lived than Charles E. Bolton," wrote the reporter. "He has known him intimately and never knew a breath of suspicion to light on him. Bolton was a genial, affable man, never could be induced to taste a glass of liquor, never smoked nor kept any but the best company and was known as an honest, straightforward man. To both gentlemen Bolton's arrest and confession was almost impossible of belief."[2]

Meanwhile, George Hearst's *San Francisco Examiner* began a journalistic campaign against Jim Hume and Harry Morse, one that would foreshadow several decades of extraordinarily irresponsible yellow journalism. The editors of the *Examiner* were consumed by jealousy over the coverage by its bitter rival, the *San Francisco Call*. The *Call* had a distinct advantage because its managing editor, Boyd Henderson, was a close friend of Harry Morse. Before meeting Morse, the thirty-nine-year-old Henderson had led an adventurous career as a reporter for the *New York Herald*. He had once been imprisoned in Cuba while attempting to interview rebel forces fighting against Spain. He also spent time with the Lowry band of Lumbee Indians who fought a guerilla campaign in North Carolina, and reported their activities in dispatches to the *Herald*. Henderson then came west to California, where, in 1874, he rode as a correspondent with then-sheriff Morse on his epic manhunt for the Tiburcio Vasquez gang.[3]

Many years later, a reporter for the *San Francisco Examiner* recalled that Harry Morse had promised Henderson a scoop on the arrest of Black Bart. That was true, for on November 17, the *Call* beat all the competition by publishing Morse's detailed, firsthand account of the capture. Its story filled half of the front page, under the headline, "BLACK BART, THE FAMOUS HIGHWAYMAN'S CONFESSION OF HIS ROBBERIES; HOW HARRY MORSE RAN HIM DOWN." The editors of the *Examiner* were outraged by the *Call*'s scoop. Overcome with envy, the next day they ran a prominent headline: "A COMEDY: BLACK BART'S NUMEROUS CRIMES TO GO VIRTUALLY UNPUNISHED." The newspaper declared, "The man who, according to the detectives' stories, has for ten years past made a business of plundering one of the wealthiest corporations in the state, of breaking open the United States mails, and to whose prowess twenty-three successful stage robberies are ascribed, escapes, after a so-called 'confession,' with a sentence of six years in San Quentin."[4]

The *Examiner* then proceeded to mock Morse, referring sarcastically to the "luminous spot on a soiled handkerchief, which was Harry Morse's pillar of fire by night and cloud of dust by day, leading him, after almost superhuman trials, to the presence of Black Bart." Its editors questioned Morse's accounts of the arrest, calling them "beautifully garnished romances" and claimed, "It looks as though the only feat of detective skill exhibited in the capture of Black Bart was an agreement to turn over to an informant a portion of the reward."

The *Examiner* even doubted that Boles was the notorious stage robber. "Whether the Charles Bolton who was sentenced yesterday is Black Bart remains to be proved. If he is, then the law has been tampered with. By rushing his trial through on what is virtually acknowledged to be a compromise, the United States Government was given no opportunity to prosecute on any of the twenty-three charges the detectives make against him of robbing the mails. A term of six years in prison…is a mockery of law. The only tenable explanation of such a miscarriage of justice is that Bart's prosecutors made a bargain with him whereby he received a light sentence, and they the $4,000 which he had hid in the woods near Copperopolis. What is the natural result of this perversion of justice? A few detectives divide a few thousand dollars, and by their admiring and cheerful tributes to the estimable and lofty character of a highwayman instill into the dime-novel charged heads of 10,000 youths of this city the idea that one has but to be a bold and successful robber to be able to force the united detective talent of the coast to intercede with the judges to obtain light sentences and to get two-column notices in the newspapers."[5]

The *Examiner* was far more interested in peddling newspapers than selling the truth. Plea bargains were common in California because many counties, especially in rural areas, lacked the funds to pay prosecuting lawyers to conduct long trials. Wells Fargo frequently hired special prosecutors for that very reason: to assist local district attorneys in robbery cases. But a six-year prison term was fairly typical for armed robbery, which is why Wells Fargo did not seek to have Boles charged with other holdups. Contrary to the *Examiner*'s claim, the US Government was free to prosecute him for mail robbery in Federal court, but there were very few Federal law enforcement officers in California during the 1880s, and no such charges were ever brought. Finally, the *Examiner* surely knew that stolen gold, when recovered from stage robbers, was always returned to Wells Fargo and was not divided among the arresting officers. In this case, Wells Fargo paid its reward to Harry Morse and Sheriff Thorn in the amount of $228.75 each. The Wells Fargo detectives were on the company payroll and therefore not entitled to rewards, but Thacker and Stone received reimbursement for their traveling expenses.[6]

Harry Morse was enraged when he read the *Examiner*'s story. He demanded a retraction, and the next day, to its credit, the *Examiner* published Morse's response. "No one could have been more astonished than Captain Stone and myself were when we read the accounts," he wrote, "and it was a mystery to us who could have given such a contorted statement to the press. As far as I am concerned, I make no pretension to great detective ability in the Black Bart case. A robbery was committed; a handkerchief was left behind by the robber, upon which was a laundry mark; the laundry was found whose mark it was; the name of the party whose laundry mark it was obtained; he was well known and was easily found and taken into custody. Now, any man with ordinary common sense could have done that. The robber's room was searched, in which sufficient evidence was found to warrant a conviction. Bart was taken to the vicinity of the robbery and identified by several men who saw him in the immediate scene of the robbery. All the evidence was written out and read to him. He saw at once that the chain of evidence was complete against him, and like a sensible man, he confessed.

"The simple facts above stated are true. No informer gave him away for a consideration. No inducements were held out to him to make him confess. He was simply told that a confession and restitution of the property stolen would likely be taken into consideration by the court and go in mitigation of his sentence; that the court, if he pleaded guilty, could not take judicial notice of the fact that he had committed other robberies. No bar-

JOHN BOESSENECKER COLLECTION.

Detective Harry Morse in 1885.

gain of any kind or promises were made to Black Bart. He made the confession of his own free will and accord. He was told that the confession of robberies made prior to October, 1880, were outlawed [the statute of limitations had expired and prevented prosecution for those crimes]; and as no indictment was found against him for them, he could not be convicted of them upon his own statement that he did them. He talked freely about them and acknowledged many of them. He also acknowledged writing the Black Bart poetry, and quoted some that he had written and intended to leave at the scene of his last robbery on the 3rd instant, but on account of the shooting at him he had to beat a hasty retreat, and so failed to leave it. His handwriting found in his room was identical with that of the poetry written on the company's waybill. He stated to me that he had taken the name Black Bart from Caxton's story of 'Summerfield.' If Bart denied his identity as Black Bart to the judge and stated that this was his first robbery, his object in so doing must have been to get a light sentence."[7]

Charley, resting in his jail cell, was unhappy when he read Morse's angry letter to the *Examiner*. A reporter went to the city prison and questioned him about Morse's statements to the newspapers. The newspaperman wrote, "He said he never told Morse or admitted to him anything about any other robberies than the Copperopolis affair, and never for a moment told him that he was Black Bart." Boles was eager to answer the journalist's questions about Morse.

"I haven't anything to say against Morse, of course, not at this time, but I consider his card just now to be in very poor taste, to say the least. All we said together on that ride over the mountains was said in a joking sort of way. I don't say who gave the thing away. I have read the published accounts and all that I have seen thus far are just a pack of lies." Charley, of course, did not explain how a detective's description of the capture of a stage robber could be "in very poor taste." But plainly he feared being prosecuted for the other stage holdups.[8]

Harry Morse's claim that no promises were made to Black Bart was certainly not true, for there is no doubt that Charley made a plea bargain. The *Examiner* promptly responded to Morse by attacking both the detective and the *Call*. It declared that the *Call* "indulged in the very ridiculous statement that 'the search for and capture of Black Bart by Harry Morse is conceded to be the best piece of detective work done in San Francisco in many years.' It might be well to wait till it is settled just how Bart was captured. The long-winded and romantic version put forth on behalf of Morse in the *Call* of Saturday has already become laughable. Morse himself says, 'I make no pretension to great detective ability in the Black Bart case,' and that 'any man with ordinary common sense' could have done as much as he did. It has further been shown that Bart confessed to Thorn, not to Morse. The extent to which the handkerchief figured in the case is not yet clear. It is asserted positively that the first information of Bart's return to the city came from Sacramento. As to the claim that the absurdly light sentence inflicted on the robber was not the result of any promise or bargain, his evidence may be worth considering. The *Alta* notes him [Boles] as saying to its reporter, 'They promised to get me a light sentence if I restored the stolen property, and on that condition I led them to the place where I had the treasure cached.' The *Chronicle* quotes him as saying to its reporter, 'They agreed that they could get me a light sentence, but only on condition that I restored the stolen treasure.'"[9]

Yet the *Examiner*, in its zeal to discredit Morse, published a wholly unsubstantiated claim that the arrest was based on an informant's tip that "came from Sacramento." That was not the only fiction created by the *Examiner*. It also reported that Boles was a member of the family of Samuel Bowles, a prominent Massachusetts newspaper publisher, that he served as a captain in the army under General Philip Sheridan, and that he got the name Black Bart from a novel by Edward Bulwer-Lytton. As we have seen, the *Examiner* even created the widely believed legend that Boles had once been a country schoolteacher in Northern California, and turned to stage robbery after he was fired for playing poker. However, when several other dailies repeated the myth, the *Examiner* promptly debunked its own story, stating, "He never taught school in this state, as has been incorrectly reported." The *Examiner's* editors, however, failed to remind their readers that they had fabricated the schoolteacher yarn two months before Black Bart's arrest, and published it again after he was jailed.[10]

Thomas Ware was also upset with the *Examiner's* attack on Morse, for the story implied that he was the informer who turned in Black Bart for a share of the reward. Ware promptly wrote to the newspaper, "In the Sunday issue of the *Examiner* there appeared an article concerning the arrest of C. E. Bolton, intimating the probability that he was 'given away' to the detectives by one of his friends. As I am the person who introduced him to Mr. Morse, those who do not know me may suspect that I am the 'friend' alluded to. Nothing could be more unjust. In order to show how innocently I was led into giving what information I did concerning Mr. Bolton, I here desire to state the true manner by which the laundry mark on the handkerchief led to his arrest.

"The handkerchief was never shown to me, but was taken to the laundry, where the washing was done, and there identified by Mr. Ferguson, the proprietor, as the mark of C. E. Bolton, sent from my office at 316 Bush Street. Morse then came to me and inquired if I was proprietor of the place and agent for the laundry. I told him I was. He then asked if I would be good enough to let him look at my book for the name of a gentleman who he understood had been getting some washing done here; said he understood the gentleman was a mining man, and being a mining man himself he desired to see him on business. I asked what name he wanted to find? He said Bolton. 'Why, certainly,' said I. 'I know Mr. Bolton well. He is in the city now; just arrived from his mine two days ago, and if you will call later you will probably meet him here, for he is an old acquaintance of mine and makes this his headquarters when in the city.'

"After asking numerous questions about his mine, etc., he left, saying he would call later, and in about an hour after he returned and said he would like to have a little private talk with me if I could spare a few moments from my business. I consented, and we started down the street together, but before he had time to divulge whatever it was he wanted to say to me, fortunately for the detective, but unfortunately for poor Bolton, he rubbed right by us and spoke to me before we noticed him. I then hailed him and told him the gentleman wished to see him. Then turning to the stranger, I said, 'I don't know your name, sir.' 'Hamilton is my name,' said he. I then introduced Mr. Bolton, and they walked down the street together and I returned to my business, not dreaming of the trap that had been set for him and knowing nothing of his arrest til late the next day. I have known Mr. Bolton intimately for seven years and had the most unbounded confidence in his honor and integrity, and did not, and could not believe him guilty until he made the confession."[11]

The *Examiner* even attacked the *Call* for its story about the crowd that visited Boles in jail. The *Call*'s first-page account appeared under the title, "THE BLACK PRINCE—A DISTINGUISHED RECEPTION TENDERED A POPULAR HERO." Yet the headline and comments in the story were plainly sarcastic, referring to a "reception" in the jail cell and calling Boles "the object of almost breathless interest." At the same time, the *Call*'s account made clear that the stage robber was no hero. But that was an insignificant detail to the *Examiner*, which declared, "The *Call* yesterday described the prisoner as 'The Black Prince' and 'a popular idol,' which seems to be an effort to further lionize a wretched robber and cause foolish boys to seek to imitate his crimes."[12]

The *Examiner's* editors conveniently forgot what they had published just two months earlier, before Black Bart had been caught. "In his methods of practicing his profession he has been a close follower of his romantic forerunner, Robin Hood," the *Examiner* had declared. "His treatment of stage passengers, especially ladies, has been unexceptionably polite and courteous and betrays indubitable evidences of his having imbibed deeply lessons of the traditions of the 'Knights of the English Road.'" Then, when Black Bart was captured, the *Examiner* began its front-page story by declaring that he was a fitting subject "for the novelist of the future" and compared his "bold deeds" to those of "Claude Duval and other noted robbers of days gone by." The *Examiner*, of course, did not bother to explain how there was any difference between the *Call's* description of Bart as the Black Prince and the *Examiner's* comparison of him with Robin Hood and Claude Duval.[13]

The *Examiner* next sought to ignite a controversy over who was entitled to credit for the arrest. "The details of his capture have been sufficiently narrated, but not enough said about Sheriff Thorn's connection with the case," its editors declared. "It was he who gathered the strongest evidence against Black Bart, which would have told [convicted him] in court, and it was upon his informing Bart what could be proven against him that the confession was obtained. This evidence was positive testimony as to his identity near the scene of the robbery." The *San Francisco Chronicle* then interviewed Thorn and headlined its account, "BLACK BART'S CAPTURE: THE CREDIT DUE TO SHERIFF THORN AND J.N. THACKER." Its story proclaimed, "The credit of the capture and conviction would seem to belong to Thorn and Thacker instead of to Hume and Morse, and doubtless both men are sorry they trusted the latter to the extent of letting them have the handkerchief, by which they gained so much advertising as great detectives."[14]

Sheriff Thorn's hometown newspaper, the *Calaveras Chronicle*, quickly joined the fray. "In all the published accounts of the capture and subsequent confession," it declared, "the name of Harry Morse figures very prominently. From reading the city papers one would be led to believe that Morse, and Morse alone, discovered the clews and worked up the evidence that eventually led to the capture." The newspaper, which was politically aligned with Thorn, insisted, "In this case the man who played the least important part comes near getting the lion's share of the honor. Our efficient sheriff, Ben K. Thorn, and detective Thacker were among the first to arrive on the scene after the robbery was committed, and to these gentlemen is due the credit of working up the case."

The *Calaveras Chronicle* then complained about the coverage

JOHN BOESSENECKER COLLECTION.

Ben Thorn, the noted pioneer sheriff of Calaveras County. He engaged in a war of words with Harry Morse over the capture of Black Bart.

of several other San Francisco newspapers. "They have told, in glowing language, how Morse consumed four hours in trying to get the prisoner to acknowledge having committed the robbery, but they say not a word about Sheriff Thorn and Captain Stone entering the room at this time. Yet this happened, and more than that. Thorn, in less than half an hour, did what Morse failed to do in four hours: convinced Bolton that his case was hopeless, that the chain of evidence against him was complete, obtained a confession from the robber, together with a promise to show the officers where the stolen treasure was hidden."

Its editor pointed out that when a San Andreas reporter asked Boles about the interrogation, he said, "I felt confident that I had a good case until Thorn reviewed the evidence he had against me. Then I saw he had me, and I gave in." The Calaveras newspaper concluded, "To Sheriff Thorn is due the credit of obtaining from C.E. Bolton, alias Black Bart, a confession of his crime after the San Francisco detective had failed in the undertaking. By obtaining this confession he has saved Wells Fargo & Co. the amount recovered, $4,500. He has also saved the taxpayers of Calaveras County the large expense that would otherwise have attended the prosecution of the case, a fact which our citizens are not apt to forget."[15]

As if on cue, a bitter dispute between Thorn and Morse quickly erupted. On December 5, Morse wrote a seemingly innocuous letter to the Calaveras County clerk, asking for a copy of the Black Bart court record and inquiring whether Thorn intended to claim the $300 reward offered by the state of California. Sheriff Thorn was incensed that Morse did not write to him directly. He mailed an angry missive to Morse, saying that "such a letter addressed to the county clerk of my county was a mean, cowardly, and unmanly stab at myself and unworthy of anyone making any claim to decency, much less of one whom I had always esteemed as an honorable, respectable gentleman."

Morse promptly responded, "If you are entitled to any part

of the state reward, you are entitled to the whole of it. But what you did to entitle you to any part of it, I am at a loss to understand. If any person outside myself should have the reward, John N. Thacker is that person. Certainly you did nothing to entitle you to it. In the first place you got it into your head that it was an Italian and not Boles who did the robbery, and only when Thacker came to your assistance did you change your mind in that respect. The handkerchief was in your possession at least one whole day and yet you did not discover the laundry mark upon it and which was the real clue to the identity of and arrest of Boles. It remained for Thacker to discover the mark.

"When Boles was arrested by me, you was at San Andreas and consequently could not possibly have had any hand in the arrest, although from what some of the newspapers got from or through you, one would imagine you did the whole business." Morse added, "I am very sorry you thought proper to act so cavalierly towards me, as I have always entertained the greatest respect for you, and not for a thousand reward would I act that way towards you." The detective concluded, "Just as soon as the reward is received I will forward the whole of it to you, and you can do with it what you please. I would advise you, however, to give it to Thacker as he is entitled to it, and not yourself."

An enraged Thorn fired back in language more colorful than accurate. "Your communication to hand. It is one which no gentleman would ever write. To say that it is impudent, insolent, malicious, and malignant but partially designates it. It is venomous, false in detail, and under any other circumstances would have been ignored by me as the scurrilous exhalation of an illiterate and pusillanimous brain. But notwithstanding your profuse assurances that I would receive the entire state reward, some considerable time has elapsed and it has not been forthcoming. It is hardly possible that the expense incurred in collecting it absorbed the entire amount."

Thorn then provided a long account of his work on the case,

and dismissed out of hand the fact that Morse had captured Black Bart. "Why was Captain Stone called in? Who took Boles into custody and delivered him to the station house? Who escorted him to San Andreas if not the man who arrested him, Captain Stone?" The sheriff even claimed, without evidence, "The herculean task of visiting ninety-one laundries existed only in the fertile and imaginative brain of a *Call* reporter, and the laundryman who really found it is entitled to the credit, and you had very little to do with the matter. And in this connection, I would suggest, Harry, that you remunerate him liberally, if you have not already done so. I will satisfy myself in regard to the matter when I receive my share of the state and government reward."[16]

In the end, Thorn's claim for the state reward failed, for it was clear that Morse had captured Black Bart. On December 29, 1883, the California state controller paid Harry Morse the entire $300 reward. The unsavory dispute between the two lawmen tarnished the extraordinary teamwork that had been the hallmark of the final manhunt. Hume, Thacker, Morse, Stone, and Thorn, with the assistance of Reason McConnell and Jimmy Rolleri, had collected evidence, interviewed witnesses, and put together a criminal case that convinced Charles Boles to plead guilty. They all deserve credit for putting an end to the greatest stage robbing spree in American history.[17]

17

San Quentin Sojourn

Charley Boles, accompanied by Sheriff Thorn, walked through the entrance of San Quentin prison on November 21, 1883. Thorn also had a second prisoner in his charge, a Chinese man named Ah Sam who had been convicted of grand larceny in Calaveras County. Unlike Black Bart, Ah Sam's prison term was only one year. San Quentin's main gate passed through the middle of the three-story guards' quarters, which in turn formed part of the wall around the prison. It had an inner and outer gate, connected by a short corridor. To the right of the gate was a door that led to the warden's office. Ben Thorn stepped inside with his two prisoners and was greeted by Captain Charles Aull. The latter had resigned from his job as a Wells Fargo detective and now was San Quentin's turnkey, or deputy warden. Aull was delighted to see the mysterious stage robber who had several times given him the slip.

"Bart, old boy, it's taken you a long time to get here," he greeted Boles jocularly.

"Yes, that's so," Charley responded. "But I wouldn't be here now if Mr. Thorn hadn't pointed the place out to me."

Later, *The Wasp*, San Francisco's famed satirical magazine, claimed that Boles also quipped to the prison officials, "This is the last stage in my career."[1]

Charley removed his diamond ring and stickpin and handed them to Sheriff Thorn with the request that he deliver them to his friend Thomas Ware in San Francisco. He also gave Thorn his gold cane as a souvenir, but the sheriff insisted that he keep it. Then Boles was booked into the prison as C. E. Bolton and assigned convict number 11,046. Charley, perhaps facetiously, gave his occupation as "laborer." Aull had him examined, and found that he had a scar on the right top of his forehead—courtesy of George Hackett's shotgun. His Civil War wounds were also evident, as recorded in the prisoner register: "scar on left wrist, gunshot wound right abdomen." Aull also noted that he had a "tattoo shield, right upper arm," which was probably also a relic of his wartime service.[2]

As was customary, Captain Aull ordered that his whiskers be shorn. Charley objected, to no avail. A San Francisco police detective, who happened to be present, observed, "He was shaved, against his will, as he did not like to sacrifice his mustache." Then Boles and Ah Sam were taken to the prison clothing shop, run by James Dods, a fellow convict. Dods was the former treasurer of Alameda County, serving a five-year term for embezzling public funds. As another witness reported, tongue in cheek, "Mr. Dods does not study to please his customers and does not seem to care whether he retains trade or not, for he gave Bart a pair of pants a world too wide and carelessly permitted Ah Sam to put on his shirt. Bart objected to taking the garment after it had enveloped the Chinaman but had to do it, Mr. Dods compromising with him for this mishap by giving him a better fit in pants."[3]

After Charley had donned his new suit—a set of woolen

prison stripes—Aull sent him to work in the sash and door factory. In that era of low taxes and minimal government, San
Quentin was expected to support itself. The prison had opened
in 1852 with a single stone cellblock, constructed by the prisoners. During the ensuing years, the convicts built an outer wall,
two more cellblocks, and numerous prison buildings. Some of
San Quentin's one thousand five hundred prisoners worked in
the brickyard, located just outside the wall, while others labored in workshops inside the prison. Prison-made bricks, doors,
sashes, and window blinds were sold to builders in San Francisco
and the Bay Area. A busy jute mill manufactured burlap bags
that were marketed to California's wheat farmers. Other convicts
worked in the prison laundry, the shoe shop, or the tailor shop,
making the striped wool prison uniforms worn by all inmates,
or in the bakery and kitchen, preparing meals for the inmates.

The guards were impressed by Charley Boles, for he was far
removed from the typically illiterate, hardened, and quarrelsome
convict. "Black Bart," said one of the prison officials, "is socia-
ble, a fine conversationalist and talks freely on any subject with
which he is acquainted. He does not look like a criminal, and
he does not associate with criminals. He is not a drinking man,
and in society would pass for an honest, intelligent granger, or a
retired miner, who had made his fortune, and was well satisfied
with the world." A reporter who visited San Quentin added,
"The guards pronounce him the best man physically that has
been sent to the institution for some years. He takes his confinement philosophically, and seems determined to reap every
advantage of the Goodwin Act, by exemplary conduct and hard
work." The Goodwin Act was a state law that provided credits,
called "coppers" by the cons, that reduced a prisoner's sentence
for good behavior.[4]

Charley did not enjoy the heavy labor of the sash and door
factory, and Captain Aull soon assigned him to lighter duties
in the prison laundry. That favorable treatment by prison offi-

WILLIAM B. SECREST COLLECTION.

Charles Aull. As a Wells Fargo detective, he hunted Black Bart; as deputy warden of San Quentin, he supervised the robber's imprisonment.

cers soon engendered jealousy among his fellow convicts. One of them complained to a *San Francisco Call* reporter. "The men who have been convicted of the highest crimes are always the most popular, over there among the prisoners, and the officials too, and if they have coin as well, there is no end of favor shown 'em. Just take Black Bart as a sample. He sticks up stagecoaches single handed. You newspaper gents give him whole columns for a send-off. He blows his own trumpet, and struts around as a swell highwayman. The prisoners at San Quentin look at him with a wish that they'd gone in for the same big game, and the officers of the prison gather him in as a pet lamb, and appoint him right off as head man of the laundry, where he gets lots of pickings, where he sits around in a private office, and has his meals cooked by his own Chinaman—one of the prisoners, of course—on his private stove."[5]

Soon after Charley entered the prison, his family and old friends began to learn of his arrest. Whether the Boles family

first read about it in the newspapers or were contacted by journalists is unknown. However, within a few weeks, Hiram Boles,
who still lived in Jefferson County, New York, wrote to him at
San Quentin and asked if he was his long-dead older brother.
On December 20, 1883, Charley responded, "Yes, tis only too
true. I am your brother, lost and in disgrace. Let this suffice for
the present. Your once loved brother, C.E. Boles." Charley's
Civil War comrades in Illinois were astonished when they heard
about his imprisonment. An Illinois journalist who interviewed
his old captain, Christian Riebsame, wrote, "Mr. Riebsame was
perfectly astounded at the information, and could scarcely believe it at first." Riebsame offered Boles effusive praise for his
courage in combat and added, "I have never seen him since the
regiment was mustered out, and I have never heard of him until
the information you have brought me."[6]

Mary Boles was even more stunned than Riebsame, and overcome with shame. She wrote to the San Francisco police, according to Jim Hume, "making inquiries to ascertain if it was
really her long lost husband. A photograph was forwarded to
her and she at once identified it as the likeness of her missing
husband." Probably through the city's police, Mary learned that
Jacob Pike was one of Charley's closest friends in San Francisco.
In December, she wrote him a long letter, saying that she could
prove that she was Boles's wife. Mary said that she had not heard
a word from him in twelve years and begged Pike to send her
any money her husband had. She also asked him to send her his
diamond ring as well as any cash Boles may have received from
the sale of his photographs in San Francisco. Mary's sense of humiliation was so great that she closed her note by asking Pike to
keep her identity a secret. He disclosed the letter to the newspapers, but honored her desire for anonymity. However, snoopy
reporters would figure out who she was and where she lived.[7]

At first Charley seemed to have no interest in contacting Mary
or his family. As he got used to confinement, his waggish sense
of humor returned. On January 10, 1884, he penned a missive

to Reason McConnell. "Dear Sir, You will please pardon me for this long delay in acknowledging your 'kind compliments' so hastily sent me on the 3d of November last, but rest fully assured, my dear sir, that you are remembered, and with nothing but the most friendly feelings, as a man having done your whole duty to your employer, yourself and to the community at large. I have often admired your fine qualities as a driver, and only regret that I am unable to compliment you on your marksmanship. I would like to hear from you, however, if consistent with your wishes, and, my dear sir, you have my best wishes for an unmolested, prosperous and happy drive through life. I am, dear sir, yours in haste. B. B." Then Charley added a postscript: "But not quite so much of a hurry as on a former occasion."

McConnell was both amused and relieved by Charley's letter. A newspaperman talked with the jehu and wrote, "The letter from Bart has been a consolation to Mrs. McConnell and her friends, who feared that the robber would seek revenge upon McConnell when he regains his liberty. Mr. McConnell, in his answer to the gentlemanly road agent, states that he is happy to know that Bart feels kindly towards him, notwithstanding their little controversy in November last." Boles also sent a humorous note to Rolleri, addressing him as "Young Jimmy" and complimenting him on his marksmanship. Charley remarked that Rolleri was a better shot than McConnell and he assured the youth that he held no grudge against him.[8]

Wells Fargo officials quickly rewarded McConnell, Rolleri, and several others who had materially aided in the capture of Black Bart. They paid McConnell $105 and offered Rolleri a job as a shotgun messenger, but his mother thought it was too dangerous and forbade him to accept it. Wells Fargo then presented Jimmy with a newly designed Colt-Burgess lever-action rifle. The gun turned out to be defective, for when he fired it, the barrel blew up in his hands. Company officials replaced it by sending him a Winchester rifle with a silver plaque on the stock, inscribed, "From Wells Fargo & Co. to James Rolleri, Jr., for meritorious conduct, November 3, 1883." The rifle was destroyed when the Rolleri family's hotel in Angels Camp burned down in 1938. The Wells Fargo men did not forget Donna McCreary, who, five years earlier, had provided Jim Hume with her meticulous description of Black Bart. When she visited San Francisco as the newlywed Donna Vann, they presented her with several gifts, including an expensive silk dress.[9]

Within six months of Charley's entering San Quentin, a correspondence began between him and his wife and family in Hannibal. Jim Hume later explained that Mary wrote to the

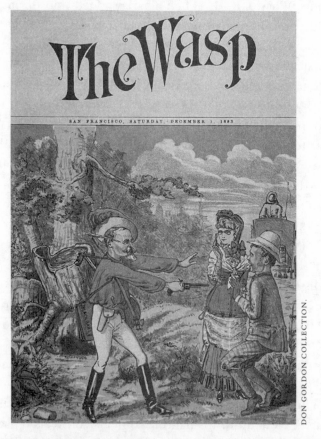

In 1883 San Francisco's satirical magazine The Wasp featured Black Bart on its cover as a cartoonish but romantic highwayman.

San Francisco police, who apparently forwarded her letters to the prison. Mary was so delighted by the discovery of her long-missing husband that she decided to buy a railroad ticket and visit him in San Quentin. That did not happen, explained Hume. "She wished to come out here, but friends persuaded her that that could do no good." Nonetheless Charley was soon corresponding regularly with Mary and his daughters, though only a handful of his letters have survived. He quickly learned that his eldest daughter, Ida, then twenty-seven, was unmarried and living in Hannibal. Eva, twenty-five, also lived in Hannibal with her railroad engineer husband, Oscar James, and their one-year-old son, as did the youngest daughter, Lillie, age twenty-three.[10]

Charley's first known family letter, written to his son-in-law Oscar James, was dated July 24, 1884, eight months after he had entered San Quentin. Apparently Oscar had been in ill health and had written to Boles and berated him for abandoning his family. Charley's response provided a rare but fascinating glimpse into his life and his character. "You will please accept my most sincere gratitude for your long and very interesting letter received several days ago," he began. "My dear son, I was very much gratified to hear of your improved health and brighter prospects for the future generally. I only hope it may continue to improve and that the bright star of hope may never wander so near the horizon again, but that it may remain high in the Heavens where its reflected light may gladden your heart and hearthstone to the last day of your life. I am indeed very sorry you have no reason to be proud of your connection with me, but hope and believe you have good and sufficient reason to be proud of my child, and judging from yours and her letters, you will never have reason to regret your choice.

"You say you are a Democrat—that makes no difference with me. I take it for granted that you are a Democrat for the same reason that I am a Republican and any man that is not willing to concede to his fellow man that which he claims for himself is neither an honest man nor a gentleman. I am a Republican simply because I think they are and always have been nearer right than their opponents and if you are a Democrat for the same reason, I am sure I shall be the last man in the world to object. But if I was an American citizen I might argue the point with you, but as I am not, I will not interfere with American politics.

"I have always followed my honest convictions of right and duty in all such matters. I enlisted and went into the war for the preservation of the Union, believing it my duty to do so and I never have seen the moment since I signed my name for that purpose that I have regretted doing so and I never expect to. I knew what to expect when I enlisted and I was not disappointed. I left behind all that was dear to me on earth (you may doubt this in the light of the past years). All I can say is, ask my Mary and those that know me best and even your Eva, little as she was when I left. I fancy even she can remember some little acts of parental affection on my part and while I was doing duty in the field, my noble and loving wife was doing equally important duties at home caring for our little ones and besides working one or two days in each week, making up clothing, preparing provisions, etc., for our noble boys in hospitals, sick or suffering from cruel gunshot wounds. And I never shall cease to love her for that noble work for I know the work of those tender hands gladdened the heart of many a noble sick or wounded comrade in the time of their greatest sorrow.

"I know you will, and have probably asked yourself the question many times—how could he leave his family if he loved them as he pretends. And no one can come so near to answering that question satisfactorily as my dear wife. She knows my nature, my disposition and temperament and knew exactly my circumstances and what I most desired to accomplish. The one great object of my life was to give my children a good education and make them as comfortable and happy as possible. Not having the wherewith to do this, I never saw a moment's real enjoyment except in their company and when I would for the time being forget my future prospects, and only think of the present, and this of course was but momentary. I therefore concluded to try once more (while my children were yet small) my fortune in the mines of Montana but was very unfortunate, but sent every dollar I could raise to my loved ones as they no doubt believe. And had I been even moderately successful I should have returned and today would be a happy man with a good, tender, loving family around me, instead of occupying a cell in a penal institution.

"No man ever done harder work—more earnest or more honest work than myself, and endured the most wonderful hardships and privations in an honest endeavor to better my condition, but all to no purpose. To be sure, I might have worked for wages and supported my family, but I did not go there for that purpose. More wages would not compensate me for being absent from my family, and besides, steady employment was out of the question, for placer mines all shut down early in the fall and remained so until about May. Yet I dreamed of nothing criminal or dishonest, neither did I for a long time after I ceased to correspond with my family and had left Montana, and I wish to say right here that I never have committed any crime worthy to be considered a crime compared with that of ceasing to correspond with my own loved family—but not that the crime for which I was convicted was bad enough and I realize the enormity of the crime as thoroughly as any man, but the above I consider the crowning mistake of my life and the source of all the sorrows of myself and those of my loving family, and that will haunt me to the grave. Aside from these two things I sometimes feel that I have done more good in the world than harm for so many, very many times, I seen the grateful eyes fill with tears and the quivering lips stammer a thank or God bless you, for some little charity I happened to be able to bestow, and I can truly say that no other investment ever paid me one hundredth part as well."[11]

Charley's letter was alternatively forthright, emotional, manipulative, and extraordinarily dishonest. Though he expressed
justifiable pride in his Civil War service, not once did he apol-
ogize for abandoning Mary and letting her raise their three
daughters in poverty. Every detail of his existence, after he left
the Montana gold fields in 1871, belied his statement, "The one
great object of my life was to give my children a good education and make them as comfortable and happy as possible." And
his closing assertion, "I have done more good in the world than
harm," must have left Oscar James scratching his head. Mary
and her daughters, however, were eager to forgive him. They
corresponded regularly, and Mary even mailed him several photographs, including a group image of the family.

On October 21, 1884, Charley wrote them a grateful letter
in reply. "My dear and loving family, I have received two letters, one from Mama and one from Ida since I wrote last and
the photograph of my whole darling little family in one group.
Great Heavens, only think, all on earth, yet dear to me, grouped
together in this little circle, a union of tender loving hearts, to
benefit and happiness of all. What a magnificent picture and
what a holy lesson it teaches. An example of affection, love and
constancy rarely equaled and never excelled and it is impossible
with the language at my command to give you full credit for
the heroic exertions put forth for the promotion of each other's
happiness under the most discouraging circumstances and it is
especially so with you, my own loving Mary, for you had the
care and responsibility of training and guiding our tender lives
in the direction you desired them to be taken, and of each other,
and for this I am so profoundly thankful that I can never find
words to fully express my gratitude.

"My darlings when I got those photos, I could do nothing
but sit and look and gaze at them for hours. I would try to put
them away and the first thing I would know I would be gazing into those dear eyes again that seemed as though they must

MARC C. REED COLLECTION.

Charley's wife, Mary Boles, seated left, and their daughters, about 1885. Ida Boles is seated at right, and standing left to right are Eva and Lillian. This is probably a copy of one of the photos they sent to Charley in San Quentin.

speak and let me know how deeply I had wronged them. Although after careful search I could find nothing in their expressions except a look of, 'My dear father I forgive you and love you as fondly and tenderly as when I was a prattling happy child basking in the sunlight of your affections over 17 years ago.' This I read in each kind eye and treasure it up in the sunniest brightest and warmest niche in this poor unworthy heart, there to remain while I have a heart to beat and a brain to think. If you could know how much I have looked at those pictures and how I cherish the three little tots, last seen May 1st, 1867, and look first upon one and then the other you may possibly imagine something near the train of thought they set in motion."[12]

A month later, Charley wrote again. "My dear Mary & loving family, I wrote last night but failed to send it as useless and now feel in a different mood consequently I will try again and I will start by thanking you for all your loving letters." After mentioning letters he had received from his daughter Lillie and brother Hiram, he described his prison life. "I have just come from supper. Had soup, tea, milk, bread, butter, roast beef, squash fried and boiled potatoes, pickles, macaroni, and a nice dish of bread pudding to wind up on and this is our usual bill of fare and same thing Sundays. And when the gas [light] is turned on it almost makes me think of being in town at a regular restaurant and do you not think I appreciate it to the fullest extent and perhaps you would be surprised to know that I wear the same clothes that you saw me in my photo or nearly so. The same coat, vest, hat, shirts, collars, cuffs, but prison pants, but they would never attract the least attention anywhere only where the people are accustomed to seeing them on prisoners.

"So you see there is nothing to be desired considered as a prisoner. Now do not make up your mind that this is the lot of all prisoners. But they are all treated humanely. Yes my dear family I am wearing the very identical laundry mark on my shirts, collars and cuffs every day that led to my capture and imprisonment and this is a facsimile of it—F.X.O.7. That simple little thing changed me from a respectable honored citizen, to a notorious outlaw and villain in the twinkling of an eye in the estimation of the people. But my dear family in reality I have not changed in the least. I did allow myself to go along under the strongest protest of conscience and under the most extraordinary circumstances. But my principles and habits are the same as when I was your honored protector—never having done any man a personal wrong or deprived him of a farthing. My own dear family, I am very proud of you when I think of your heroic exertions in this cold world in support of each other and I love you more every letter I read from you for I discover new beauties of character and nobleness in every one of your affectionate letters to me."[13]

Perhaps not surprisingly, Charley insisted that he had been driven into a life of stage robbery when he said, "I did allow myself to go along under the strongest protest of conscience and under the most extraordinary circumstances." Mary believed him wholeheartedly, but his daughters would prove to be more cynical. His youngest, Lillie, was then working in a wig shop in Hannibal. One of Charley's surviving letters to his family rambled from mawkish sentimentality over Eva's one-year-old son Albert, nicknamed Bertie, to waggish interpretation of the Bible, and finally to his balding pate.

"Bertie, my darling little pet, I would like to bite you," he began. "I think you must [be] sweet enough to eat. Kiss your venerable grand papa good night and go to sleep, you fat rascal. Well, Oscar, I have got around to you and what shall I say. I can only say I am heartily glad you are getting the best of your troubles. I think I have reason to thank you for your uniform kindness to all those that are dearer than life to me. This I know will sound very thin to you, but it is truth nevertheless, but Eva will stand by Moses notwithstanding his conspiracy to rob the Egyptians of their gold and silver raiment. Well, I don't know that I blame the Israelites much, for their Lord told them to do it and that he would give them favor in the sight of the Egyptians so they could borrow everything they wanted and they did borrow and then lit out. Just as naturally as the Jew and gentile does now in the 19th Century, but I promised to drop this, so please excuse me.

"Well, let everyone enjoy their opinion to the fullest extent is my motto. I am extremely glad to know that you and Eva are so happy in your relations with each other, and my sincere wish and belief is that it may continue through life and that there may never a cloud cross the pathway of your happiness and that you may succeed in all business undertaking, but [I] would like to see you settle permanently somewhere if it were in accordance with your wishes.

"Lillie darling, why don't you chip in, or are you listening and taking items [notes]? I would like to be there now. I think you would soon have a wig customer. You are dealing in wigs, bangs, frizzes, mustaches, and the like, are you not? You ought to be able to get up a pretty good dude and dudine by this time. I suppose you have some of that breed in Hannibal, as well as we have in San Francisco, in fact. What would a city be without them.

"Well, gather around for I have but a short time longer to talk. Good night Oscar, good night dear Eva, good night my darling Ida, good night loving daughter Lillie. I sent Bertie to bed some time ago. Now, my own dear Mary, draw up your chair a little closer for I want to tell you how much I love all our darling children just gone to rest. But my main object is to tell you before we retire how dearly I love you for all you have done for me and our sweet little ones and to ask again your pardon for the wrong I have wrought. I hear the echoing answer 'I forgive' and my dear, I will love you while life lasts. Good night, Your Charles."[14]

One of Mary's closest friends was Linda Bills, her former neighbor in Decatur who was the widow of Charley's Civil War comrade Reuben Bills. Linda had remarried, to a prominent farmer, Henry F. Wedgewood, of Delphos, Kansas. Early in 1885, Lillie Boles moved four hundred miles west to Delphos, where she got work and lived with the Wedgewoods on their farm. Charley began writing regularly to Lillie in Delphos. That fall, Eva and her little son, Bertie, fell seriously ill, and Lillie returned to Hannibal to care for them. As the two recovered, her father sent a caring note. "My Dear Daughter Eva, I don't know when I have experienced so much relief mentally as I did on the occasion of receiving your kind and loving letter giving the glad news of your returning health and that of your darling babe, for I had feared it was much worse and I do really hope by this time your recovery has become perfect. I suppose your darling sister Lillian has left you and I know how much you will miss her.

"It always gave me the greatest satisfaction to hear of the perfect harmony existing between my dear daughters and their mother and if possible my love has been made stronger for you on that account. My dear Eva and Ida I want you (as I know you will) to keep a kind loving watch over dear mama's comfort. I love you darlings for the grand display of affection always shown for her, each other, and your unworthy father. But, my darlings, I will love you always and under all circumstances through life. No matter what, the fondest affection of your father's heart will always be first for his dear Mary and loving children, next for those that have shown friendship and sympathy under these terrible circumstances. I am, my dear family, as ever your affectionate father and husband, C.E. Boles."[15]

For Charley, as the dreary weeks, months, and years drifted slowly by, that regular exchange of letters provided the brightest and most hopeful light of his San Quentin sojourn.

18

I Have Abandoned Crime of Every Kind

Charley Boles proved to be an ideal but aloof convict. As a result of good behavior, he was moved from the prison laundry to a choice job as an assistant in the pharmacy. Charley was supervised by the San Quentin physician, Thomas B. Eagle, and its pharmacist, Dr. Dudley Fuller. They had something in common with the highwayman, for both had served in the Union Army during the Civil War. The two doctors found Boles reliable and responsible and thought highly of him. A journalist who later interviewed San Quentin officials wrote, "His prison life was uninteresting. He obeyed all the rules of the institution promptly, and was in all respects a model prisoner. He was secluded in his habits, and avoided being seen as much as possible. Whenever any curious visitor tried to get a glimpse of him he became enraged. He did not consider himself an ordinary convict, and avoided all intercourse with his fellows."[1]

Indeed, Charley was no ordinary convict. In January 1884, just two months after Boles entered the prison, the country's biggest publisher of dime novels, Beadle & Adams of New York, released a corker. It was sensationally titled, *The Gold Dragon; or, The California Bloodhound: A Story of Po-8, the Lone Highwayman.* Its author, a thirty-one-year-old Bostonian named William H. Manning, was a prolific writer for Beadle & Adams. Other than the fact that the protagonist was Black Bart, *The Gold Dragon* was rank fiction and had no connection to the highwayman's story. Nonetheless, countless boys must have gobbled up the dime novel, for timeworn copies exist to this day.

Boles had no role in the book's production, and he assiduously sought to avoid publicity. The *San Francisco Examiner* later claimed that "certain detectives"—whom it did not name— "extended him their sympathy as well as their unbounded friendship and aid in his hour of need if he would only write a book narrating his romantic and eventful career—the book to be subject to the supervision and inspection of these detectives, that they might embellish it and show themselves to the world as the most useful as well as the most wonderful of men. They intended having this book published, and predicted for it an immense sale, from which they expected to realize—well, simply fortunes. When this project was suggested to Mr. Bart, he not only treated it with contempt, but expressed astonishment that honorable men should seek to engage in such disreputable business."[2]

The only writing Charley did was in letters to his wife and daughters. He also wrote to his sister Maria and her minister husband, Thomas Bradshaw, at their home in Reno. But not surprisingly, they wanted nothing to do with him. Boles later complained about that snub in a note to Mary. "Only think of a once loving sister, only a few miles away, and never bestowed a line, or likely a thought, on her once loved brother simply because he was in trouble and in need of a sister's sympathy."[3]

Mary, in one of her letters, revealed to Charley how her brother Henry and his wife had defrauded her out of her home

The dime novel about Black Bart, published two months after he entered San Quentin.

in Hannibal. Boles then fired off a letter to his sister-in-law demanding that the property be returned. Henry Johnson, in turn, mailed an angry note to the warden of San Quentin, demanding to know if "convicts were allowed to send out abusive letters." Captain Aull then ordered Boles into his office and told him that "he would not be allowed to write any more such letters."

According to one of Charley's friends, he told Aull, "You will not be called upon to pass out any letters for me, but you can't dictate to me what I shall write to anybody. I will write what I please. When my letters come to you for approval, you can pass judgment upon them, but not otherwise. I believe you are not warden of this prison."

The friend explained, "Then Aull put on his official dignity, and said he would not be talked to in that way."

To that, Boles supposedly responded, "You have sent for me and opened a conversation. If you don't want to be talked to in my way, you can close the interview by sending me away, but while I am here I will say just what I mean."[4]

Jim Hume also described to the newspapers what he called Charley's "villainous letter," but said nothing about Boles being disrespectful to Aull, who was one of the Wells Fargo detective's closest friends. Given that Boles kept his desirable job as assistant in the prison pharmacy, and that Aull was a strict disciplinarian who spent two decades running San Quentin and Folsom prisons, it is highly improbable that Black Bart gave him any back talk. Either way, Mary never received the Hannibal property back from her brother and sister-in-law.[5]

Mary counted the weeks and months as she eagerly awaited her husband's return. In 1886, Hume corresponded with her nephew Charles E. Booth, who, ironically enough, was a pharmacist, albeit in Minnesota. Booth wrote to the Wells Fargo detective, "She worships her erring husband yet, and says that she will forgive him for the cruelty done her, as she thinks some unseen, irresistible power must have led him to his course of crime; but I consider him to be a rascal to leave his family unprovided for as he did. Still, if it is the wish of his family to have him join them again, and there is any of the sunny side of life left for them, I hope he may live long enough to atone for some of the misery he has caused them."[6]

During his term in San Quentin, Charley Boles was perhaps its most notorious convict. Less known at that time was Bill Miner, who, a hundred years later, would be immortalized in the popular 1982 film *The Grey Fox*. Beginning in 1866, Miner had served several terms in San Quentin for highway robbery. In 1881, following a spree of stage holdups in California and Colorado that left two of his gang dead at the hands of a lynch mob, Miner was finally captured by Wells Fargo's Charles Aull. He served nearly twenty years in San Quentin before he was released and went to the Pacific Northwest, where he became Canada's most infamous train robber. Miner's many exploits had made him a leader among the convicts, and in San Quentin, he got to know Charley Boles. He was so impressed that he once said, "There's only one man I can take my hat off to, and that's the fellow down in the medicine shop, Black Bart."[7]

Next to Black Bart, Jimmy Hope was the most infamous prisoner in San Quentin. Like Boles, he was a gentleman robber, and the two became well acquainted. Hope, seven years younger than Boles, had a long career as a bank burglar and stole more money than many Western bandit gangs combined. Beginning in the late 1860s, he pulled numerous East Coast bank jobs and escaped from jail and prison. His biggest heist took place in 1878, when he and his gang made off with almost $3 million from the Manhattan Savings Bank in New York City. Hope was captured and imprisoned, but he managed to escape to San Francisco. In 1881, he and an accomplice tunneled under a San Francisco bank vault. But much to their chagrin, the ever-alert police captain Isaiah Lees was waiting for them with a squad of shotgun-wielding detectives. This escapade landed Hope in San Quentin for five years. The veteran burglar was released in 1886, but he would reappear prominently in the story of Black Bart.[8]

On Christmas Eve of 1886, a reporter visited San Quentin to witness the annual Convicts' Ball, a "stag dance" in which some prisoners dressed as female dance partners. Although it was, as the journalist noted, San Quentin's "chief social event of the year," Charley Boles was nowhere to be seen. The reporter got an interview with one of his convict friends, Bob Darr, a saloonkeeper serving a life term for murder. When asked about the infamous road agent, Darr answered, "He ain't down here tonight. He keeps up his style, and don't run with the boys.

He's up in [cell] 53 now, and is just as tony as ever. Bart was a slick operator, but he ain't responsible for all that's laid to him."

"How about the twenty-nine stages?" the newspaperman asked.

This photo of Charley Boles was taken in San Francisco just before he entered San Quentin prison.

"Well, now. I'll just tell you about that. Wells, Fargo's agent got leave to interview Bart, and he showed Bart a list of twenty-nine stage robberies and gave Bart a song-and-dance about how he'd like to make things square for himself with the company, and would see that Bart didn't get things socked to him too heavy, if Bart would acknowledge a few extra stage rackets that had never been traced up. 'I'm agreeable,' says Bart. 'Chalk off the whole batch to me, if you like.' Bart was always friendly like that, and so he got the whole lot laid off on him."[9]

Darr's story about the stage holdups undoubtedly came from Boles himself. This was not the last time this story would surface. One of Charley's friends later claimed that Hume had a private interview with Boles in San Quentin. The detective supposedly said to him, "Now this thing is all over, Bart, and nothing that you say can make any difference to you, but you can help me out. I have on my books a long list of robberies that nobody has been arrested for. You can admit to me that you committed them, and I can cross them all off."

According to this account, Charley refused, and Hume pleaded with him, saying, "What difference does it make to you? All I want is to clear up my books and square myself. If you will say that you did them I can make my record clear. It will help me with the company. Now here's one case. I know you did that."

"Yes," Boles supposedly responded. "I did that one, if that is any consolation to you. And as for the rest, you can scratch off whatever you like. I don't care what you do. If you want to clear up your books that is your business."

There can be little doubt that Charley made this claim to fellow convicts as well as to friends in San Francisco. Yet there was ample evidence connecting him to all twenty-nine stage holdups. His same comrade also claimed, "The detectives and Captain Aull were very anxious to get hold of Bart's diamonds and jewelry, and tried all ways to get them. They came to him with a nice story about his biggest diamond. They said it was a family heirloom, that tender and romantic associations were connected with it, and that the lady to whom it belonged was very anxious to recover it. It was a pretty tale, but it was a lie. Bart happened to know that the diamond had been sent with a lot of others for selection, and was being returned to the diamond merchant when he confiscated it. He wouldn't give it up, and he allowed the schemers to see his contempt for them."[10]

Jim Hume promptly debunked the story. "False, all false," he declared. "The truth of the matter is this. A diamond ring worth $200 had been purchased by a man at Quincy for his daughter. This was sent to him by Wells Fargo & Co. on a valuation of $100, and Black Bart secured it among other valuables when he robbed the stage. Subsequently the purchaser removed to Inyo County, and hearing that Black Bart had been apprehended, offered to pay the company the $100 they had paid for the loss of the ring if we could secure it. I saw Black Bart about the matter and he said he had disposed of it. I saw the party referred to by him, but he denied that he was in possession of stolen property. That ended the matter. Heirloom indeed. I never thought of making such a representation."[11]

Charley was deeply humiliated by his incarceration and invariably shied away from those who tried to see him. A reporter who joined a prison tour in 1887 wrote, "Black Bart, the Po8, was visited at the drug shop, where he is employed. He is very shy of visitors and, as soon as he perceived the party, took his hat and disappeared." However, another journalist who toured San Quentin five months later had better luck, writing, "He is extremely averse to conversing with strangers and as a general rule contrives to be very busy when visitors are about. Black Bart has gained the respect of the doctor and apothecary by close attendance to his duties and has become sufficiently acquainted with the art of compounding prescriptions to enable him to take a position in a drug store." The reporter managed to talk with Boles briefly and noted that "he does not look to be over forty-five," even though he was then fifty-eight. "Being questioned as to what pursuit he intended to follow on his release, he replied that he thought he would settle down somewhere as a drug clerk. Bart has never received a visitor since his arrival at San Quentin."[12]

Charley's closest friend in San Quentin was a notorious high-wayman and murderer who went by the name of Charles Dorsey. As Jim Hume explained, "Dorsey had the reputation, deserv-edly, of being a bad man, the worst man of all the 1,200 in that prison." The principal thing the two convicts had in common is that both fought in the Civil War. Dorsey was a former Confed-erate soldier who claimed to have ridden with William Clarke Quantrill's guerilla band. He said that after the infamous 1863 massacre in the antislavery town of Lawrence, Kansas, he fled west and adopted the alias of Dorsey. "My true name I have never divulged," he once declared.

Dorsey first entered San Quentin in 1865 on a burglary charge. Released two years later, he made a major blunder by pulling a holdup in El Dorado County, where Jim Hume was undersheriff. Hume and other officers captured him, and he was sent back to San Quentin. The desperado was in and out of prison in the 1870s and finally took part in a bloody stage rob-bery near Nevada City in 1879. Dorsey shot and killed a pas-senger and fled to Union City, Indiana, where he used some of the loot to buy a saloon and a lumber company. Finally, in 1882, he was located and captured by Wells Fargo's Charles Aull and Captain Isaiah Lees of the San Francisco police. The arrest cre-ated a sensation, for Dorsey had hoodwinked everyone in Union City into thinking that he was a wealthy businessman. The de-tectives returned him to Nevada City, where he was convicted of murder and sentenced to life in San Quentin.[13]

The killer did share one other trait with Boles. As a reporter who interviewed Dorsey in prison observed, "He is unusually intelligent and a most interesting conversationalist." No doubt he and Charley enjoyed swapping Civil War tales. And, as it later turned out, they also discussed the best places to rob a stage-coach. Dorsey's other close prison friend was George Shinn, leader of a gang that had pulled California's first train holdup in 1881. Dorsey took Charley into his confidence and told him that he and Shinn were planning an escape. Boles had no wish to break out, but he kept the plan to himself. Shinn was a trusty, or trusted convict, whose job was to drive a supply wagon in and out of the prison. On the afternoon of December 1, 1887, Shinn started for the prison gate. It was raining heavily, and he had a large tarp covering the wagon bed. As the wagon passed through the yard, Dorsey leaped unnoticed into the bed and hid under the tarp. Shinn drove out the gate and past the unsuspecting guards to the prison wharf. There the two escapees commandeered a rowboat and crossed San Francisco Bay. The fugitives made their way to the Sierra foothills of Amador County, where they hid out in an isolated shack. Despite a persistent manhunt, Dorsey and Shinn stayed hidden and avoided capture.[14]

Less than two months later, Charley Boles prepared to leave San Quentin the legal way. He received credits for good behavior, which shortened his sentence. Boles had served four years and two months when his term expired on January 21, 1888. At eight that morning, he stepped into the warden's office, where he shook hands with the prison officials and received their congratulations. From there he went to the clerk's office. The prison

San Quentin prison as it appeared at about the time of Charley's release in 1888.

clerk gave him $5 in traveling expenses and returned his gold cane, silver watch, and gold collar buttons and cuff links. When Boles stepped outside the main gate, he was greeted by a reporter for the *San Francisco Examiner*, who asked if his term had seemed like a long one.

"Not very long to look back on," Charley replied, "but it was an awful long time in passing."

The journalist wrote that Boles was nervous and apparently feared that Federal officers were waiting to arrest him for robbing the mails. When asked about that, Charley changed the subject and remarked that his wife and daughters lived in Missouri and that he planned to take a train to St. Louis on February 4. The reporter noted, "He did not say what his plans for the future were, but said that he had had enough of stage robbing."

"Will you write any more poetry?" asked the newspaperman.

"Didn't I tell you," Charley answered with a laugh, "that I had abandoned crime of every kind?"[15]

Boles then departed for San Francisco by train and ferry. A *San Francisco Chronicle* reporter met him when he landed at the ferry building and observed that "he presented a splendid appearance after his long confinement and was in a very cheerful mood. His gray mustache and chin whiskers bore evidence of the careful nursing they had received during the past two months of the road agent's imprisonment. Bart was neatly attired in a well fitting suit of dark material and a derby hat sat jauntily upon his iron gray locks."

In response to the journalist's questions, Charley said, "Since my incarceration I have understood that a great many people were of the opinion that I had taken to the road because of domestic difficulties. Such, I assure you, however, is not the case. I have for many years had a faithful wife, who has been true to me at all times and she still clings to me. I have also three daughters, who have now grown to womanhood, who entertain only the most tender feelings for me. They have been well brought up and received all the benefits of a first-class education, and I look forward to a very happy reunion with my family.

"It has also been said that during my criminal work I have been guilty of robbing people outside of the corporation of Wells Fargo & Co. That I positively deny. I never at any time injured any person outside of the express people and Wells Fargo & Co. are the only persons living to whom I owe one quarter of a dollar. I know that the mail bag which was on the stage that I stopped near San Andreas—and of course you are aware that it is the only stage robbery with which I have been connected— was cut open when found, but I tell you truthfully that I did not cut it. I never intended to tamper with the mail or to injure private individuals in any respect. The mail bags which were rifled must have been cut open by the stage driver or some of the numerous detectives who were hunting so arduously for me."

The newspaperman concluded his report, "When asked as to his future movements, Black Bart said that as yet he had not decided upon any definite plan of action. He thought that he would remain here four or five days and then go East. The general tenor of his conversation warranted the inference that the lone highwayman was well off in this world's goods and could travel with comfort in any direction which took his fancy."[16]

Yet Charley was certainly not well off, and his statement that he only robbed Wells Fargo was hardly true. As Jim Hume once pointed out, "In the popular mind, Black Bart, as he so romantically styled himself, has come to be regarded as a sort of modern Robin Hood, a stage robber of heroic mold, a gallant free lance, who never robbed the passengers or the poor, but confined his attentions entirely to wealthy corporations such as Wells Fargo & Co. This is a delusion. He is, in fact, the meanest and most pusillanimous thief in the entire catalogue, for by his own statement he made all his large hauls from the mail, which he always rifled, and from which, excepting his last robbery, he always obtained more than from the express, and by so doing he robbed the most needy, those who, to save a small express charge, used the mails as a means of transmitting their money.

"From these hard earnings Black Bart, with his boasted magnanimity, realized his largest revenue. When the express is robbed the shippers are reimbursed as soon as the amount is known; but for the people who entrust their money to the United States mails, in the event of a robbery there is no redress. Their loss is irrevocable. The [Federal] government never repays them or makes the slightest effort to recover the money or discover the offender." Hume also explained that Federal law officers rarely investigated stage robberies. "Since I have been with Wells Fargo & Co., the express has been robbed 353 times, and I judge the mail has been robbed on about 200 of these occasions, and I have never known of the government paying out a cent to detect the robbers, nor have I known of a United States officer going out to investigate, excepting perhaps on one or two occasions years ago. If the 'boys' would confine themselves to the mail and let Wells Fargo & Co. alone they would have a comparatively safe and probably more lucrative calling."[17]

Charley, following his interview, left the reporter at the ferry building and boarded a streetcar down Market Street. He soon arrived at the Nevada House, a lodging place at 132 Sixth Street, between Howard and Mission. It was run by his friend Emily Burling, his former landlady at the Webb House. Despite his notoriety, she was loyal to Charley and let him stay there. Boles spent much of the next week in his room, too ashamed to be seen by his friends and acquaintances. His embarrassment knew no bounds when, a few days later, he found himself the subject of a long poem written by Ambrose Bierce, the celebrated humorist. Bierce published it in his regular column, "Prattle," in the *San Francisco Examiner*. One particular stanza surely rankled Black Bart.

What's that? You ne'er again will rob a stage?
What! Did you do so? Faith, I didn't know it.

Was *that* what threw poor Themis in a rage?
I thought you were convicted as a poet.[18]

Despite Charley's many promises to return to Mary and their daughters, he was having second thoughts. Ten days after his release, on January 31, 1888, he wrote to his family. "My dear loving wife and children: After waiting all these days hoping to be able to comply with your wishes and my own most ardent desires, I most sincerely regret that I must disappoint you. My dear it is utterly impossible for me to come now. Oh, my constant loving Mary and my darling children, I did hope and I had good reason for hoping to be able to come to you and end all this terrible, terrible uncertainty, but it seems that it will end only with my life. Although I am free and in fair health, I am most miserable. My dear family, I wish you could give me up forever and be happy, for I fear I shall be a burthen to you as I live no matter where I am. My loving family I would willingly sacrifice my life to enjoy your loving company for a single week as I once was. I fear you will blame me for not coming but Heaven knows it is an utter impossibility. I love you but I fear you will not believe me and I know the world will scoff at the idea and I am not prepared to prove my assertions. I am too sensitive for this world and not fit to try the next.

"I have not called on any of my old friends and have only met by chance those I have seen. They seemed delighted to meet me and have had many invitations to call on them but I feel as though it would not be right to handicap them with my company, notwithstanding their earnest requests. Oh, my dears, you cannot tell how I feel with the papers making all kinds of remarks about me and reported interviews that never took place. It is simply astonishing what nonsense they will put into one's mouth, but the trouble is they will make him swallow it for it goes to the world and if he should pay any attention to it, to try to correct through the press, they would only double the dose.

"All this you may have seen, 'tis all bosh. But the fact of my not being able to come home is the greatest disappointment to me almost of my life. As you know I have tried to point out to you that it would be better for me to stay away and do all I could for you, and I really thought so, and I am afraid you may think I did and do not intend to come home at all. But if I thought I should never see you again, miserable as I feel, I know my miseries would be increased beyond endurance. Now my dear when I can come I cannot tell. But if I live you will surely see me before another Christmas anyhow and if possible sooner. Oh my dear family how I would like to be able to come now and it was the hopes of this that have kept me silent so long."[19]

But Charley's letter left out one crucial detail. The reason he could not return to his family was that he intended to resume his career as a stage robber.

19

Black Bart Robs Again

When Charley wrote the letter to Mary and his daughters, he was on his way to the Sierra Nevada foothills to see Charles Dorsey, his fugitive chum from San Quentin. Prior to Dorsey's prison break, he and Boles had agreed to meet on February 1, 1888, at a railroad crossing just west of Newcastle in Placer County. It was a remote spot, thirty miles northeast of Sacramento. Their planned rendezvous was to take place just one day after Boles penned that plaintive note to his family.

Dorsey and his partner, George Shinn, had laid low after their San Quentin escape two months earlier. The pair had made their way to the mining camp of Ione in Amador County, where they built a wood shanty in the brush outside of town. According to Shinn, who later made a detailed confession to Hume and Aull, the two left their shack on January 28, 1888, and walked fifty miles north to Newcastle. At the appointed time, they met Black Bart at the railroad crossing. Shinn later said that Boles and Dorsey first stepped aside and held a whispered conversation. Then the two openly discussed plans for a holdup spree. As Shinn explained, "Their calculations were to go and rob the Sonora stage and get some money and then, after that, they were to put up some other jobs. My understanding was they were to go East and rob a train or something of that kind."

After they finished talking, Shinn told Boles that his boots were worn out by their long flight from San Quentin. Because Shinn was afraid he would be recognized, he gave Charley some money and asked him to buy a new pair. Boles agreed and hiked several miles west to Rocklin, where he bought a new pair of shoes and a supply of food. When he returned, the three talked again and agreed that Boles would meet them in one week at the Amador County fairgrounds in Ione. Dorsey also gave him detailed directions to their shanty near Ione. The trio separated, but on the designated day, Charley failed to appear at the fairgrounds. Recalled Shinn, "I never saw Black Bart again after I left him below Newcastle, and if Dorsey had seen him after that I think he would have spoken of it."[1]

The notorious Charles Dorsey was Boles's closest comrade in San Quentin.

Boles, always a loner, had second thoughts about taking on a pair of partners. He boarded a train for San Francisco and returned to Emily Burling's Nevada House. Charley promptly wrote another letter to Mary, insisting that he would return to her. "I got a letter the other day from the manager of the Oakwood Theatre and Dietz Opera House, saying he had a chance to make some coin. He requested me to give him my address so he could see me and arrange [it]. He claims to have known me well in former years around the stock boards. But I cannot, of course, lend myself to any dime museum racket. My stay in the city has been quiet, and if the papers would let up, I would not care so much, for I can't strike back very well. Now, my dear, I hope you will not think, or attribute my not coming home to any lack of desire on my part, or lack of affection for any of you, for I appreciate your wonderful constancy and affection above all things—it's all I have to console me in my lonely, lonely hours. All other relations are as 'ropes of sand.'

"Oh, my dear how I do hope you may retain your health until I can come to you. I think this climate would suit you much better than Missouri. Now, my dear, take good care of yourself and don't worry about me for I shall do the best I can. But, oh, my dear, how I do regret not being able to come to you. My dear, the clouds look dark and gloomy and the real struggle of life is at hand and I must meet it and fight it out. It will not be long at the longest, but it promises to be a terrible struggle. Let come what will, I must see my own loved Mary and our loving children once more if it is but for a day or an hour— only to see you face to face and imprint a kiss on each of your constant, faithful, loving lips and look into the depths of those tender, loving eyes and then see and read for myself written in tears of love and sympathy these words: 'My dear husband, my dear father, I forgive you.' When that time comes—then, and not until then, can I expect the first ray of sunlight to enter my poor bleeding, desolate heart. Now, my dear Mary and loving children, may God bless you. Good night. Charles."[2]

Boles, much to his chagrin and annoyance, was shadowed by detectives whenever he left the Nevada House. Meanwhile, Mary wrote back to him and enclosed a recent clipping from the *Hannibal Courier.* The story included comments that she had made to the newspaper about his stated desire to return to his family, as well as some complimentary remarks by the editor. Charley promptly responded to his wife, expressing gratitude plus a mixture of low spirits, bitterness, and anger toward the detectives and prison officials. "I have made no effort to avoid them or any one else yet," he wrote, "but when I do Mr. Detective will find his hands full to keep track of me. Not that I care for anything only this contemptible annoyance by his constant presence, and I know too if they can they will put a job on me if I remain among them, thinking that my having served a term it will be easy to fasten the second on me. But I don't propose to allow them to succeed in anything they can concert against me.

"Now my dear I hope you can see the necessity of the move I am about to make. My Dear you certainly can forego getting letters every week or two for awhile, and then my Dear as I said before I will come to you if I live. My Dear I got the paper you sent me and thank you a thousand times for it, for I wish everybody knew all the circumstances under which our terrible trouble was brought about, and I thank you for your statement and feel grateful to the publishers for their kind words of encouragement and only wish the world at large could find it in their hearts to deal with me in the humane, sensible, and lenient manner the editor of the *Courier* has done. For such language appeals directly to all that is manly and worth redeeming in the human character, and I most heartily appreciate the kind and lenient sentiments therein expressed.

"My loving Mary, if we had come in contact with nothing but such sentiments in the past years of my life it would have saved me from a life of sorrow, sadness, and disgrace, and you from a life of unutterable sorrow and hardship, and our loving children from a life of Poverty, Humiliation, and Care. But the future must be attended to and let the past take care of the dead past… My dear family I am completely demoralized, and feel like getting entirely out of reach of everybody for a few months and see what effect that will have. Oh my dear family how little you know of the terrible ordeal I have passed through, and how few of what the world calls good men are worth the Giant Powder [dynamite] it would take to blow them into eternity. Thousands that under your everyday life you would call good nice men are until the circumstances change to give them a chance to show their real character. I have reference now to those that have charge of our public institutions. For instance you might go about them as a visitor and meet men there that you would think the very essence of official purity. But go into the hospital and there see what they are doing for those that need their care, and you will find 99, yes 99 in every hundred that would not turn his hand over to save a prisoner's life. But why talk about that. I am disgusted with those things. I must now close after telling you again not to worry about me, and all may come out better than I expect, at least I hope so. Now may Heaven bless you and all our loved ones. Good Night. Your unhappy, unworthy husband."[3]

Jim Hume, who had engaged detectives to shadow Black Bart, later said, "He came to San Francisco and remained here a couple of weeks. He left San Francisco early in February, went to Modesto, Madera, and Visalia." Charley actually departed the bay city about February 7, and made his way south through the San Joaquin Valley. On February 22, local officers in Merced recognized him from his photograph. He was not wanted, and the lawmen left him alone. Boles then boarded a train and continued south a hundred miles to the farming town of Visalia, arriving the next day. He got a room at the Visalia House, where he registered as "M. Moore" from San Francisco. Charley stayed four days and checked out on February 27, leaving his valise behind. According to a Visalia reporter, he told the hotelkeeper that "he might call for it sometime or ask to have it forwarded to him, or he might never call or send for it." Hume later obtained the valise from the hotel man. He explained, "The valise was found to contain canned meats, sugar, coffee, and crackers, which Boles, or Bart, as we generally call him, had evidently procured for the purpose of camping out in the mountains. Among the few articles of clothing was a linen cuff with the cabalistic laundry mark F.X.O.7."[4]

Charley vanished for a few months, but in May, he was spotted in Fresno and several other towns in the sprawling San Joaquin Valley. From there he drifted north to Redding, where he walked thirty miles east to Bullskin Ridge, west of the settlement of Montgomery Creek. This was about five miles from the spot where he had held up Louis Brewster's stage in 1881. At ten o'clock on the night of July 27, 1888, Dan De Forrest was at the reins of the Redding-bound stage. As he urged his team

JOHN BOESSENECKER COLLECTION.

The valise that Boles left behind at the Visalia House. It was later displayed by Wells Fargo at the Chicago World's Fair in 1893.

up Bullskin Ridge, a lone masked bandit, wielding a shotgun, appeared in the moonlit road.

"Halt!" Boles shouted. De Forrest pulled on the reins, and Charley ordered, "Throw out the box, mail bags, and brass lock."

The jehu knew exactly what he wanted, for the registered mail was carried in canvas and leather bags secured by brass locks. He responded by saying there was nothing in the mail sacks. De Forrest later said that the highwayman warned him "that if he did not do as commanded the top of his head would be shot off."

After he threw down the Wells Fargo box, and the mailbags, the road agent told him, "Drive on."[5]

Boles made off with $30 from the Wells Fargo box and almost $400 from the mail. Local law officers hunted for the robber in vain. Jim Hume looked into the holdup and concluded that the culprit was Black Bart. Meanwhile, Charley stayed out of sight for the next few months. Hume believed that he had left the state. The detective later said that Boles "has resumed his former mining operations and is again prospecting for bullion in our treasure boxes. He is too subtle and keen to risk suspicion by selecting any small town as a place of residence, for the reason that his frequent absences would be noted and discussed, and he would naturally desire to avoid particulars in regard to his trips, his mine, etc., and as it is a well known fact this is much more difficult to accomplish in a small town than in a city where one scarcely knows the name of his next-door neighbor, much less his business, habits or pursuits. For these reasons we believe that he has selected some such city outside of the state of California, as Denver, Kansas City, Omaha, Salt Lake, Tucson, or even Chicago or St. Louis, and, without creating surprise or suspicion, makes these periodical trips for the purpose of cleaning up his mine and replenishing his exchequer, and then returns to lead the same apparently innocent, blame-less life which he pursued in San Francisco."[6]

Whether Boles actually left California is uncertain, but it is just as likely he hid out in a camp in the Sierra Nevada. He reappeared a few months later, on November 8, 1888, on the stage road below Downieville, in the Sierra Nevada Mountains. Late that morning, reinsman Carl Johnson was urging his stage team up Ditch Hill, about three miles west of Goodyears Bar. His coach had left Downieville and was on the way to Nevada City, forty miles southwest. Today the winding stage road is the aptly named Highway 49, which connects many of the famed mining towns of the gold rush. Johnson had proceeded about seven miles from Downieville, and was slowly moving up the Ditch Hill grade, when the lone road agent appeared from be-hind a tree, a gun at his shoulder.

"Hi there," he called out sarcastically. "Hands up!"

Johnson reined in his team and pulled back on his brake. As his two passengers gaped open-mouthed, Charley issued his time-honored order. "Hand out the mail."

Johnson threw down two bags, but Boles knew he was hold-ing out.

"Now the other one," he snapped.

After Johnson complied, Black Bart demanded, "Give me the express."

The driver tossed down one Wells Fargo box, but once again, Charley had done his homework. "I want the other box also."

Johnson threw it out, but it landed near the stagecoach wheels. One passenger tried to exit the stage and move the strongbox out of the way. "Stay where you are," Boles shouted. "Now drive on and be damned quick about it!"

Johnson cracked his whip and the stage rattled off. At the next stop, two miles down the road, he reported the affair. Very quickly a posse of lumberjacks and sawmill workers grabbed guns and horses and raced to the scene. But the mysterious road agent had vanished into the heavy timber. Word was sent to Jim Hume, and he quickly deduced that the bandit was Black Bart. He also reported that Wells Fargo had lost $800 in coin plus a gold bar worth $2,200.[7]

Charley was not done with stage robbing. Following his usual route, he walked out of the Sierra foothills, then crossed the Sacramento Valley and the Coast Range to Mendocino County. Twelve days later, on the early afternoon of November 20, 1888, he stationed himself at the top of a hill a few miles north of Black Bart Rock, where he had stopped Alex Fowler's stage ten years before. At three o'clock, he stepped in front of a Ukiah-bound coach driven by Sam Haskett and covered him with a shotgun. Haskett readily complied when told to throw out the express and the mail. "The box never felt so light to me," he later said jokingly.

A posse soon rode to the scene, where they found the road agent's abandoned shotgun and axe. The possemen followed a set of tracks to a ranch nine miles distant and arrested the owner. They thought his boots matched the bandit's boot prints, but a judge set the man free for lack of evidence. Jim Hume then arrived in Ukiah and looked into the case. Although no witnesses to the last three holdups could identify the lone highwayman, Hume had no doubt that he was Black Bart. He also revealed that Boles had escaped with $685 from Wells Fargo and $1,000 from the mail. Once again, just as he had done ten years earlier, Hume hired the mountaineer and hunter Buck Montgomery to track the bandit. Montgomery rode to the holdup site, picked up the trail, and for ten days painstakingly followed it across the Coast Range. He tracked Black Bart to the Southern Pacific Railroad depot at Arbuckle, in the Sacramento Valley, and reported to Hume that the road agent had boarded a train and vanished two days before he got there. Jim Hume was so impressed with Montgomery's man-hunting skills that he offered him a job as a Wells Fargo special officer and shotgun messenger. Four years later, Montgomery was murdered by the notorious Ruggles brothers when they held up his stage near Redding. An enraged mob of Montgomery's friends then broke into the county jail, dragged out John and Charlie Ruggles, and hanged them both in one of California's most famous lynchings.[8]

Buck Montgomery's report was the last sighting of Black Bart in California. His total haul in the three stage robberies was just over $5,000, a small fortune in that era. On November 30, Hume issued an $800 reward notice for Boles, offering $300 from Wells Fargo, $300 from the state, and $200 from the US post office. Newspapers had a field day with the story. "BLACK BART. THE POET AT HIS OLD TRICKS ON THE PUBLIC HIGHWAY," trumpeted the *Sacramento Record-Union*. Proclaimed the *San Francisco Chronicle*, "BOLD BLACK BART. THE POET ROBBER AGAIN AT WORK." The story was news on the East Coast as well. "BLACK BART. THE KING OF HIGHWAYMEN AT LARGE ONCE MORE," read the headline in the *Philadelphia Times*.[9]

Almost immediately, Hume was swamped with reports of Black Bart sightings in San Francisco. "I have received scores of letters about Black Bart," he told a reporter, "and many of them stated that he was in town. Several of the writers declared that they had seen him. They are mistaken. In San Francisco are two solid businessmen whose appearance is so much like that of the robber that when I send a man to look after Bart I tell him to get a look at these men, in order to know the robber if he sees him. All of these people have seen one of these gentlemen. Black Bart is not in San Francisco. I have men out looking for him, and from their reports I feel pretty sure that we will catch him, and, what is more, that we have evidence enough now to convict him."[10]

In Hannibal, someone showed Mary Boles an interview with Hume in the *San Francisco Chronicle* in which the detective described how Charley had abandoned his wife and allowed her to raise their daughters alone in a life of poverty. Hume also explained that Black Bart's "bosom companion" in prison was the notorious Charles Dorsey. Mary was furious and dashed off a letter to the *Chronicle*'s editor. "I have just finished reading your long article of November 28th about C. E. Boles, and I drop my work to tell you that falsehood, base falsehood, runs all through it, from the time it pretends that he wrote an unkind word to any one of his family here. It is true that he did write once to my sister-in-law here in Hannibal, who had cheated me out of my home here, and I presume he did say some pretty sharp things to her, and she certainly deserved it, for bad as he has done he would scorn to stoop to the deed she has to account for. Now about my husband rejecting the friendship of his family. Not for one moment has he ever done it, to our most certain knowledge...

"Every one of us here believe today that Hume & Co. are after an innocent man now, for he has told us over and over again that while God gave him breath he would never lift his hand to do a dishonorable act to disgrace us further; and we know he refused to write a history of his life while at San Quentin, which probably would have been a source of quite a good sum of money in the end, simply, as he said, because he had done enough to make us unhappy; and for the future, if left alone, he would do all in his power to aid us and not disgrace us further... Now, as to making bad friends, I know that his most valued friends in San Quentin were Dr. Eagle and the druggist Fuller, from the former of whom I have received the most kind letter, speaking very highly of my husband while under him."[11]

By this time, every stagecoach holdup on the West Coast was being blamed on Black Bart. California saw numerous stage robberies in 1888, including half a dozen or more by lone bandits. The culprit in several of the attacks was Ham White of Texas, who held up more than twenty coaches in his long career. Unlike Boles, White was no long-distance walker. Lame in one leg from a deadly Texas gunfight in 1875, he always rode a horse to and from his holdups. But like Black Bart, he had an ironic sense of humor. On November 15, 1888, during a heavy rain storm, White stopped a stagecoach from Paso Robles to San Luis Obispo on the Central Coast of California. He got only a pit- tance from the passengers and less than $50 from the Wells Fargo box. The next morning, as the driver was passing the holdup site on his return trip, he spotted a Wells Fargo money envelope pinned to a roadside tree. The jehu stopped to investigate and found a poem scribbled on a scrap of paper inside the envelope:

Lo! Here I've stood, while wind and rain
Have set the trees a-sobbin'.
And risked my life for that damned stage
That wasn't worth the robbin'.

At the bottom it was signed, "Black Bart, Po8." The news- papers widely reprinted the poem, and despite the protestations of Hume and Thacker, journalists insisted that Black Bart was the culprit. In fact, Boles was then on his way to Mendocino County to rob the Ukiah stage, three hundred miles to the north. Ham White managed to elude lawmen, then boarded a train to Arizona Territory. Just eight days later, he held up an Arizona stagecoach. He was soon captured and sent to Yuma prison. He never admitted pulling the Paso Robles stage holdup, and ever since his clever imitation poem was accepted as writ- ten by Boles himself.[12]

The new rash of holdups revived public interest in Black Bart. On December 2, the *San Francisco Examiner* devoted half a page to a purported interview with the fugitive bandit. The *Examiner*'s new owner, William Randolph Hearst, was already developing his mastery of faked interviews and bogus "news" stories. Hearst claimed that one of his reporters managed to lo- cate Boles after taking a railroad trip, followed by a twenty-five

mile horseback ride to a secret mountain location. The correspondent asserted that he almost drowned while fording a creek
and was rescued by a stranger who turned out to be Black Bart.
Though the *Examiner's* account was utterly preposterous, the
"interview" with Bart actually contained a great deal of fac-
tual information. The reporter told how Boles had once settled
in Iowa, how he had left to pursue mining in Montana, how
Mary had been swindled out of her home, and how his father
had died and left some money to Mary and the girls. These facts
most likely came from one or more of Charley's San Francisco
friends, such as Thomas Ware and Jacob Pike, who were in a
position to provide truthful information about the road agent's
personal history.[13]

The phony interview also contained numerous criticisms of

JOHN BOESSENECKER COLLECTION.

A contemporary newspaper illustration of Black Bart with his shotgun.

Jim Hume and claimed that he had lied about Black Bart's background and criminal career. The next day, Hume—no shrinking violet—railed against the *Examiner*. "The article is a tissue of falsehoods from beginning to end," he declared to a reporter for the *San Francisco Chronicle*. "The man who wrote it is a dirty, contemptible, lying cur. I repeat it—he is a dirty, contemptible, lying cur!"

"What do you particularly object to in the article?" asked the *Chronicle* man.

"I object to all of it. In the first place the writer of the article never saw Black Bart, and the twaddle it contained was therefore manufactured out of whole cloth. Secondly it was written solely to injure my reputation as a private citizen and detective."[14]

In fact, the *Examiner* ran the story not to defame Hume but to sell newspapers and make money. And not all newspapermen were as disreputable as William Randolph Hearst. The following week, the *Hannibal Journal* conducted an authentic interview about Black Bart. The editor assigned one of his writers to talk with Mary Boles. Writing in the third person, the journalist described his visit to her humble home in Hannibal. "Ascending the stairway of a neat frame tenement house at No. 117 Market Street, the reporter knocked at the door of the only room in which a light was burning, but the lady who came to the door said that Mrs. Boles lived just across the hall, but as the rooms were dark she supposed that the lady was not at home. The newsman, however, ventured to knock at the across-the-hall door and his perseverance was rewarded by the appearance of a lady whom above all others he was just then most anxious to see."

Mary greeted the reporter and said, "Pardon me, I was sitting at the window thinking, and had really not noticed that it had grown so dark."

She lit a lamp, and in response to the newsman's question about Charley, responded, "Yes, I knew, or almost knew, what you wanted before you told me, but I absolutely know nothing more about my husband's whereabouts than is known to the public generally. The last letter I received from him was February 21, and in that he said that if his life was spared, he would be with us by Christmas at farthest, and when I opened the door in response to your knock, I would not have been greatly surprised to find him in the hall, and oh how unspeakably happy I would have been to find him there."

"You have heard, Mrs. Boles, that your husband is charged with having returned to his old business of stage robbing since his release from prison?"

"Oh yes, sir, I have heard that, but I cannot, cannot believe that it is true. I believe, and his children believe, that he is innocent. In the very last letter we received from him he declared that he would never again be guilty of an act that would disgrace his wife and children, and I believe he has been true to that promise."

"How then do you account for his long silence?"

"He knows the detectives are again on his track, and that whether innocent or guilty, no mercy would be shown him should he again fall into their hands. You can easily see then why he dare not write, as the letter no matter where mailed, would be almost certain to fall into their hands. I believe he is engaged in mining in some secluded spot in the mountains, though of course I do not know. He may be dead. God only knows."

"Do you still hope for the promised Christmas visit from him?"

"Oh, sir, I hardly know what to look or hope for. If he is alive and not pursued by the detectives I believe he will come. I know that he still loves us. The evidence in my possession shows beyond all doubt that he is still as devoted to us as he was when we last saw him twenty years ago. A gentleman wrote to me soon after he was first captured that all my old letters and the little pocket bible I sent him when he was in the army were found on his person. And then, too, my husband wrote me about the same time that he still had the letters and the bible and that all the gold in California would not buy them, though some of the letters were worn into shreds. Oh, sir, do you believe that he would have taken such care of my letters if he had ceased to love me? No, no, that could not be. If you would read the letters he has written to me since his release, you could but see the spirit of devotion that pervades them all.

"Then again," Mary continued, "in all the accounts that appeared in the newspapers about his robberies, it was never even hinted that there was a woman associated with him. To the contrary, it has been repeatedly said that he was unlike all other men of his class in that respect. And there is another peculiarity about his history. He has never been charged with robbing a stage passenger or an individual. I remember reading of one case where a frightened lady handed him her watch and purse, but he handed them back to her and told her not to be alarmed, and that she had nothing to fear at his hands. It has been said that his depredations and robbing were confined exclusively to the Wells Fargo express company. I do not say this to excuse him, for God knows that he has enough to answer for. But oh, sir, he has some noble traits of character, and if they would only let him alone, I know that he would henceforth lead an honorable life. Here is a letter from the physician of the prison in which he was confined three years, and you can see how highly he was esteemed, even under the unfortunate circumstances then surrounding him.

"Once, since his release, he wrote to me that it would probably be better for him to go off somewhere and never come near us again, as our association with him might disgrace us all. I wrote to him in return that we loved him as dearly as ever, and were willing to follow him to the ends of the earth. In answering this letter, he said that he once more had something to live for, and God helping him, would henceforth live for his wife and children." Before the reporter departed, Mary showed him several letters she had received from Charley soon after his release. The newspaperman closed his account by remarking, "She is thoroughly lady-like in her bearing and manners and impressed the *Journal*'s representative most favorably."[15]

But Mary's effort to paint Charley as a devoted husband fell flat. It had been more than ten months since his release from San Quentin, and he still had not appeared at her Hannibal doorstep. Contrary to her claims, his depredations had not been confined exclusively to Wells Fargo. He had stolen thousands of dollars from the US mails and had also committed petty burglaries by stealing tools and clothing from remote ranch houses. And Mary's assertions that Charley did not have another woman were wrong, for California newspapers had reported that he had two mistresses, one in San Francisco and another in Sacramento.

Jim Hume may also have been wrong about Boles making his headquarters in a distant city, for he surfaced once more in California. His pals Charles Dorsey and George Shinn had fled to Chicago, where they worked at odd jobs and burglaries. In 1889, Dorsey and Shinn returned to California, where they pulled several saloon holdups and stage robberies. No doubt inspired by Black Bart, on July 31, 1889, Dorsey and Shinn stopped a coach driven by Charley's nemesis, Reason McConnell, on Funk Hill. After blowing up the Wells Fargo safe with dynamite, the two fled forty miles north to their old hideout near Ione. As Shinn later revealed, "After robbing the Sonora stage, we went to the camp, and hanging on a hook Dorsey found a piece of paper, and looking it over, he observed upon it the words, 'B.B.O.K.' [Black Bart is O.K.] He said that the words were in Black Bart's handwriting, and that during our absence he had been to the camp. We left Bart's notice where we found it, and Dorsey stuck one up to let Bart know we had been to the camp. We came back in six weeks and the notices were still in the same place. Dorsey destroyed them."[16]

Shinn also said, "When we robbed a stage we never would

touch the mail bags, because Black Bart had always told Dorsey that the mail bags never carried anything worth taking." Yet that was the opposite of what Boles had told Jim Hume.

Charley, no matter where he hid out, remained an inveterate newspaper reader. He soon learned the fate of Harry Roberts, his old Montana mining partner. Roberts had stayed in Silver Bow, where he gave up gold mining and became a teamster boss, hauling ore from the mines. In May 1889, following a drunken saloon quarrel, he shot and killed a fellow teamster. The fifty-seven-year-old Roberts was tried, convicted, and sentenced to death. Four months later, his legal hanging on the gallows in Butte was prominently featured in newspapers throughout California and the West. For Boles, it may have been a sober reminder of what fate held in store for him if he continued his career as a highwayman. There is no record of Black Bart ever robbing again.[17]

Mary Boles never wavered from her firm conviction that Charley would come back to her. In another letter she sent to the *San Francisco Chronicle*, Mary insisted, "I am convinced that he never thought of deserting me when he left Montana for California after the most severe struggle against the drought of that year and the one before. As to him not sending money to us, he well knew I would rather suffer want than be supplied with a dollar that did not come honestly."[18]

But Mary's beliefs were simply delusional. Her blind faith that he would return was based entirely on the empty promises in his letters. Charley's correspondence revealed him as a selfish, manipulative liar, for Mary and her daughters never saw him again. And that was the greatest crime he ever committed.

20

Myth and Mystery

Black Bart vanished completely, and the mystery surrounding his life, his criminal career, and his abrupt disappearance only deepened in the months and years that followed. That void was filled with countless wild yarns and fictional stories. Though Charley left rhymes at only two holdup sites, a myth quickly grew that he graced every robbery with his poems. In 1882, before he was even captured, several journalists falsely asserted that he mailed "clever verses" to Northern California newspapers. In 1889, a man in Cloverdale who claimed to be a friend of Boles said, "Bart used to leave one of these tracts with every coach that he held up. I know where twenty or thirty of them can be found. Some of the people who own them have them framed, and would not sell them for $50." The fable spread, and over the years, innumerable authors and magazine writers claimed that Bart left poetry at the scene of every stagecoach robbery.[1]

The concept of a poet highwayman long captivated the public. No sooner was Boles locked up in San Quentin than "new"

Black Bart poems began to appear. In 1884, the *Washington Star* of Washington, DC, printed a dramatic interview with Daniel Shealy, reportedly a stage driver in Copperopolis. Shealy described how he was robbed by Black Bart, who left behind some clever doggerel:

> Once I toiled for gold in ditches.
> Now with ease I amass riches.
> Daniel, now I'm on this lay,
> I'll come again another day.

Shealy claimed that soon after, Black Bart robbed his stage again, stealing the driver's gun and leaving behind another poem:

> Daniel, it grieves me to say it.
> Next time you attempt to play it,
> Buy an overcoat of pine,
> And I'll send the corpse in time.[2]

Yet as we have seen, Black Bart never robbed a coach driven by a man named Shealy. In fact, there was no stage driver in California by that name. The jehu, the interview, and the two poems were the product of the fertile imagination of the Washington journalist who concocted the story. Four years later, a Philadelphia newspaper claimed that one of Bart's rhymes was found in San Quentin prison:

> I'm sorry I spent my time
> Ripping up this mail.
> I didn't find money enough
> To buy a feeding for a quail.

The same story claimed that Bart "was of Mexican parentage and possessed the straight, lithe figure of that race. His glossy hair grew long and full like a silken veil over his shoulders." Its writer spun a long-winded yarn in which the bandit played a round of poker, and lost, to a stage passenger, all in the middle of a holdup. The fictional passenger was, not surprisingly, a charming young schoolteacher. As late as 1934, an amateur historian produced what he claimed was a newly discovered Black Bart poem. Though a fabrication, it was undeniably funny.

> I rob the rich to feed the poor,
> Which hardly is a sin.
> A widow ne'er knocked at my door
> But what I let her in.
> So blame me not for what I've done,
> I don't deserve your curses,
> And if for any cause I'm hung,
> Let it be for my verses.[3]

One of the earliest and most enduring Black Bart fables was that Wells Fargo paid him to stay away from its express shipments. This story first appeared in 1883, just days after Boles entered San Quentin. A newspaper reported, "Some think that he will be pardoned out in a short time and enter the service of Wells Fargo & Co. in the capacity of a detective." The story resurfaced in 1887 when another daily repeated a rumor "that on the expiration of his sentence he will he taken into the employ of Wells Fargo & Co. as a private detective."[4]

The *San Francisco Examiner* went one better, declaring that Boles, soon after his prison discharge, told a friend, "I'm a detective myself now, and I've just received my first month's salary." He then purportedly displayed $125 in gold and silver coin. Another journalist tried to confirm the story, and asked Wells Fargo's chief detective, "Is it true, Mr. Hume, that Black Bart, after his release, was in the pay of your company?"

The exasperated lawman denied it, saying, "I am astonished at your asking such a question."[5]

James B. Hume, about 1890.

JOHN BOESSENECKER COLLECTION.

In 1893, a Los Angeles newspaper claimed that Wells Fargo "now pays him a salary to report at their main office each day, which is the only duty he has to perform. The company evidently believes that the cheapest way is the best." The story continued to spread, and in 1909, another Los Angeles journal ran the headline "THREE THOUSAND A YEAR JUST FOR BEING GOOD," and announced that Black Bart reported once a month to Wells Fargo headquarters in San Francisco. "For ten years past he has been receiving $250 monthly from the big corporation and all in the world he has to do for the money is keep honest." Given that Charley would then have been eighty years old, he could hardly have posed any further risk that would justify such an expense.[6]

The fable about Wells Fargo giving pensions to bandits existed long before Charley's capture. As early as 1875, newspapers reported that the express company paid Nevada stage robber Jack Harris "a certain salary a month to let their stages alone." And thirty years later, when Charley's San Quentin comrade Jimmy Hope died in New York City in 1905, East Coast journals claimed that banks had paid him a pension to refrain from robbing them. If financial institutions really did that, the famed Pinkerton's National Detective Agency, which specialized in protecting banks and capturing bank robbers, would have gone out of business.[7]

Another enduring myth about Black Bart is that he pulled all his robberies with an unloaded shotgun. This tale seems to have had its origins in an 1888 article in the *San Francisco Bulletin*, which reported, "It is not even known that his celebrated shotgun was ever loaded, as no one ever heard him discharge it." The story gained more credence in 1909, when a writer for the *Overland Monthly*, a hugely popular Western magazine, declared, "Black Bart never took a human life. He never fired a bullet, for the simple reason that he did all his work with an unloaded shotgun." In the years that followed, the authors of dozens of books and magazine articles consistently repeated this yarn. It even made its way into otherwise reliable histories of the American West.[8]

However, as we have seen, after Boles robbed George Sharpe's Camptonville stage in 1881, the jehu reported, "There was a double-barreled muzzle-loading shotgun in his hands. I could see the caps on the nipples." There would be no reason for Black Bart to place percussion caps on an unloaded shotgun. And after stopping Clint Radcliff's stage near Jackson in 1883, Charley accidentally discharged his shotgun as the reinsman drove off. Most convincingly, Boles himself admitted that his shotgun was loaded. During his first newspaper interview, while he was in the San Andreas jail, the reporter asked him if his gun had been loaded with buckshot. "Yes," Charley responded. "Of course when a person goes into that line of business he must be prepared for emergencies."[9]

Black Bart's shotgun itself became a topic of interest. Soon after his arrest, Nathaniel Curry, one of San Francisco's best known firearms dealers, claimed that Boles had purchased a custom-made shotgun from him. Charley told Curry that he needed the gun for duck hunting. A journalist who spoke with Curry reported, "Black Bart used a special kind of cartridges, and a number of shells loaded to his order can be seen in Curry's store." Over the years, various old-timers each claimed to have found one of Bart's shotguns. Given that Boles used several different guns and left his weapon behind at a few robbery sites, those claims could be true—or not. The only known, authentic Black Bart shotgun is the one he left in the hollow tree on Funk Hill after his last holdup. Wells Fargo displayed it at the Chicago World's Fair in 1893. The company's successor, American Railway Express, presented the gun in the 1920s to W. Parker Lyon, who later featured it in his huge Pony Express Museum in Southern California. Today the shotgun is on display at the Autry Museum of the American West in Los Angeles.[10]

Soon after Boles was released from San Quentin, a tradition surfaced in which stage drivers—long known for spinning colorful yarns for passengers—began making false claims that they had been robbed by Black Bart. In 1888, a whip named John Holmes told the San Francisco Examiner that Black Bart had robbed his stage at Berry Creek on the route between Oroville and Quincy. But the Examiner—never one to get in the way of a good story—could easily have learned that the reinsman in that 1878 holdup was Charles Seavy, and that Bart had never robbed Holmes's stage. In San Francisco in 1894, a former jehu, Josiah "Old Josh" Quincy, boasted that he once "looked down the barrel of Black Bart's gun and through cool nerve escaped with his life." But no driver by that name was ever stopped by Black Bart.[11]

In old age, Billy Hodges, who once drove stagecoaches into Yosemite, told newspapermen that in 1875, he had been the first jehu held up by Bart. That dubious honor, however, fell to John Shine. Hodges also said that Black Bart had robbed his coach a second time in 1883—also a fantasy. Sandy Hobbs, another old-time stage driver, hit hard times after 1900 and landed in numerous California jails for public drunkenness. He claimed that he had been held up by bandits many times and had killed a stage robber in 1885, but his tales were fabrications. Hobbs even insisted that Black Bart had robbed his coach in 1886, a time when the road agent was safely locked up in San Quentin. As late as 1953, Charlie Lambert, a well-known reinsman in Mendocino County, recalled that he had been held up by Black Bart near Willits in the 1890s. But the eighty-four-year-old pioneer may simply have been forgetful, because his stage had actually been robbed in 1891 by Harry Miller, son of Joaquin Miller, the famed "Poet of the Sierras," and not by Black Bart.[12]

Many places in California claim connections, sometimes fictional, to Black Bart. Still standing in the historic Calaveras County gold rush town of Murphys is the Murphys Hotel, one of the oldest still operating in California. Among the famous guests reported to have stayed there were Mark Twain, Horatio Alger, Ulysses S. Grant, John Jacob Astor, and Henry Ward Beecher. In the 1930s, someone discovered that a man named "Carlos E. Bolton" had signed the hotel's register three times in 1880. A popular history writer then seized on that coincidence, declaring, "Bart had once signed himself 'Carlos Bolton.' Perhaps he had drunk an extra cup or two of coffee that day. Surely he must have had one small moment of delight when he meditated upon that fine romantic fillip to his own plain 'Charles.'" Ever since, operators of the hotel, local historians, and writers of tourist guidebooks have reveled in the belief that Black Bart once luxuriated in Murphys.[13]

The fact is that Carlos Bolton had no connection to Black

Bart. His full name was Carlos Edson Bolton, born in Vermont in 1847. He served as a teenage soldier in the Union Army during the Civil War, then married and came to California in the 1870s. Bolton settled in Columbia, a gold town thirteen miles south of Murphys, where he worked as a machinist in local mines. He later opened a restaurant in Sonora, but it failed, and he filed for bankruptcy in 1880. The next year, he moved to Idaho, where he became a prominent mine owner and justice of the peace. He opened Bolton's Hot Springs, a hotel and resort near Hailey, Idaho. Bolton's wife died in Idaho, and he moved to Arizona Territory in 1907. Eight years later, he was appointed a US land commissioner and handled homestead claims until his death in Arizona in 1920. Carlos Bolton was a highly respected pioneer, as far removed from a stage robber as could be imagined.[14]

There are many more myths. One holds that Black Bart always walked because he was afraid of horses. This is a modern invention, routinely included in books that mention him. But there isn't a shred of evidence that Boles was afraid to ride horseback. He walked to and from his holdups because that made it easier for him to avoid detection. Yet another legend is that he stopped twenty-three or twenty-eight stages. The actual number was thirty-two, twenty-nine of them before he entered San Quentin and three more after he was released. That made him, by far, the most prolific stage robber in American history. Even the Jesse James gang held up no more than half a dozen stagecoaches. And countless writers since 1883 have claimed that the rewards for Black Bart totaled $18,400. That yarn was spun by a journalist who took the actual reward of $800 and multiplied it by twenty-three, which was the number of holdups Boles had initially been accused of committing.

Over the years, Black Bart's euphonious name inspired both copycat bandits and characters in popular culture. In the 1880s and '90s, newspapermen—tongue in cheek—often referred to unidentified stage robbers as "Black Bart" or "a disciple of Black Bart." The most notorious of these bandits was an Austrian immigrant, Reimund Holzhey. In 1889, he robbed several stagecoaches and two railroad trains in Michigan and Wisconsin. Newspapers were quick to dub him "Black Bart." In his final holdup, Holzhey shot and killed a stage passenger, then was captured and sentenced to life in prison. Two years later, journalists nicknamed Ham White, the prolific stage robber of Texas, California, and Arizona, "Black Bart the Second."[15]

During the 1930s and '40s the poet-highwayman's popular appeal continued to grow, and his story was included in numerous books about California, Wells Fargo, and the Wild West. In 1948, the film *Black Bart* was released, starring Dan Duryea as the slippery stagecoach robber. Like most Hollywood westerns, it was fiction and had little to do with Black Bart except for its title. In this rendering, Boles is an outlaw who abandons his gang, goes to California, and embarks on a spree of stage holdups. Finally he stops a coach that happens to carry his old bandit partners as well as the famed performer Lola Montez, played by the sultry Yvonne De Carlo. Bart and Lola form an attachment, and following a series of improbable adventures, he is killed by a posse. The film was a success and revived so much interest in Black Bart that the following year, Wells Fargo Bank offered a reward to anyone who could prove what happened to the mysterious bandit. The reward was never paid.[16]

By that time, Mary Boles and her daughters were long gone. Mary had stayed in Hannibal, still calling herself a widow. In 1893, daughters Ida, Eva, and Lillie made a trip to Chicago to see the World's Fair, known as the World's Columbian Exposition. Among the lavish exhibits was a large display by Wells Fargo & Company, featuring scores of photos and artifacts from its romantic history on the frontier. Mary's daughters were stunned when they stumbled across a wanted poster for Black Bart, along with his shotgun from Funk Hill and the valise he had aban-

PHOTO BY JOHN BOESSENECKER.

During the 1890s, Mary Boles lived in this house, located at 715 Center Street in Hannibal, Missouri.

doned in Visalia. The items had been kept by Wells Fargo detectives and were prominently displayed. Years later, Mary's granddaughter said that the three sisters had been humiliated by the discovery. "They never let on that they were looking at their own father's belongings," she recalled. "They felt very keenly the, to them, unnecessary disgrace he had brought to them."[17]

Mary, in her final years, convinced herself that Charley had committed suicide. In 1895, she moved to Salt Lake City, where she lived with Ida and Ida's husband. Suffering from heart disease, Mary died there on March 9, 1896, at the age of fifty-seven. Ida and Eva were with her at the end, and Eva brought Mary's remains back to Hannibal, where she was buried. The Boles sisters did not suffer the same delusion as did their mother. They fully understood that their father had abandoned them, and they felt very bitter toward him. Nonetheless, when Eva spotted a newspaper photo of an unknown elderly man who had been found living in San Francisco in 1903, she thought it was her father. Eva boarded a train for California, but on her arrival, she quickly learned that the man was not Charles Boles.

Charley's daughters made no effort to conceal from their own children the family's connection with Black Bart. All three women lived quietly and respectably. Ida outlived her mother by only three years, dying in Salt Lake City in 1899. Eva spent her life in Hannibal, where her husband, Oscar, died in 1891. She raised two children and worked for almost forty years in the insurance and real estate business, dying of cancer in 1922. Lillie stayed in Delphos, Kansas, where she married a prominent wheat farmer in 1890. She and her husband had one daughter and moved to Oklahoma, where Lillie died in 1929.[18]

Eva was not the first member of the Boles family to try to locate her father. In the early 1890s, Charley's nephew Claude Boles, son of his brother Hiram, moved to Reno, where he lived with Charley's sister Maria and her husband, Thomas Bradshaw. By that time, Bradshaw had become a land specu-lator. He also owned a real estate agency in Reno, and Claude went to work for him as a clerk. In 1893, Claude took a train to San Francisco, where he interviewed police officers and de-tectives in an effort to locate Black Bart. He was unsuccessful, but wrote to a friend that he "felt certain his uncle was in Old Mexico." In the end, no one in the family ever discovered the fate of Charles E. Boles.[19]

In the decades that followed, many stories circulated about Black Bart's demise. One of the most widely published accounts is that he died in New York in 1917. This yarn had its origins in a popular history volume published in 1939. Its author wrote, "A New York newspaper carried an account of the death of Charles E. Boles in 1917," but he admitted that it was "an unsupported story." In fact, it was entirely unsupported. Whoever recalled and recounted the obituary in the 1930s managed to get few of the details right. The news item was actually published in 1914, and the departed was Charles Edwin Bolles, aged sixty-seven, who lived in Brooklyn, New York. Bolles was certainly

not Black Bart, for he had been a well-known New York photographer since 1879.[20]

Perhaps the most dramatic story of Black Bart's death is that
in 1888, a masked, shotgun-wielding highwayman stopped a
coach on the Geiger Grade, between Reno and Virginia City,
Nevada. The Wells Fargo messenger promptly opened fire, and
the road agent dropped dead in the road, riddled with buckshot.
The local sheriff investigated and found several men who identified the dead man as Black Bart from the highwayman's photographs. With no other evidence, the body was buried next to
the wagon road. Allegedly the Wells Fargo messenger reported
the killing, but somehow Jim Hume never received word of the
incident. If such a shooting had actually occurred, the Reno
newspapers would have given it front-page coverage, but they
published not a word. In fact, no fatal stage holdup took place
anywhere near the Geiger Grade in 1888, nor for ten years afterward. Though romantic and exciting, the story was manufactured out of whole cloth.[21]

In recent years, several self-published books about Black Bart
have been released, and the author of each claims to have discovered the highwayman's true fate. One alleges that Bart was
actually Alvy Boles, a blacksmith in Yreka, California, who
died in 1890. That tale is readily debunked because Alvy Boles
personally signed the voters' registration roll in Yreka in 1884,
when Black Bart was behind bars in San Quentin. Plainly they
were two different men. Another writer claims that Charley
Boles, upon his release from San Quentin, went to Jackson,
in Amador County, where he befriended a stage driver, Pete
Podesta. Boles purportedly confided in Podesta and told him
many details of his life. The author claims that Jim Hume hired
Boles as a Wells Fargo detective and even had him investigate a
California train robbery in 1888. One major problem with the
story is that Pete Podesta and Reason McConnell were friends,
and McConnell, who became a Wells Fargo shotgun messenger

in 1890, often rode guard on Podesta's stage. In 1899, the pair were badly wounded when bandits opened fire on their coach. But McConnell, in his memoirs, says nothing about Podesta befriending Black Bart, an important detail he would not have ignored. And given that numerous people in the area, including McConnell and Sheriff Ben Thorn, knew Boles by sight, this tale can also be chalked off as a fable.

Yet another volume contends that Boles, after leaving prison, assumed the name Charles Wells and worked as a pharmacist's assistant at a drugstore in Marysville, dying there in 1914. This yarn—based on a bit of local folklore from the 1980s—gained traction in 2017 when Marysville cemetery officials unwisely put a marker on Wells's grave, with an inscription stating that he was Black Bart. Yet contemporary newspaper accounts state that Charles Wells was a farmer, not a pharmacist. And the drugstore where he allegedly worked and roomed, at 400 D Street in Marysville, was just one block from the residence of George Hackett, the Wells Fargo special officer and shotgun messenger who wounded Black Bart in 1882. It is hardly possible that both Wells and Hackett could live near each other in a rural town of less than four thousand people without the Wells Fargo officer ever seeing and recognizing the famous highwayman. This story is also, unfortunately, rank fiction.

As early as 1889, Jim Hume was overwhelmed with such spurious sightings of Black Bart. In response, he issued a circular in which he provided the road agent's description and pointed out, "During his incarceration at San Quentin he was seen and noted by nearly every sheriff there officiating in the State and could hardly fail to be recognized by any one of them in the event of a chance meeting. He would be known by all convicts who were at the penitentiary during the time of his imprisonment, and all these facts lead to the conclusion that it is highly improbable that he has chosen this state as a place of residence." Two years later, Hume reiterated his statement by telling a California re-

The grave of Mary Boles in Hannibal, Missouri.

porter, "Bart is not in the state and he's not likely to come back either. Every now and then we hear stories to the effect that he has been seen hovering about certain camps and interior towns in the vicinity of stage roads, but the stories were given birth in the fertile imagination of some romancer. These stories have never worried me any, because I know that Bart has long since given up operations on this side of the Rockies. I know a great deal more about him than I would care to talk about."[22]

But whatever Hume may have known about the bandit's later life, he took it with him to the grave in 1904. John Thacker, however, was not so reticent, for he became responsible for creating a popular fable that Black Bart spent his final years in China, Japan, or Australia. This story began on July 1, 1889, when Thacker told a newspaperman that, a few weeks earlier, Boles had boarded a steamship in Victoria, Canada, bound for

China. Thacker said that he got his information "through a police official from a man who said he recognized Bart, and was positive it was he who left on the China steamer." Eight years later, the detective offered more details about Boles. "He went to Utah and then up to Montana and then to Hailey, Idaho," Thacker explained. "I think he had some business to settle there. Anyhow he was straight as a string. Finally he made a bee line for Vancouver, and I saw him board the steamer *Empress of China* for Japan. He is in that country now."

But Thacker's information was thoroughly garbled. It was true that on June 4, 1889, a man named C. E. Bolton had boarded a steamer in Victoria, Canada. But that Bolton was a well-known travel writer and lecturer. And his destination was not China, but Seattle, eighty miles south through the Puget Sound. The Canadian informant who saw the steamer's manifest simply assumed that C. E. Bolton was Black Bart. Thacker was undoubtedly misquoted about watching Boles board the steamship, for in his initial statement, he said he had received his information secondhand from the police official. Last, Thacker's suspect in Hailey, Idaho, was none other than Carlos E. Bolton, who owned and operated Bolton's Hot Springs, five miles from town. Detective Thacker had simply received misidentifications of Black Bart that, due to the slow and unreliable communication of the era, were never investigated or confirmed.[23]

There is one account of Black Bart's fate that does not entirely strain credulity. As Claude Boles concluded in 1893, it is possible that Charley ended up in Mexico, perhaps with his prison chum Jimmy Hope. The famed bank robber was released from San Quentin in 1886 and then was extradited to New York to face charges of jail breaking. In 1889, a judge set him free, but gave him two days to leave the state. Hope promptly boarded a steamer bound for San Francisco by way of the Isthmus of Panama. He still had some of the fortune he had stolen from banks. San Francisco police detectives waited for Hope at the wharf, but when his scheduled steamship arrived, the noted thief was not aboard. Apparently he had disembarked in Central America or in Mexico. The following year, Hope's son Johnny, one of his bank robbery gang, was released from prison and told journalists that he would join his father, who was then running a cattle ranch. In one interview, Johnny Hope said that the ranch was in South America, and in another, he said it was south of the border.[24]

Next, in the fall of 1892, a visitor arrived in San Francisco and told a reporter for the *San Francisco Bulletin* that while passing through Durango, in central Mexico, he had accidentally met Black Bart. He said that he immediately recognized the former bandit because he had known him in Iowa many years before. He told the journalist, "Bolton is quite prosperous. In addition to a saloon and fandango house which he runs in Durango, Bart is interested with Jimmy Hope, the notorious despoiler of the Manhattan Bank, New York City, in an extensive cattle range near Durango from which both derive a lucrative living." But the accuracy of the story was called into doubt by its use of the name Bolton. If the man had been acquainted with Charley in Iowa, he would have known him as Boles, for the highwayman did not use the Bolton alias until long after he abandoned his family. And further, the visitor claimed that Black Bart told him that "a woman betrayed him" in San Francisco and she had been paid $30,000 to turn him over to the detectives. That claim, of course, was totally baseless.[25]

However, in 1902, some slight support for the story surfaced. W. B. King, a Wells Fargo detective assigned to the company's operations in Mexico, told a newspaperman that in about 1897, he had spotted Black Bart working at a mine near Durango in central Mexico. King claimed that he carefully watched the suspect and identified him by sending photos to Wells Fargo headquarters. The detective's story was credible up to that point. But it lost plausibility when King declared that he then arrested the bandit, had him extradited to the US, and received a $20,000 reward. That too never happened. But a year later, in 1903, a newspaper in Santa Rosa, California, reported that Boles "was in Arizona or New Mexico, aged and respected, his identity not known, a man of family in affluent circumstances, an extensive stock range being his realm." This could also be dismissed as another wild yarn, except the newspaper provided some accurate details about Boles's background and said that its informant, who lived in Santa Rosa, had been a fellow volunteer in the 116th Illinois. That man was undoubtedly Charley's friend Dr. Joseph Hostetler, the surgeon for the 116th, and it is possible that Boles wrote to his old Civil War comrade and boasted of the success that had so long eluded him.[26]

So, did Black Bart use his stolen loot to acquire a ranch in the American Southwest or in Mexico? Did he live out his final years in quiet anonymity as a prosperous cattleman? Surely that is how Charley Boles would have wanted his story to end. Perhaps some day the truth will out, but until then, the fate of Black Bart, the poet highwayman, remains one of the great mysteries of the Wild West.

★ ★ ★ ★ ★

Acknowledgments

I have collected bits and pieces of information about Black Bart for more than fifty years. In 1990, I provided research, documents, and other help to Bruce Levene, who, with his coauthor, the late William Collins, wrote the first biography of the noted highwayman, entitled *Black Bart: The True Story of the West's Most Famous Stagecoach Robber*, published in 1992. In the next few years, two more biographies appeared: the late George Hoeper's *Black Bart: Boulevardier Bandit* (1995) and Laika Dajani's *Black Bart: Elusive Highwayman-Poet* (1996). Each book provided new information about Charley Boles's mysterious life.

With the advent of online genealogical data banks, digital newspapers, and other historical records, I was able to locate a great deal of additional source material that shed new light on Black Bart and his career. But this book could not have been written without the groundbreaking work contained in the three volumes mentioned above. I owe a deep debt of gratitude to each of these authors, and especially to Bruce Levene, who was kind enough to provide me with many of the research materials he used in writing his 1992 book. This volume is therefore dedicated to Bruce Levene with many thanks for his unselfish assistance.

I also owe a great debt to the wonderful staff of the Wells Fargo History Museum in San Francisco, who first welcomed me as a teenager in the late 1960s and provided documents and encouragement to a young aficionado of the Old West. Irene Simpson Neasham (1916–2006) was its director for three decades. She and her assistants, Merrilee Gwerder Dowty and the late Elaine Gilleran, helped me more times than I can recall. Many thanks are also due to my old friend, the late Dr. Robert J. Chandler, Senior Research Historian for Wells Fargo Bank from 1978 to 2010. Bob was always there to track down an obscure document or answer my never-ending questions. Thanks also to Marc C. Reed, who researched Black Bart more than thirty years ago. Marc tracked down the very rare photos of Mary Boles and her daughters that appear in this volume, and was kind enough to provide copies of documents and review the Civil War chapters for me.

My great pal, the late William B. Secrest, was the leading authority on crime and law enforcement in frontier California. Bill shared his research with me, and I have cited several of his numerous books in the notes to this volume. Richard H. Dillon was another friend who has passed on. Dick encouraged me as a young writer, and his book *Wells Fargo Detective: A Biography of James B. Hume* provided essential information about Black Bart. Another old friend, Don Gordon, is a dedicated Wells Fargo historian and collector. Don and I visited some of the many sites of Black Bart's stage holdups, and he helped greatly with my research.

I also owe a huge debt of gratitude to Joanne Penn of Norwich, England. She is the daughter of my friend and colleague, Chris Penn, also of Norwich, who is a well-published authority on the history of the Wild West. Joanne did extensive genealogical work and uncovered the family history of Charles E. Boles in Norfolk, England. The late Dick Reames, great-great-grandson of Charles Boles, was kind enough to let me interview him in 1993 and to acquire from him a collection of original letters written by Boles to his family. Those letters are quoted in this book. Peter Pike Jr. graciously shared with me information, photographs, and two books he has produced about his great-grandfather, Jacob Pike, who was Black Bart's friend in San Francisco.

The late Lorraine Kennedy of the Calaveras County Museum in San Andreas assisted me many times over the years. I am grateful to the helpful staffs of the California State Archives in Sacramento, the California State Library in San Francisco, and the Bancroft Library at the University of California, Berkeley. I would also like to thank my fellow members of the Wild West History Association for their friendship and support. Its bimonthly journal and annual rendezvous are highly recommended. I encourage anyone interested in the history of the Old West to join this organization.

To my agent, Claire Gerus, and my editor, Peter Joseph, assistant editor Grace Towery, editorial assistant Eden Railsback, and copyeditor Jennifer Stimson, many thanks for all their efforts connected with this book. And last, I am ever grateful to my wife and chief literary critic, Marta Diaz, for her love, advice, and support.

Endnotes

Chapter 1

1   James M. Hutchings, *In the Heart of the Sierras*. Oakland, CA: Pacific Press Publishing (1888), p. 212.

2   John Shine, Databases of Illinois Veterans Index, at www.ancestry. com; *A Memorial and Biographical History of the Counties of Merced, Stanislaus, Calaveras, Tuolumne, and Mariposa, California*. Chicago, IL: Lewis Publishing Co. (1892), pp. 389–390; "John Henry Shine," *Successful American*, vol. 7, no. 4 (March 1903), p. 199.

3   C.A. Gillingham, Wells Fargo agent, to Leonard F. Rowell, Assistant Superintendent of Wells Fargo, July 26, 1875, Wells Fargo Bank History Department, San Francisco, CA; San Francisco (CA) *Examiner*, July 27, 1875; San Francisco (CA) *Call*, November 17, 1883; New York (NY) *Sun*, reprinted in Monongahela (PA) *Daily Republican*, December 28, 1883; William Collins and Bruce Levene, *Black Bart: The True Story of the West's Most Famous Stagecoach Robber*. Mendocino, CA: Pacific Transcriptions (1992), pp. 19–22; George Hoeper, *Black Bart: Boulevardier Bandit*. Fresno, CA: Word Dancer Press (1995), pp. 1–5.

4   Los Angeles (CA) *Times*, February 2, 1930.

5   On Ben K. Thorn, see John Boessenecker, *Badge and Buckshot: Law-lessness in Old California*. Norman, OK: University of Oklahoma Press (1988), chap. 3. On James B. Hume, see Richard Dillon, *Wells Fargo Detective: A Biography of James B. Hume*. New York, NY: Coward-McCann (1969).

6   John Boessenecker, *Shotguns and Stagecoaches: The Brave Men Who Rode for Wells Fargo in the Wild West*. New York, NY: St. Martin's Press (2018), pp. xi–xix.

7   Marysville (CA) *Daily Appeal*, December 29, 1875; San Francisco (CA) *Examiner*, December 29, 1875; Laika Dajani, *Black Bart: Elu-sive Highwayman-Poet*. Manhattan, KS: Sunflower University Press (1996), p. 36.

8   Albany (OR) *Cultivator*, June 8, 1876; Marysville (CA) *Daily Ap-peal*, June 14, 1876; Sacramento (CA) *Daily Union*, June 9, 1876; Portland (OR) *Oregonian*, June 27, 1876; Collins and Levene, *Black Bart*, pp. 59–61; Dajani, *Black Bart*, pp. 36–37.

9   Santa Rosa (CA) *Sonoma Democrat*, April 9, 1870; Petaluma (CA) *Weekly Argus*, August 10, 1877; San Francisco (CA) *Chronicle*, November 14, 1883; Santa Rosa (CA) *Press Democrat*, November 15, 1964; Collins and Levene, *Black Bart*, pp. 65–68; Hoeper, *Black Bart*, pp. 9–10. Nu-merous modern accounts state that the holdup took place on Meyers Grade Road, an inland wagon route in the hills southeast of Fort Ross. That is contradicted by Ash Wilkinson's original report, given here, which was published in the Point Arena (CA) *News*, and reprinted in the Petaluma (CA) *Courier*, August 16, 1877. Timber Gulch, the cor-rect site of the holdup, should not be confused with Timber Cove, which is located two miles north of Fort Ross.

Chapter 2

1   Joanne Penn, "What was the True Identity of Black Bart?" at www.norfolkrecordofficeblog.org. Ms. Penn is the first genealogist to un-cover the correct family history of Black Bart. Most of the fam-ily members, including John and Leonard, spelled their surname "Bowles." Charles used the "Bowles" spelling until the 1850s, after

which he consistently signed his name "Boles." For sake of consistency and to avoid confusion, the name is spelled "Boles" in the narrative. Some recent accounts claim Charles's middle name was Earl, but there is no proof, only speculation based on the fact that one of his nephews was named Earl.

2 Bury (UK) *Bury and Norwich Post*, August 4, 25, 1830.

3 Bury (UK) *Bury and Norwich Post*, August 25, 1830; Naturalization record, Leonard Bowles, August 8, 1836, on www.ancestry.com; Collins and Levene, *Black Bart*, p. 40; Dajani, *Black Bart*, p. xiv.

4 San Francisco (CA) *Chronicle*, January 6, 1884; San Francisco (CA) *Examiner*, December 3, 1888.

5 Watertown (NY) *Northern State Journal*, October 11, 1848; Stockton (CA) *Evening Mail*, November 17, 1883.

6 John Boessenecker, *Gold Dust and Gunsmoke: Tales of Gold Rush Outlaws, Gunfighters, Lawmen, and Vigilantes.* New York, NY: John Wiley & Sons (1999), pp. 2–4.

7 William Boles, Iowa Marriage Records, July 4, 1841, on www.ancestry.com; San Francisco (CA) *Chronicle*, January 6, 1884; Collins and Levene, *Black Bart*, p. 42.

8 San Francisco (CA) *Chronicle*, January 6, 1884.

9 San Francisco (CA) *Chronicle*, January 6, 1884; Washington (DC) *Weekly National Intelligencer*, February 7, 1852.

10 San Francisco (CA) *Chronicle*, January 6, 1884; San Francisco (CA) *Daily Alta California*, May 14, June 15, 1852; Sacramento (CA) *Daily Union*, May 15, 1852. The date and place of death of Robert Boles are unknown.

11 California state census, 1852, Placer County, on www.ancestry.com; Auburn (CA) *Placer Herald*, August 20, 1853; San Francisco (CA) *Chronicle*, November 28, 1888; Collins and Levene, *Black Bart*, p. 43.

12 Boessenecker, *Gold Dust and Gunsmoke*, pp. 322–326.

Chapter 3

1   Iowa Marriages Index, Charles Boles and Mary E. Johnson, at www. ancestry.com; New Oregon (IA) *Plaindealer*, June 23, July 7, 1896.

2   New Oregon (IA) *Plaindealer*, June 29, October 19, 1860; Cresco (IA) *Howard County Times*, December 20, 1888; Collins and Levene, *Black Bart*, pp. 43–44.

3   US Census Population Schedules, Alexandria, New York, 1860; warranty deed, Charles E. Boles to Mary Boles, May 11, 1860, courtesy Marc C. Reed; Collins and Levene, *Black Bart*, p. 44.

4   Decatur (IL) *Herald and Review*, December 9, 1888; Decatur (IL) *Daily Review*, April 30, 1979; Collins and Levene, *Black Bart*, pp. 43–44; Dajani, *Black Bart*, p. 2.

5   Naturalization record, Leonard Bowles, August 8, 1836, on www. ancestry.com; Naturalization record, John Bowles, April 15, 1851, on www.familysearch.org; Charles E. Boles to Oscar James, July 24, 1884, reprinted in Dajani, *Black Bart*, pp. 114–116.

6   Nashville (TN) *Daily Union*, March 18, 1864; Collins and Levene, *Black Bart*, p. 45; Jane Martin Johns, *Personal Recollections of Early Decatur*. Decatur (IL): Daughters of the American Revolution (1912), p. 201.

7   Thomas Littleton, quoted in Dajani, *Black Bart*, p. 3.

8   Alton (IL) *Evening Telegraph*, November 28, 1883; Chicago (IL) *Tribune*, June 20, 1907; John Foster, quoted in Dajani, *Black Bart*, p. 7.

9   Johns, *Personal Recollections of Early Decatur*, p. 202; William Craig to Levica Craig, December 14, 1862, Ohio State University Library, at www.ehistory.osu.edu.

10 Reuben Bills to Linda Bills, November 12, 1862, quoted in Dajani, *Black Bart*, p. 7.

11 Reuben Bills to Linda Bills, December 14, 1862, quoted in Dajani, *Black Bart*, p. 9.

12 William Marsh to his brother, September 15, 1862, quoted in Peter R. Wells, "Lincoln's Boys: The Enlisted Men of the Illinois Infantry

in the Civil War," unpublished thesis, Illinois Wesleyan University (1987), p. 64.

13 Wayne C. Temple, ed., *The Civil War Letters of Henry C. Bear, A Soldier in the 116th Illinois Volunteer Infantry*. Harrogate, TN: Lincoln Memorial University Press (1961), p. 6.

14 Reuben Bills to Linda Bills, December 16, 1862, quoted in Dajani, *Black Bart*, p. 9.

15 Woodstock (IL) *Sentinel*, February 11, 1863.

16 Reuben Bills to Linda Bills, January 3, 1863, quoted in Dajani, *Black Bart*, p. 9.

17 Temple, ed., *The Civil War Letters of Henry C. Bear*, pp. 22–24.

18 Decatur (IL) *Daily Review*, October 26, 1910.

Chapter 4

1 Chicago (IL) *Tribune*, January 26, 1863.

2 Temple, ed., *The Civil War Letters of Henry C. Bear*, p. 29.

3 Decatur (IL) *Weekly Republican*, April 21, 1887; Decatur (IL) *Herald and Review*, July 27, 1913.

4 Chicago (IL) *Tribune*, January 26, 1863.

5 Decatur (IL) *Herald and Review*, December 9, 1888, September 26, 1902, July 27, 1913.

6 Temple, ed., *The Civil War Letters of Henry C. Bear*, pp. 32–35.

7 Hillsboro (OH) *Highland Weekly News*, April 2, 1863; Decatur (IL) *Herald and Review*, October 7, 1887.

8 Chicago (IL) *Tribune*, April 4, 1863; Elliot G. Storke and L. P. Brockett, *A Complete History of the Great American Rebellion*, Vol. II. Auburn, NY: Auburn Publishing Co. (1865), pp. 883–886.

9 Decatur (IL) *Herald and Review*, December 9, 1888, December 1, 1907.

10 *Illinois at Vicksburg*. Chicago, IL: The Blakely Printing Company (1907), p. 25.

11 Charles Affeld diary, April 30, 1863, at www.taylors-battery.com.

12 Chicago (IL) *Tribune*, May 8, 1863.

13 Charles Affeld diary, May 7–15, 1863, at www.taylors-battery.com.

14 Sergeant Stephen A. Rollins to his parents, July 20, 1863, at www. battleofchampionhill.org.

15 Osborn H. Oldroyd diary, May 16, 1863, at www.battleofchampion-hill.org. Oldroyd later became an authority on Abraham Lincoln and wrote several books about him. His huge collection of Lincoln memorabilia is displayed in Ford's Theatre in Washington, DC.

16 Bloomington (IL) *Pantagraph*, June 5, 1863.

17 Steven E. Woodworth, Charles D. Grear, eds., *The Vicksburg Assaults, May 19-22, 1863*. Carbondale, IL: Southern Illinois University Press (2019), pp. 13–14.

18 Temple, ed., *The Civil War Letters of Henry C. Bear*, p. 41; William T. Rigby, *Siege and Defence of Vicksburg and the Vicksburg National Military Park*. Chicago, IL: Illinois Central Railroad Company (1909), pp. 10–11.

19 Christopher R. Gabel, *The Vicksburg Campaign, November 1862-July 1863*. Washington, DC: Center of Military History (2013), pp. 53–55.

20 Charles Affeld diary, May 22, 1863, at www.taylors-battery.com.

21 Chicago (IL) *Tribune*, June 6, 1863; Thomas Mears Eddy, *The Patriotism of Illinois: A Record of the Civil and Military History of the State in the War for the Union*, Vol. 1. Chicago, IL: Clarke & Co. (1865), pp. 468–469; Rigby, *Siege and Defence of Vicksburg*, p. 17; "General Thomas Edwin Greenfield Ransom," *Illinois Central Magazine*, vol. 3, no. 4 (October 1914), p. 13.

22 Alton (IL) *Evening Telegraph*, November 28, 1883.

Chapter 5

1   Alton (IL) *Evening Telegraph*, November 28, 1883; Napa (CA) *Register*, November 23, 1883.

2   Richard Puffer to his sister, May 28, 1863, quoted in Wells, "Lincoln's Boys," p. 62.

3   Nashville (TN) *Journal*, July 10, 1863.

4   Canton (MO) *Press*, August 28, 1903; Eric Michael Burke, "Soldiers from Experience: The Emergence of Tactical Culture in Sherman's Fifteenth Army Corps, 1862-63," PhD dissertation, University of North Carolina at Chapel Hill (2019), p. 304.

5   Bloomington (IL) *Pantagraph*, November 28, 1883; Collins and Levene, *Black Bart*, p. 46.

6   William Craig to Levica Craig, July 11, 1863, Ohio State University, at www.ehistory.osu.edu.

7   William Craig to Levica Craig, April 15, 1864, Ohio State University, at www.ehistory.osu.edu.

8   Milwaukee (WI) *Daily News*, December 2, 1863; Decatur (IL) *Herald and Review*, January 24, 1904; Storke and Brockett, *A Complete History of the Great American Rebellion*, pp. 1119–1121; *Soldiers' and Patriots' Biographical Album*. Chicago, IL: Union Veteran Publishing Co. (1892), p. 204.

9   Mark Grimsley and Todd D. Miller, eds., *The Union Must Stand: The Civil War Diary of John Quincy Adams Campbell*. Knoxville, TN: University of Tennessee Press (2000), p. 137.

10 *Reminiscences of the Civil War from Diaries of Members of the 103rd Illinois Volunteer Infantry*. Chicago, IL: Press of J.F. Leaming (1904), p. 27; Grimsley and Miller, *The Union Must Stand*, p. 138.

11 Decatur (IL) *Herald and Review*, July 7, 1913.

12 Decatur (IL) *Herald and Review*, December 9, 1888.

13 Alton (IL) *Evening Telegraph*, November 28, 1883; Decatur (IL) *Her-*

ald and Review, December 9, 1888, December 1, 1907; Private John Foster, quoted in Dajani, *Black Bart,* p. 7.

14 William Craig to Levica Craig, June 23, 1863, April 3, 1865, Ohio State University, at www.ehistory.osu.edu.

15 William Craig to Levica Craig, February 10, 1864, Ohio State University, at www.ehistory.osu.edu.

16 Charles E. Boles to Oscar James, July 24, 1884, reprinted in Dajani, *Black Bart,* pp. 114–116; Charles E. Boles family tree, on www.ancestry.com.

17 *Reminiscences of the Civil War from Diaries of Members of the 103rd Illinois Volunteer Infantry,* p. 52.

18 Louisville (KY) *Courier-Journal,* May 19, 1864; Washington (DC) *National Tribune,* February 10, 1910.

19 *Transactions of the McLean County Historical Society,* Vol. 1. Bloomington, IL: Pantagraph Printing Co. (1899), p. 432.

20 Decatur (IL) *Herald and Review,* December 9, 1888; Collins and Levene, *Black Bart,* p. 48.

21 New York (NY) *Times,* December 23, 1864; Edward Schwabe Jr., "The March to the Sea: The Operational Role of Sherman's Right Wing," thesis, Naval War College, Newport, RI (1986), pp. 22–23.

22 W. F. Hinman, *Camp and Field: Sketches of Army Life Written by Those Who Followed the Flag.* Cleveland, OH: N. G. Hamilton Publishing Co. (1892), p. 465.

23 William Craig to Levica Craig, April 3, 1865.

24 New York (NY) *Times,* December 23, 1864; Isaiah L. Reed, "Men with Deadly Rifles Outclass Fort's Monster Cannon," at www.historynet.com.

25 Stockton (CA) *Evening Mail,* November 17, 1883; Hannibal (MO) *Journal,* December 13, 1888.

26 Decatur (IL) *Herald and Review,* October 6, 1887, December 9, 1888, August 16, 1903.

27 William Craig to Levica Craig, April 9, 1865, Ohio State University Library, at www.ehistory.osu.edu.

28 Chicago (IL) *Tribune*, June 16, 24, 1865.

Chapter 6

1 San Francisco (CA) *Examiner*, December 2, 1888; Decatur (IL) *Daily Republican*, November 27, 1883.

2 San Francisco (CA) *Daily Alta California*, February 12, 1866; San Francisco (CA) *Examiner*, April 3, 1887.

3 Boles was back in New Oregon by December 22, 1866, when he signed a legal document there. See Laika Dajani, "Black Bart," *Quarterly of the Tuolumne County Historical Society*, vol. 34, no. 3 (January–March 1995), p. 1174.

4 C. E. Booth to James B. Hume, April 26, 1886, reprinted in San Francisco (CA) *Bulletin*, January 21, 1888; Cresco (IA) *Howard County Times*, April 3, 1867, December 20, 1888; Collins and Levene, *Black Bart*, pp. 49–50.

5 Helena (MT) *Post*, September 21, November 2, 1867; Collins and Levene, *Black Bart*, p. 50.

6 US Census Population Schedules, Silver Bow, Montana Territory, 1870; Helena (MT) *Post*, November 9, 1867, November 27, 1868; Butte (MT) *Miner*, August 24, 1889.

7 Butte (MT) *Miner*, August 24, 1889, September 14, 1900.

8 Charles E. Boles to Mary Boles, April 4, 1869, copy courtesy of Bruce Levene. Edited versions of the letter appear in San Francisco (CA) *Chronicle*, December 12, 1888, and Collins and Levene, *Black Bart*, pp. 50–51.

9 Leona Middleton to George Ezra Dane, April 12, 1935, quoted in Dajani, *Black Bart*, p. xv. Leona Middleton was Charley's great-granddaughter.

10 Deer Lodge (MT) *New North-west*, June 8, 1877.

11 US Census Population Schedules, New Oregon, Iowa, 1870; San

Francisco (CA) *Chronicle*, November 28, 1888, December 12, 1888; Charles E. Boles family tree, on www.ancestry.com.

12 Cresco (IA) *Howard County Times*, September 7, 1871, July 7, 1948; Booth to Hume, April 26, 1886, in San Francisco (CA) *Bulletin*, January 21, 1888.

13 Lowville (NY) *Lewis County Democrat*, March 27, 1872; Lowville (NY) *Journal and Republican*, April 3, 1872.

14 *Estate of John Bowles*, Jefferson County, New York, Wills and Probate Records, on www.ancestry.com; Albany (NY) *Daily Argus*, October 24, 1872; Collins and Levene, *Black Bart*, pp. 51–52, 183–184.

15 Stockton (CA) *Evening Mail*, November 17, 1883; San Francisco (CA) *Chronicle*, November 28, 1888.

16 Stockton (CA) *Evening Mail*, November 17, 1883.

17 San Francisco (CA) *Examiner*, December 2, 1888.

Chapter 7

1 Sacramento (CA) *Record-Union*, November 17, 1883.

2 Henry S. Brooks, *A Catastrophe in Bohemia*. New York, NY: C. L. Webster & Co. (1893), pp. 82–84.

3 San Francisco (CA) *Call*, reprinted in St. Louis (MO) *Globe-Democrat*, November 21, 1883.

4 Sacramento (CA) *Daily Union*, November 4, 1874; Stockton (CA) *Independent*, March 24, 1875; Stockton (CA) *Daily Evening Herald*, March 24, 1875.

5 San Francisco (CA) *Call*, November 17, 1883.

6 Collins and Levene, *Black Bart*, pp. 69–70.

7 San Francisco (CA) *Examiner*, April 3, 1887; Sacramento (CA) *Bee*, November 15, 1883.

8 Chico (CA) *Weekly Butte Record*, August 3, 1878; Quincy (CA) *Feather River Bulletin*, August 3, 17, 1878; Oroville (CA) *Weekly Mercury* Au-

gust 2, 9, 1878; Oroville (CA) *Butte County Register*, August 2, 1878; Collins and Levene, *Black Bart*, pp. 71–73; Hoeper, *Black Bart*, p. 43.

9   Oroville (CA) *Weekly Mercury*, August 2, 1878; Quincy (CA) *Feather River Bulletin*, August 3, 1878. Previous accounts incorrectly identify the driver as D. E. Barry or Dan Barry; his name was David Emerson Berry (1823–1887) who lived in nearby Strawberry Valley. Chico (CA) *Weekly Butte Record*, April 30, 1887.

10   Quincy (CA) *Feather River Bulletin*, August 3, 10, 17, 1878; Marysville (CA) *Daily Appeal*, August 4, September 13, October 18, 1878; Sacramento (CA) *Daily Union*, August 15, September 12, 1878; Chico (CA) *Weekly Butte Record*, October 26, 1878.

11   Wells Fargo reward notice, 1878, Wells Fargo Bank History Dept.

12   Ukiah (CA) *City Press*, October 4, 11, 1878; Cloverdale (CA) *News*, October 12, 1878; San Francisco (CA) *Bulletin*, October 8, 1878. In about 1950, a state highway crew removed Black Bart Rock when they straightened the road. A tall rock outcropping, situated four and a half miles north near Ridgewood Summit, was then falsely dubbed Black Bart Rock by local boosters and is known by that name to this day. It has no connection with Black Bart. However, as recounted in Chapter 19, Black Bart did rob a stage near Ridgewood Summit on November 20, 1888.

13   Cloverdale (CA) *News*, October 12, 1878.

14   San Francisco (CA) *Examiner*, June 30, 1921; Dajani, *Black Bart*, pp. 48–49. Most accounts state incorrectly that Donna McCreary (1860–1941) was then only fourteen. Her correct dates of birth and death are in the California Death Index at www.ancestry.com.

15   Cloverdale (CA) *News*, October 12, 1878; San Francisco (CA) *Bulletin*, October 8, 1878; San Francisco (CA) *Chronicle*, November 28, 1888.

16   Lida Hume, typescript of diary, 1932, Wells Fargo Bank History Dept.; Ukiah (CA) *City Press*, October 11, 1878; San Francisco (CA) *Examiner*, June 30, 1921.

17   James B. Hume to Lida Munson, October 5, 1878, quoted in Dajani, *Black Bart*, pp. 50–51.

18 Boessenecker, *Shotguns and Stagecoaches*, pp. 179–180.

19 San Francisco (CA) *Examiner*, June 30, 1921.

Chapter 8

1 California State Archives, San Quentin Prison Register: Hugh De Tell, alias David Granard and David Gramon, convict nos. 719, 1750, and 2511; Walter Sinclair, alias William Harris and Frederick Smith, convict nos. 1819 and 2843.

2 The Osgood Toll House still exists and has been moved to the Lake Tahoe Historical Society Museum in South Lake Tahoe.

3 Sacramento (CA) *Daily Union*, August 5, 6, 1867.

4 San Quentin Prison Register, Hugh De Tell, alias George Martyn, convict no. 3628, and Walter Sinclair, convict no. 3627; Dillon, *Wells Fargo Detective*, pp. 108–109.

5 Dillon, *Wells Fargo Detective*, pp. 24–35.

6 Boessenecker, *Badge and Buckshot*, pp. 141–152; Boessenecker, *Shotguns and Stagecoaches*, pp. 15–30, 116–120.

7 John Boessenecker, "The Bride and the Brigand," *Wild West Magazine*, vol. 30, no. 4 (December 2017), pp. 64–69.

8 Boessenecker, *Shotguns and Stagecoaches*, pp. 121–122.

9 Sacramento (CA) *Daily Union*, October 18, 1871, February 11, 1875; Healdsburg (CA) *Russian River Flag*, December 21, 1871, November 26, 1874.

10 Wells Fargo & Co. reward notice, January 20, 1879, California State Library, Sacramento, CA.

11 San Jose (CA) *Mercury-News*, June 24, July 3, September 12, 1879, November 20, 1883; San Francisco (CA) *Call*, October 10, 11, 1905.

12 Dajani, *Black Bart*, pp. 21–22; San Francisco (CA) *Examiner*, November 17, 1879.

13 John Boessenecker, ed., *Against the Vigilantes: The Recollections of Dutch*

Charley Duane. Norman, OK: University of Oklahoma Press (1999), pp. 29–35, 191; San Francisco (CA) *Bulletin*, November 17, 1883; San Francisco (CA) *Call*, November 17, 1883.

14 US Census Population Schedules, San Francisco, CA, 1880; San Francisco (CA) *Chronicle*, March 2, 1879; San Francisco (CA) *Examiner*, July 13, 1881.

15 Hubert Howe Bancroft, *Popular Tribunals, Vol. II*. San Francisco, CA: The History Company (1887), p. 125; Boessenecker, *Shotguns and Stagecoaches*, pp. 85–86.

16 Marysville (CA) Daily Appeal, June 24, 26, 1879; Oroville (CA) *Butte County Register*, June 27, 1879; Hoeper, *Black Bart*, p. 18.

17 Red Bluff (CA) *Daily People's Cause*, October 27, 1879; Redding (CA) *Independent*, October 30, 1879; Fort Jones (CA) *Scott Valley News*, October 30, 1879; Collins and Levene, *Black Bart*, pp. 84–85; Dajani, *Black Bart*, pp. 52–56.

18 Collins and Levene, *Black Bart*, pp. 86–87; Dajani, *Black Bart*, p. 56; Hoeper, *Black Bart*, pp. 19–20.

19 Dillon, *Wells Fargo Detective*, p. 168.

20 Yreka (CA) *Journal*, reprinted in Red Bluff (CA) *Daily People's Cause*, November 15, 1879.

21 San Francisco (CA) *Daily Alta California*, November 28, 1883.

Chapter 9

1 San Francisco (CA) *Daily Alta California*, November 14, 1883.

2 Stockton (CA) *Evening Mail*, November 17, 1883; San Francisco (CA) *Call*, November 15, 1883.

3 Auburn (CA) *Placer Herald*, March 11, 1876; Sacramento (CA) *Daily Union*, April 1, 1916.

4 Peter Pike Jr., ed., *Memoir and Writings of Jacob M. Pike*. Centralia, WA: Gorham Printing (2020), pp. 14–19, 89–95. On the 1856 lynchings in Coulterville, see San Francisco (CA) *Chronicle*, March 13, 1892.

5   Pike, *Memoir and Writings of Jacob M. Pike*, pp. 29–30; Peter Pike Jr., *California Bound*. Centralia, WA: Gorham Printing (2018), pp. 31–32.

6   Stockton (CA) *Evening Mail*, November 17, 1883.

7   Sacramento (CA) *Daily Union*, September 9, 1913.

8   Edward Byram, *Journals*, vol. 3, pp. 62–68, author's collection. On Isaiah W. Lees, see William B. Secrest, *Dark and Tangled Threads of Crime: San Francisco's Famous Police Detective Isaiah W. Lees*. Sanger, CA: Word Dancer Press (2004).

9   *Chronological Record of the Police Department of San Francisco*. San Francisco, CA: Board of Police Commissioners (1896), pp. 2, 4; San Francisco (CA) *Daily Alta California*, November 14, 1883; San Francisco (CA) *Bulletin*, January 21, 1888; San Francisco (CA) *Call*, April 25, 1894; San Francisco (CA) *Chronicle*, April 13, 1886; San Francisco (CA) *Examiner*, September 20, 1891.

10 *Chronological Record of the Police Department of San Francisco*, pp. 2, 4, 5; San Francisco (CA) *Chronicle*, February 17, 1874; San Francisco (CA) *Examiner*, November 17, 1883; San Francisco (CA) *Call*, September 16, 1895, June 13, 1903; San Francisco (CA) *Bulletin*, November 17, 1883; Secrest, *Dark and Tangled Threads of Crime*, pp. 179, 238–241.

11 Edward Byram, *Journals*, vol. 2, p. 250, author's collection; Stockton (CA) *Evening Mail*, November 17, 1883; San Francisco (CA) *Examiner*, November 17, 1883; San Francisco (CA) *Call*, November 17, 1883.

12 San Francisco (CA) *Call*, November 15, 1883; Eugene T. Sawyer, "Old Time Minstrels of San Francisco," *Overland Monthly and Out West Magazine*, vol. 81, no. 6 (October 1923), p. 7.

13 San Francisco (CA) *Call*, November 15, 1883; Grass Valley (CA) *Morning Union*, August 29, 1882, November 17, 1883; *Langley's San Francisco Directory*. San Francisco, CA: The Directory Publishing Co. (1882), p. 710.

14 Petaluma (CA) *Weekly Argus*, July 23, 1880; Petaluma (CA) *Courier*, July 28, August 4, 1880; Mendocino (CA) *Beacon*, July 31, 1880; Sonoma (CA) *Democrat*, July 31, 1880. In later years, some local his-

torians conflated Black Bart's 1877 Timber Gulch holdup with the 1880 Meyers Grade holdup and erroneously wrote that both robberies had taken place on Meyers Grade.

15 Sonoma (CA) *Democrat*, July 31, 1880; Mendocino (CA) *Beacon*, August 7, 1880; Petaluma (CA) *Weekly Argus*, August 13, November 5, 1880. Based on the arrest of Lane Nelson and the mistaken belief that there were three robbers, several writers, unaware that the charges were dismissed, concluded incorrectly that Nelson, not Black Bart, was guilty of this robbery. In fact, Boles later confessed to Jim Hume that he had robbed this stage.

16 Chico (CA) *Weekly Butte Record*, September 11, 1880; Collins and Levene, *Black Bart*, pp. 93–96.

17 Wells Fargo & Co. reward notice, October 23, 1880, Wells Fargo Bank History Dept.; Shasta (CA) *Courier*, quoted in Marysville (CA) *Evening Democrat*, February 4, 1888.

18 Portland (OR) *Oregonian*, September 20, 1880; Collins and Levene, *Black Bart*, pp. 97–101.

19 Medford (OR) *Mail Tribune*, December 18, 1960.

20 Red Bluff (CA) *Sentinel*, June 26, 1880; Tehama (CA) *Tocsin*, October 30, 1880; Collins and Levene, *Black Bart*, p. 101. On Charles Aull, see William B. Secrest, *Lawmen and Desperadoes*. Spokane, WA: Arthur H. Clark Co. (1994), pp. 25–30.

21 Yreka (CA) *Journal*, November 24, 1880; Sacramento (CA) *Daily Union*, November 22, 1880.

Chapter 10

1 Mark Twain, *Old Times on the Mississippi*. Toronto, Canada: Belford Brothers (1876), pp. 10–11.

2 Booth to Hume, April 26, 1886, in San Francisco (CA) *Bulletin*, January 21, 1888.

3 San Francisco (CA) *Chronicle*, November 28, 1888; San Francisco (CA) *Examiner*, April 3, 1887; Collins and Levene, *Black Bart*, pp. 183–184.

4   Census Population Schedules, Hannibal, MO, 1880; *Hannibal City Directory*. Hannibal, MO: Winchell & Ebert (1875), pp. 13–14, 64; Hannibal (MO) *Clipper*, December 10, 1874, January 13, 1875; San Francisco (CA) *Chronicle*, November 28, 1888; Collins and Levene, *Black Bart*, p. 210.

5   *Hannibal City Directory*. Hannibal, MO: Hannibal Printing Co. (1881), p. 41; San Francisco (CA) *Examiner*, July 13, 1881.

6   Redding (CA) *Independent*, September 1, 1881; Stockton (CA) *Evening Mail*, September 1, 1881.

7   Redding (CA) *Shasta County Democrat*, October 12, 1881; Chico (CA) *Semi-Weekly Enterprise*, October 14, 1881; Collins and Levene, *Black Bart*, pp. 107–111.

8   Chico (CA) *Weekly Butte Record*, October 22, 1881.

9   Marysville (CA) *Daily Appeal*, October 13, 1881; Boessenecker, *Shotguns and Stagecoaches*, pp. 230–232.

10 Redding (CA) *Independent*, quoted in Sacramento (CA) *Daily Bee*, October 24, 1881.

11 Oroville (CA) *Weekly Mercury*, October 28, 1881; Sacramento (CA) *Union*, November 18, 1881, February 14, 1882; Red Bluff (CA) *Tehama County Daily Republican*, November 26, 1881. On Samuel P. Haslett (1835–1906), see Baltimore (MD) *Sun*, January 10, 25, 1906.

12 Sacramento (CA) *Bee*, November 24, 1883; San Francisco (CA) *Call*, August 14, 1892, January 17, 1909.

13 Marysville (CA) *Daily Appeal*, December 17, 1881. Jim Hume later reported that the holdup took place on December 15, 1881, and that date has been used by all subsequent writers. However, contemporary newspaper accounts make it clear that the robbery took place on December 16.

14 Marysville (CA) *Daily Appeal*, December 28, 1881; Oroville (CA) *Daily Register*, June 30, 1920; Collins and Levene, *Black Bart*, p. 114.

15 Boessenecker, *Shotguns and Stagecoaches*, pp. 123–125.

16 Sacramento (CA) *Bee*, January 19, 1882; Sacramento (CA) *Daily*

Union, January 27, 1882; Cloverdale (CA) *Reveille*, quoted in Petaluma (CA) *Weekly Argus*, February 3, 1882; Ukiah (CA) *Mendocino
Dispatch Democrat*, February 3, 1882.

17 Ukiah (CA) *Mendocino Dispatch Democrat*, February 10, 1882.

18 Ukiah (CA) *Mendocino Dispatch Democrat*, February 3, 1882; Santa
Rosa (CA) *Sonoma Democrat*, February 11, 1882.

Chapter 11

1 Redding (CA) *Independent*, May 26, June 2, 23, 1882; San Francisco
(CA) *Examiner*, June 2, 1882, July 19, 1885; R. Michael Wilson, *Wells,
Fargo & Co., Report of Stagecoach and Train Robbers, 1870 to 1884*. Las
Vegas, NV: RaMa Press (2007), pp. 239–240.

2 US Census Population Schedules, Jackson County, OR, 1920 (Ora
E. Ragsdale); Sacramento (CA) *Daily Union*, August 28, 1885; Med-
ford (OR) *Mail Tribune*, June 12, 13, 1917; Jacksonville (OR) *Post*,
June 16, 1917.

3 Ukiah (CA) *Mendocino Dispatch Democrat*, June 16, 1882; Cloverdale
(CA) *Reveille*, reprinted in Burbank (CA) *Review*, June 21, 1882; Dajani, *Black Bart*, p. 66.

4 William V. Wells, *Walker's Expedition to Nicaragua: A History of the
Central American War*. New York, NY: Stringer and Townsend (1856),
pp. 34, 37; *Great Register of the County of Placer* (1877), p. 20; Grass
Valley (CA) *Union*, November 5, 1911.

5 Sacramento (CA) *Bee*, November 16, 1883. Norval Douglass's son,
Nevada County Sheriff David F. Douglass, was killed in a gunfight
with criminals in 1896, one of the state's most notorious murders of
that decade.

6 Marysville (CA) *Daily Appeal*, July 14, 1882; Quincy (CA) *Feather River
Bulletin*, December 8, 1883; John Boessenecker, "George Hackett: Terror to Road Agents," *Old West*, vol. 24, no.1 (Fall 1987), pp. 15–17.

7 Oroville (CA) *Weekly Mercury*, July 14, 1882; Quincy (CA) *Feather
River Bulletin*, December 8, 1883; Boessenecker, "George Hackett,"
pp. 15–17. In 1935, the Butte County Road Department erected a
marker at the location of the second holdup, which was then errone-

ously known as Black Bart Bend. The marker incorrectly stated that it was the location of the holdup in which Black Bart was wounded by George Hackett. In fact, that holdup took place thirty-one miles east. The marker is still standing and can be seen on the old stage road, now called Black Bart Road, at its intersection with Sandra Lane, twelve miles east of Oroville.

8   Marysville (CA) *Daily Appeal*, July 14, 1882; Boessenecker, "George Hackett," p. 17.

9   Yreka (CA) *Journal*, June 30, July 7, 1882; Chico (CA) *Weekly Enterprise*, September 22, 1882; Collins and Levene, *Black Bart*, p. 125; Dajani, *Black Bart*, p. 72.

10 San Francisco (CA) *Daily Alta California*, September 23, 30, 1882; San Francisco (CA) *Examiner*, September 23, 1882; Red Bluff (CA) *Tehama County Daily Republica*n, September 23, 1882; Dajani, *Black Bart*, pp. 74–75.

11 Cloverdale (CA) *Reveille*, November 25, 1882; Grass Valley (CA) *Morning Union*, November 28, 1882; Collins and Levene, *Black Bart*, pp. 126–128. Numerous accounts incorrectly state that this holdup took place on November 23, 1882.

12 Collins and Levene, *Black Bart*, pp. 128–129; Dajani, *Black Bart*, pp. 76–77.

13 William B. Secrest, *Perilous Trails, Dangerous Men*. Clovis, CA: Quill Driver Books (2002), pp. 66–74.

14 *Langley's San Francisco Directory*. San Francisco, CA: The Directory Publishing Co. (1883), p. 244; San Francisco (CA) *Chronicle*, March 15, 1884.

Chapter 12

1   US Census Population Schedules, Jefferson County, New York, 1850, Oneida, New York, 1880, Reno, Nevada, 1900; Hannibal (MO) *Journal*, December 13, 1888; Reno (NV) *Gazette-Journal*, August 27, 1885, June 3, 1902; Santa Cruz (CA) *Sentinel*, April 30, 1905; Reno (NV) *Nevada State Journal*, February 27, 1937.

2   US Census Population Schedules, San Francisco, CA, 1880; Grass

Valley (CA) *Morning Union*, August 29, 1882, November 17, 1883; San Francisco (CA) *Examiner*, November 19, 1883; Dajani, *Black Bart*, p. 23.

3   Wells Fargo & Co. reward notice, December 18, 1882, accessed at www.historical.ha.com; San Francisco (CA) *Examiner*, November 15, 1883.

4   Cloverdale (CA) *Reveille*, April 14, 1883; Sacramento (CA) *Daily Union*, April 13, 1883; Santa Rosa (CA) *Sonoma Democrat*, April 21, 1883; Collins and Levene, *Black Bart*, p. 130; Dajani, *Black Bart*, pp. 78–79. Jim Hume misspelled the driver's last name as Connibeck, which is not a surname, and that error has been repeated in all subsequent accounts. William Krumdick was the driver of the Lakeport-Cloverdale stage from 1883 to 1886. He died in 1887 after he was shot in a quarrel in Middletown, Lake County. Cloverdale (CA) *Reveille*, March 13, December 18, 1886; Napa (CA) *Napa County Reporter*, February 18, 1887.

5   Several writers have concluded incorrectly that the landlady at the Webb House in 1883 was Mrs. W. Warner (Mary) Henry. However, San Francisco city directories show that she was the Webb House landlady from 1879 to 1882, when she moved to Oakland.

6   Jackson (CA) *Amador Ledger-Dispatch*, June 30, 1883; Collins and Levene, *Black Bart*, pp. 131–132.

7   On Morse, see John Boessenecker, *Lawman: The Life and Times of Harry Morse, 1835-1912*. Norman, OK: University of Oklahoma Press (1998).

8   Boessenecker, *Lawman*, p. 249.

9   Napa (CA) *Napa County Reporter*, September 14, 21, 1883; San Francisco (CA) *Examiner*, September 16, 1883; Napa (CA) *Register*, September 21, 1883.

10   Sacramento (CA) *Daily Union*, September 3, November 19, 1883.

11   Reason E. McConnell, "Shotgun McConnell, The Life and Times of a Frontier Family," unpublished ms., pp. 58–59, Wells Fargo Bank History Dept.; Stockton (CA) *Evening Mail*, November 16, 1883.

12 Owen Treleaven, "Old Men in the Sun," unpublished ms., c. 1940, Calaveras County Historical Society, pp. 235, 238–241; US Census Population Schedules, Tuolumne County, CA, 1880; Collins and Levene, *Black Bart*, pp. 136–137.

13 San Francisco (CA) *Bulletin*, November 17, 1883.

14 Modesto (CA) *Bee*, November 24, 1913.

15 New York (NY) *Sun*, reprinted in Monongahela (PA) *Daily Republican*, December 28, 1883.

Chapter 13

1   New York (NY) *Sun*, reprinted in Monongahela (PA) *Daily Republican*, December 28, 1883.

2   Healdsburg (CA) *Enterprise*, July 19, 1913; *An Illustrated History of Sonoma County, California*. Chicago, IL: Lewis Publishing Co. (1889), p. 270.

3   McConnell, "Shotgun McConnell," pp. 2–38, 45–51.

4   Treleaven, "Old Men in the Sun," p. 241.

5   McConnell, "Shotgun McConnell," pp. 52–55; San Francisco (CA) *Bulletin*, November 14, 1883.

6   Treleaven, "Old Men in the Sun," p. 243; San Andreas (CA) *Calaveras Prospect*, November 9, 1883.

7   McConnell, "Shotgun McConnell," p. 56.

8   Information for Robbery, People v. C.E. Bolton, November 17, 1883, copy in Wells Fargo Bank History Dept.; San Andreas (CA) *Calaveras Prospect*, November 9, 1883; Stockton (CA) *Evening Mail*, November 16, 1883; Collins and Levene, *Black Bart*, pp. 141–143, 217.

9   Stockton (CA) *Evening Mail*, November 5, 1883; McConnell, "Shotgun McConnell," p. 57.

10 Information for Robbery, People v. C.E. Bolton, November 17, 1883,

and John N. Thacker to Orrin Langmaid, March 15, 1884, both in
Wells Fargo Bank History Dept.

11 McConnell, "Shotgun McConnell," p. 58; Information for Robbery, People v. C.E. Bolton.

12 Sacramento (CA) *Daily Union*, November 19, 1883; Collins and
Levene, *Black Bart*, pp. 152–153.

13 Reno (NV) *Gazette-Journal*, November 14, 1883; Sacramento (CA)
Daily Union, November 19, 1883.

14 San Francisco (CA) *Daily Alta California*, November 14, 1883.

Chapter 14

1 San Francisco (CA) *Call*, November, 17, 1883; Ben K. Thorn to
Harry N. Morse, 1884, Society of California Pioneers, San Francisco, CA; Dillon, *Wells Fargo Detective*, p. 177.

2 Salt Lake City (UT) *Tribune*, July 20, 1902; San Francisco (CA) *Call*,
November 17, 1883.

3 San Francisco (CA) *Examiner*, November 14, 1883; Collins and
Levene, *Black Bart*, p. 157.

4 San Francisco (CA) *Chronicle*, November 14, 1883: San Francisco
(CA) *Call*, November 17, 1883; San Francisco (CA) *Examiner*, No-
vember 19, 1883; Boessenecker, *Lawman: The Life and Times of Harry
Morse*, pp. 249–251; Collins and Levene, *Black Bart*, p. 155.

5 Boessenecker, *Lawman: The Life and Times of Harry N. Morse*,
pp. 176–178.

6 San Francisco (CA) *Call*, November 15, 17, 1883.

7 San Francisco (CA) *Call*, November 15, 17, 1883; San Francisco (CA)
Examiner, November 14, 1883.

8 San Francisco (CA) *Daily Alta California*, November 14, 1883.

9 San Francisco (CA) *Daily Alta California*, November 14, 1883.

10 San Francisco (CA) *Chronicle*, November 14, 1883.

11 San Francisco (CA) *Call*, November 14, 1883; San Francisco (CA) *Examiner*, November 14, 1883.

12 San Francisco (CA) *Daily Alta California*, November 20, 1883; San Francisco (CA) *Chronicle*, November 20, 1883.

13 Stockton (CA) *Evening Mail*, November 14, 1883.

14 San Francisco (CA) *Examiner*, November 14, 1883.

15 San Francisco (CA) *Examiner*, September 16, 1883; San Francisco (CA) *Alta California*, November 14, 1883; San Francisco (CA) *Call*, November 14, 1883; San Francisco (CA) *Chronicle*, November 14, 1883; San Francisco (CA) *Bulletin*, November 14, 1883.

16 San Francisco (CA) *Call*, November 14, 15, 17, 1883; San Francisco (CA) *Bulletin*, December 24, 1905.

17 Stockton (CA) *Evening Mail*, November 17, 1883; San Francisco (CA) *Bulletin*, January, 21, 1888; testimony of Ben. K. Thorn, People v. C.E. Bolton, Calaveras County Superior Court (1883), quoted in Collins and Levene, *Black Bart*, pp. 217–218.

18 San Francisco (CA) *Call*, November 15, 17, 1883; Stockton (CA) *Evening Mail*, November 15, 16, 1883; New York (NY) *Sun*, reprinted in Monongahela (PA) *Daily Republican*, December 28, 1883; Boessenecker, *Lawman: The Life and Times of Harry Morse*, pp. 249–251. On Black Bart's shotgun, see *Catalogue, Wells Fargo & Company Historical Exhibit at the World's Columbian Exposition* (1893), p. 29.

Chapter 15

1 Stockton (CA) *Evening Mail*, November 17, 1883.

2 Stockton (CA) *Evening Mail*, November 17, 1883; Sacramento (CA) *Record-Union*, November 17, 1883; Collins and Levene, *Black Bart*, p. 169, 219; Hoeper, *Black Bart*, p. 89.

3 Treleaven, "Old Men in the Sun," pp. 269–270. In the 1930s, Mary Anna "Mamie" Bunt (1863–1950), then Mrs. Dorsey Ramsden, described the stagecoach trip in a letter to Owen Treleaven.

4   Ben K. Thorn to Harry N. Morse, 1884; San Francisco (CA) *Examiner*, December 3, 1888.

5   San Francisco (CA) *Daily Alta California*, November 20, 1883; San Francisco (CA) *Examiner*, November 20, 1883; San Francisco (CA) *Chronicle*, November 20, 1883; Collins and Levene, *Black Bart*, p. 173.

6   San Francisco (CA) *Daily Alta California*, November 20, 1883; San Francisco (CA) *Call*, November 20, 1883.

7   San Francisco (CA) *Chronicle*, November 20, 1883; San Francisco (CA) *Call*, November 20, 1883.

8   San Francisco (CA) *Examiner*, November 20, 1883.

9   San Francisco (CA) *Call*, November 20, 1883.

10 San Francisco (CA) *Examiner*, November 21, 1883.

11 San Francisco (CA) *Bulletin*, November 20, 1883.

12 San Francisco (CA) *Chronicle*, November 21, 1883.

13 San Francisco (CA) *Chronicle*, November 23, 1883; San Francisco (CA) *Examiner*, December 3, 1888.

14 San Francisco (CA) *Chronicle*, November 23, 1883.

Chapter 16

1   Boston (MA) *Globe*, November 14, 1883; Philadelphia (PA) *Times*, November 25, 1883; Omaha (NE) *Daily Bee*, November 21, 1883. Claude Duval (1643–1670) was a famous gentleman highway robber in England.

2   Napa (CA) *Weekly Register*, November 23, 1883.

3   Boessenecker, *Lawman: The Life and Times of Harry Morse*, pp. 201–204, 328.

4   San Francisco (CA) *Call*, November 17, 1883; New York (NY) *Tribune*, January 8, 1922; San Francisco (CA) *Examiner*, November 18, 1883.

5　San Francisco (CA) *Examiner*, November 18, 1883.

6　Wells Fargo & Co. cash books, cited in Collins and Levene, *Black Bart*, pp. 175–176.

7　San Francisco (CA) *Examiner*, November 19, 1883.

8　San Francisco (CA) *Bulletin*, November 20, 1883.

9　San Francisco (CA) *Examiner*, November 21, 1883.

10　San Francisco (CA) *Examiner*, November 14, 17, 21, 1883.

11　San Francisco (CA) *Examiner*, November 19, 1883.

12　San Francisco (CA) *Call*, November 20, 1883; San Francisco (CA) *Examiner*, November 21, 1883.

13　San Francisco (CA) *Examiner*, September 16, November 14, 1883.

14　San Francisco (CA) *Examiner*, November 20, 1883; San Francisco (CA) *Chronicle*, November 21, 1883.

15　San Andreas (CA) *Calaveras Chronicle*, November 23, 1883.

16　Ben K. Thorn to Harry N. Morse, 1884.

17　California State Controller warrant no. 3146, December 29, 1883, California State Archives.

Chapter 17

1　San Francisco (CA) *Examiner*, November 22, 1883; *The Wasp*, March 12, 1887.

2　San Quentin Prison Register, convict no. 11046, California State Archives; Grass Valley (CA) *Union*, November 23, 1883.

3　San Francisco (CA) *Examiner*, November 22, 1883; Sacramento (CA) *Daily Union*, November 23, 1883; Grass Valley (CA) *Union*, November 22, 23, 1883.

4　San Jose (CA) *Daily Mercury*, February 16, 1887; San Francisco (CA) *Daily Alta California*, January 8, 1883.

5 San Francisco (CA) *Call*, quoted in Salt Lake City (UT) *Deseret News*, January 10, 1884.

6 Charles Boles to Hiram Boles, December 20, 1883, copy in Bruce Levene collection; Bloomington (IL) *Pantagraph*, November 28, 1883; San Francisco (CA) *Examiner*, December 6, 1883.

7 San Francisco (CA) *Daily Alta California*, December 22, 1883; San Francisco (CA) *Chronicle*, November 28, 1888.

8 San Francisco (CA) *Examiner*, January 20, 1884; Joseph Henry Jackson, *Bad Company*. New York, NY: Harcourt, Brace & Co. (1949), pp. 190–191.

9 San Francisco (CA) *Examiner*, November 24, January 20, 1884, December 4, 1938; Stockton (CA) *Mail*, December 17, 1883; San Francisco (CA) *Chronicle*, November 23, 1883; Treleaven, "Old Men in the Sun," p. 245.

10 San Francisco (CA) *Examiner*, November 28, 1888; Collins and Levene, *Black Bart*, p. 210.

11 Charles E. Boles to Oscar James, July 24, 1884, reprinted in Dajani, *Black Bart*, pp. 114–116.

12 Charles E. Boles to Mary Boles, October 11, 1884, original in author's collection; reprinted in Collins and Levene, *Black Bart*, pp. 181–182.

13 Charles E. Boles to Mary Boles, November 10, 1884, original in author's collection; reprinted in Collins and Levene, *Black Bart*, pp. 181–182.

14 Charles E. Boles to Mary Boles, undated letter from 1884, original in author's collection.

15 Charles E. Boles to Eva Boles James, October 7, 1885, original in author's collection; Kansas State Census, Delphos, KS, 1885, dwelling no. 173 (Lillie Boles, Henry F. Wedgewood, and Harriet Melinda Wedgewood); Dajani, *Black Bart*, pp. 106, 143.

Chapter 18

1 San Francisco (CA) *Chronicle*, November 28, 1888.

2 San Francisco (CA) *Examiner*, April 6, 1887.

3 Charles E. Boles to Mary Boles, reprinted in Hannibal (MO) *Journal*, December 13, 1888.

4 San Francisco (CA) *Examiner*, December 2, 1888.

5 San Francisco (CA) *Examiner*, November 28, 1888. Hume mistakenly told reporters that Boles wrote the "villainous letter" to his son-in-law rather than to his brother-in-law.

6 Booth to Hume, April 26, 1886, in San Francisco (CA) *Bulletin*, January 21, 1888.

7 Mark Dugan and John Boessenecker, *The Grey Fox: The True Story of Bill Miner, Last of the Old-Time Bandits*. Norman, OK: University of Oklahoma Press (1992), pp. 78–79.

8 Secrest, *Dark and Tangled Threads of Crime*, pp. 221–223.

9 San Francisco (CA) *Examiner*, December 26, 1886.

10 San Francisco (CA) *Examiner*, December 2, 1888.

11 San Francisco (CA) *Chronicle*, December 3, 1888.

12 San Francisco (CA) *Examiner*, January 24, 1887; San Francisco (CA) *Chronicle*, July 3, 1887.

13 Boessenecker, *Shotguns and Stagecoaches*, pp. 131–135; William B. Secrest, *California Desperadoes: Stories of Early California Outlaws in Their Own Words*. Sanger, CA: Word Dancer Press, (2000), pp. 109–115.

14 San Francisco (CA) *Examiner*, December 2, 1887, November 12, 1890; Secrest, *California Desperadoes*, pp. 116–117.

15 San Francisco (CA) *Examiner*, January 22, 1888; San Francisco (CA) *Chronicle*, January 22, 1888.

16 San Francisco (CA) *Chronicle*, January 22, 1888.

17 San Francisco (CA) *Examiner*, April 3, 1887.

18 San Francisco (CA) *Examiner*, January 29, 1888; Collins and Levene, *Black Bart*, p. 189.

19 Charles E. Boles to Mary Boles, January 31, 1888, in San Francisco (CA) *Chronicle*, December 11, 1888.

Chapter 19

1 San Francisco (CA) *Examiner*, November 12, 1890.

2 Charles E. Boles to Mary Boles, no date, in Hannibal (MO) *Journal*, December 13, 1888.

3 San Francisco (CA) *Chronicle*, December 11, 1888.

4 San Francisco (CA) *Examiner*, November 28, 1888; Sacramento (CA) *Record-Union*, February 23, 1888; Visalia (CA) *Tulare Times*, March 1, 1888.

5 San Francisco (CA) *Chronicle*, May 28, November 28, 1888; San Jose (CA) *Mercury-News*, May 28, 1888; San Francisco (CA) *Examiner*, July 28, 1888.

6 Sacramento (CA) *Daily Union*, November 28, 1888.

7 Grass Valley (CA) *Union*, November 11, 1888; San Francisco (CA) *Chronicle*, November 13, 1888; Chico (CA) *Weekly Enterprise*, November 16, 1888.

8 Mendocino (CA) *Beacon*, November 28, December 5, 1888; Petaluma (CA) *Courier*, December 5, 1888; Sacramento (CA) *Record*, November 28, 1888; Boessenecker, *Shotguns and Stagecoaches*, pp. 180–182, 187–194.

9 Sacramento (CA) *Record-Union*, November 28, 1888; San Francisco (CA) *Chronicle*, November 28, 1888; Philadelphia (PA) *Times*, December 16, 1888.

10 San Francisco (CA) *Examiner*, December 1, 1888.

11 San Francisco (CA) *Chronicle*, December 11, 1888.

12 Los Angeles (CA) *Herald*, November 16, 1888; Santa Maria (CA) *Times*, November 17, December 1, 1888. On Ham White, see *Mark*

Dugan, Knight of the Road: The Life of Highwayman Ham White. Athens, OH: Ohio University Press (1990).

13 San Francisco (CA) *Examiner*, December 2, 1888.

14 San Francisco (CA) *Chronicle*, December 3, 1888.

15 Hannibal (MO) *Journal*, December 13, 1888.

16 Fresno (CA) *Morning Republican*, August 2, 1889; San Francisco (CA) *Chronicle*, August 1, 1889; San Diego (CA) *Union*, November 3, 1890; San Francisco (CA) *Examiner*, November 12, 1890. In Shinn's confession, he referred to Dorsey by his other alias, Charles Thorn.

17 San Francisco (CA) *Chronicle*, May 15, August 24, 1889.

18 San Francisco (CA) *Chronicle*, December 12, 1888.

Chapter 20

1 San Francisco (CA) *Alta California*, September 23, 1882; New York (NY) *Sun*, January 12, 1889.

2 Washington (DC) *Star*, April 5, 1884.

3 Philadelphia (PA) *Times*, August 6, 1888; Auburn (CA) *Placer Herald*, February 3, 1934.

4 Reno (NV) *Weekly Nevada State Journal*, December 1, 1883; San Jose (CA) *Mercury News*, February 16, 1887.

5 San Francisco (CA) *Examiner*, December 11, 1888; San Francisco (CA) *Chronicle*, December 12, 1888.

6 Los Angeles (CA) *Herald*, October 8, 1893; Los Angeles (CA) *Evening Post-Record*, September 15, 1909.

7 Corinne (UT) *Daily Mail*, May 4, 1875; Hailey (ID) *Wood River Times*, March 26, 1891; Washington (DC) *Times*, June 11, 1905.

8 San Francisco (CA) *Bulletin*, reprinted in Los Angeles (CA) *Evening Express*, January 28, 1888; John A. Henshall, "Tales of the Early California Bandits: Black Bart," *Overland Monthly*, vol. 53, no. 6 (June 1909), p. 475.

9   Stockton (CA) *Evening Mail*, November 17, 1883.

10 San Francisco (CA) *Alta California*, December 2, 1883; Los Angeles (CA) *Times*, December 4, 1932; Greg Martin, *The Parker Lyon-Harrah's Pony Express Museum*. San Francisco, CA: Chrysopolis Press (1987), pp. 160–161.

11 San Francisco (CA) *Examiner*, reprinted in New York (NY) *Sun*, August 19, 1888; Los Angeles (CA) *Herald*, August 19, 1894.

12 San Francisco (CA) *Call*, September 4, 1910; Chicago (IL) *Inter Ocean*, June 4, 1911; Santa Barbara (CA) *Independent*, April 19, 1910; Santa Rosa (CA) *Press Democrat*, June 28, 1953; Sacramento (CA) *Daily Union*, December 9, 1891.

13 Joseph Henry Jackson, *Tintypes in Gold*. New York, NY: The Macmillan Co. (1939), p. 63; Jackson, *Bad Company*, p. 182.

14 Hailey (ID) *Wood River Times*, June 21, 1882, June 6, 1883; Windsor (VT) *Journal*, August 22, 1891; Tombstone (AZ) *Weekly Epitaph*, January 4, 1914; St. Johnsbury (VT) *Republican*, February 18, 1914; Salmon (ID) *Recorder*, August 20, 1920; Charles K. Bolton, *The Boltons of Old and New England*. Albany, NY: Joel Munsell's Sons (1889), pp. 13, 15; Carlo M. De Ferrari, "The Murphys Hotel Register," *Quarterly of the Tuolumne County Historical Society*, vol. 34, no. 3 (January–March 1995), pp. 1177–1178.

15 Roy O'Dell, "Black Bart of Wisconsin," *Wild West History Association Journal*, vol. 6, no. 1 (February 2014), pp. 33–41; St. Joseph (MO) *Daily News*, June 18, 1891.

16 Oakland (CA) *Tribune*, April 7, 1949.

17 Chicago (IL) *Tribune*, April 24, 1893; *Catalogue, Wells Fargo & Company Historical Exhibit*, pp. 14, 21, 29; Dajani, *Black Bart*, p. 133.

18 Salt Lake City (UT) *Herald*, March 12, 1896; Delphos (KS) *Republican*, May 3, 1890; Collins and Levene, *Black Bart*, pp. 209–211; Dajani, *Black Bart*, p. 133.

19 Dajani, *Black Bart*, pp. 133–135; author's interviews with Dick Reames, great-great-grandson of Charles Boles, October 1993.

20 Brooklyn (NY) *Standard Union*, October 15, 1914; Brooklyn (NY) *Chat*, October 17, 1914; Jackson, *Tintypes in Gold*, p. 92.

21 Hoeper, *Black Bart*, pp. 154–156.

22 Los Angeles (CA) *Herald*, January 27, 1889; Sacramento (CA) *Record-Union*, January 11, 1891.

23 San Francisco (CA) *Examiner*, July 3, 1889, September 9, 1897; Victoria (Canada) *Daily Times*, June 4, 1889.

24 Brooklyn (NY) *Standard Union*, December 5, 1889; San Francisco (CA) *Chronicle*, January 1, 1890; New York (NY) *World*, October 23, 1890; New York (NY) *Sun*, October 23, 1890.

25 San Francisco (CA) *Bulletin*, November 17, 1892.

26 Mexico City (Mexico) *Mexican Herald*, February 24, 1902; Santa Rosa (CA) *Republican*, reprinted in Portland (OR) *Daily Journal*, April 2, 1903.

Index